EMOCRACY

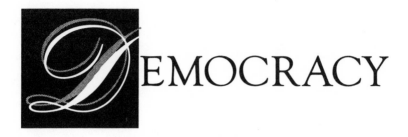

DEMOCRACY

A SHORT, ANALYTICAL HISTORY

ROLAND N. STROMBERG

M.E. Sharpe
Armonk, New York
London, England

Library of Congress Cataloging-in-Publication Data

Stromberg, Roland N., 1916–
Democracy : a short, analytical history / Roland N. Stromberg.
P.   cm.
Includes bibliographical references and index.
ISBN 1-56324-761-5 (hardcover : alk. paper)
ISBN 1-56324-762-3 (pbk. : alk. paper)
1. Democracy—History. I. Title.
JC421.S79   1996
321.8′09—dc20   95-50394
CIP
Printed in the United States of America

The paper used in this publication meets the minimum requirements of
American National Standard for Information Sciences—
Permanence of Paper for Printed Library Materials,
ANSI Z 39.48-1984.

BM (c)   10   9   8   7   6   5   4   3   2   1
BM (p)   10   9   8   7   6   5   4   3   2   1

Those who employ their pens on political subjects, free from party-rage and party-prejudice, cultivate a science which, of all others, contributes most to public utility.

—David Hume

Contents

DEMOCRACY

1

Defining Democracy

"Of the governing tendencies of the modern world by far the most important is the spread of democracy," historian H.A.L. Fisher once observed. It is possible to make this claim for other general processes, such as capitalism, secularization, rationalization, urbanization, the growth of science and technology, but Fisher's point was certainly well taken.

It is surprising how little study has been made of democratization, in comparison with the other processes. Some years ago a historian of political thought remarked on the scarcity of scholarly studies of democratic ideas.[1] If the situation has improved since then, works of synthesis are still rare. An authoritative history of democratic thought in western civilization, one that gives adequate attention to the dialectic of thought and action, seems to be lacking. Such a work would examine how the concept of democracy came into being, entered into contact with the real world, enriched or changed its meaning, was absorbed by various groups and systems, aroused utopian hopes or suffered cruel disenchantment.

The Word and Its Usage

The initial problem facing any student of democracy is how to define the term. *Democracy* is a fuzzy term. The word is all around us; it is constantly used in the news media and everyday discourse to define our own culture and to shape our policies toward others, who are said to be delinquent if they are "undemocratic" and may even need to have this nebulous entity thrust upon them by force. Democracy continues to occupy large space in headlines: it triumphs over communism, is restored in Haiti, is hailed as the master principle of our age. One of the five goals for joint action by the United States and the European Union, proclaimed in December 1995, is "development of democracy throughout the world." It is presented as a cure-all for troubled peoples and lands. But its failures or inadequacies even at home are also frequently deplored: books are written every year such as *The Betrayal of American Democracy* (William Greider). "Cry Democracy!" headlines *The Economist* (December 1987). "The main political issue in the world today is the advancement of democracy," a Polish colleague of Lech Walesa proclaimed in 1989.

But there is much confusion in usage of the term. Democracy is confused with liberalism or constitutionalism or social equality or national independence; it may be taken to mean majority rule or minority rights. The meaning varies with the time and place. Democracy is invoked as a model and used to legitimize different causes for different reasons. Democracy, Christopher Hollis once exclaimed metrically, means

> One thing at Moscow, one at Rome
> A third in Sudan and a fourth at home.

We could add other places where the word has undergone strange transformations. Throughout the world, everybody invokes it, even tyrants. In assuming absolute power, Sheik Majibar Rahman of Bangladesh explained in 1975 that banning opposition parties and strikes was necessary in order to "ensure democracy." The longtime Philippine dictator Ferdinand Marcos published a book proving that his rule was, as the title claimed, *Today's Democracy*. Communist-ruled countries called themselves "people's democracies." More recently in postcommunist Russia, members of the extreme nationalist party, which many dubbed fascist, and which in combination with ex-Communists strove to overthrow the precarious reform government of Boris Yeltsin, called themselves (ironically?) the Liberal-Democrats.

Politicians typically mouth the word *democracy* when (as is often the case) they can think of nothing else. Democracy is a hurrah word. A British politician of the late nineteenth century said that, when asked a hard question at a public meeting, his habit was to mention the name of Gladstone, the popular Liberal party leader; this gave him time to think because it set off five minutes of cheering. Much the same is true of democracy. At the extreme limits of vagueness, we find the word used simply as a synonym for good, as when, for example, the Russians are said to behave "undemocratically" when they wage war on Chechnya (as if democratic governments never went to war). Or general histories of the United States are titled, for example, "The Making of a Democracy." William L. O'Neill calls his book on the United States in World War II *A Democracy at War*.

Definition of the term has often depended on local conditions and special circumstances. For example, when in the 1980s the old British Liberal party merged with elements from the right wing of a bitterly divided Labour party, who called themselves Social Democrats, the new party decided to adopt the name of Liberal Democrats. (Social Democrat was the name of the pre-1914 Marxist parties, including Lenin's in Russia, but in British usage it tended to convey more democrat than socialist.) The term *democrat* for the British was a symbol that invoked a sense of being progressive yet moderate, committed to public welfare yet not dogmatically socialist. It was also a title extracted from the names of the two merging parties. One would have had to follow the intricacies of British politics over a long period of time to understand this meaning fully. "Every term," G.K. Chesterton remarked, "comes to us coloured from all its adventures in history." Democracy's adventures have been unusually long and varied.

But today one often meets the term *liberal democracy*.[2] Two things are vaguely conflated that once were seen not only as different but as antagonistic. (The point is discussed further below.) "Democracy," the London *Economist* (1995) opined, "is not just a matter of casting ballots, important though that is. It is also about free speech, religious tolerance and the rule of law." In popular western usage today, liberal democracy may often be about all these things, but historically as well as conceptually each is a separate thing. Religious toleration and freedom of the press arose at separate times, both long before there was any democracy in the sense of allowing people to cast meaningful ballots. Constitutionalism, or "the rule of law," has even more ancient roots. These things would not have been called democracy prior to the late nineteenth century at the earliest.

Using a word so indiscriminately risks turning it into a nonsense syllable. One may feel, as J.R.R. Tolkien remarked about freedom, that "the word has been so abused by propaganda that it has ceased to have any value for reason." Or as a scholar recently remarked in a book about another much-used and abused political term, *fascism*, "The history of the term is replete with examples of definitions according to political expediency." Like fascism, democracy is "a semantic jungle." It is a "worn-out term," or as philosopher John Austin snapped, "a useless word." Contemporary academics concerned with analyzing the processes of government or the nature of society tend to avoid the term or show their embarrassment by putting it in quotation marks. It is too hopelessly vague, and professors, who must aspire to the status of scientists nowadays, have to come up with other terms, such as *pluralism*, which to be sure turn out to be almost equally unmanageable. Political scientists discuss more specific processes and institutions, such as pressure groups, political parties, the organization of policy making and decision making, the composition of elites, the workings of bureaucratic machinery. Democracy is too "open" a concept for them to feel comfortable with it. A standard treatise about the British political order published in 1974 (by Richard Rose, a distinguished academic) did not have the word *democracy* in its index. Democracy is not relevant to the real processes of government, declared W.H.C. Eddy in his *Studies in Democracy* (1966).

Simone Weil (1937) had earlier cited the indiscriminate use of this term (along with capitalism, fascism, and communism) as evidence for "the end of social intelligence." Scholars might take democracy for granted as, in some sense, the larger structure, but even here they have preferred to discuss more specific "civic cultures" that differ in subtle ways from one democratic country to another; each political community develops its own special customs or conventions that enable the system to work.

Of course, in having varied and shifting meanings, democracy is like many terms in daily use that are central to our practical thinking. The philosopher Max Scheler once observed that "[t]here is not . . . an accepted definition of mathematics, physics, or chemistry, not to mention biology and the human sciences." Along with other words, such as *art* and *social justice* and *Christianity*, democracy is one of the words W.B. Gallie called "contested concepts" the nature of which is to be essentially undefinable. While being familiar to everyone and usually eliciting a strong emotional response, such terms have no clear, single meaning.

People often assume that these nebulous entities, among which democracy is numbered, are good things; few attack art, social justice, democracy, or Christianity as ideals, though of course they may and usually do attack particular artists, reformers, proclaimed democrats, nominal Christians. These symbols may thus function as "ideal types" against which we measure reality, without expecting that the real world will attain the ideal. These words are essential precisely because they elude definition: "The value of the term," Peter Calvert writes of a somewhat similar case (*The Concept of Class*), "lies in the fact that the task [of establishing a precise meaning] is impossible." Chesterton pointed out that "the indefinable word is the essential one." Philosophers have noticed that such terms as *love, blue, good* cannot be defined because they are irreducible; we can only point to them. Perhaps democracy is such a case.

In any event, despite its hopeless ambiguities, the term continues to be vigorously active. The historian's task is to dissect the layers of meaning that past experience has deposited on it. The critical intelligence may dismiss the term *democracy* as cant, or avoid it as lacking clarity, but it survives in our culture as a word loaded with the freight of past experiences, hopes, failures, an essential counter in the community's discourse.

Confusion with Other Ideas

In popular parlance, democracy has become confused or amalgamated or overlaid with other ideas. There is a puzzling conflation of things logically separate or even contradictory in what is commonly called democracy. It is, for example, often assumed that equality and democracy are identical. A section in a recent book about the French Revolution by a well-known scholar is titled "Democratization: The Quest for Equality."[3] But equality and democracy are certainly not, on the face of it, the same. Democracy may be seen as a subbranch of equality. The nineteenth century, it has been said, was about equality. Equality of rights spelled liberalism, equality of votes democracy, equality of goods socialism. Other equalizing demands came from women and ethnic minorities. People who wish to define democracy as a social principle, broader than a political process, usually seem to mean more nearly social equality. But an egalitarian society could be politically most undemocratic, in the sense of being ruled by a despot or an oligarchy. Such was evidently the approximate condition of nineteenth-century Serbia, a peasant society without class distinctions, ruled by a strong king, with no elected legislature. This seems a rather normal pattern for a premodernized people. Russia, widely considered to have had the most despotic government in Europe, was socially in some ways more democratic than Western Europe: there were few social gradations, and the vast majority were equal if only in their servitude.

Conversely, a socially undemocratic society, defined as one with unequal classes or status groups—unequal in prestige, wealth, or both—could have a popularly elected government. This was not unlike Great Britain in the late nineteenth century. It seems indeed to have been taken for granted at one time that social and political democracy were *inversely* proportionate. A considerable body of thought followed the thinking of Montesquieu in holding that unless there was an aristocracy, the king would become a despot, as in the Orient; only the nobility, in a society of graded ranks, could check the sovereign. One had to choose between social inequality and political tyranny.

The extensive literature on the subject of democracy frequently presents the argument that democracy depends on there being social inequality. Equality of condition is not what the masses of people want; they want the opportunity to rise, and there must be a top to which to rise. When unlimited equality of opportunity is granted, the result is usually a most unequal distribution of wealth; the more talented or aggressive clamber to the top over the bodies of the less advantaged and thus create a plutocracy. Such was the case in the greatest example of successful democracy, the United States of America.

Thus there is a contradiction between democracy and actual equality.

A confusion exists between democracy and liberalism. Both were great nineteenth-century terms; the philosopher-historian Benedeeto Croce, who thought that history was the story of liberty, held that *liberty* was the great word of the nineteenth century. Today democracy tends to be used, as a *New York Times* writer recently used it in talking about China, to mean human rights. Governments that forbid public protest and censor the newspapers are called undemocratic. But defined as majority rule or government by popularly elected representatives, democracy is not the same thing as liberty and may clash with it. In the early nineteenth century, democracy was commonly seen as an enemy of liberty. It was once almost axiomatic that the two things are irreconcilably opposed; so argued a whole library of nineteenth-century writings, led by W.E.H. Lecky's massive historical analysis *Democracy and Liberty* (1896), virtually every page of which argued for the eternal opposition between them. As Whigs, the English liberals all the way into the nineteenth century were strongly antidemocratic. They stemmed from the noble lords who had resisted the king in 1688. Disraeli called them a Venetian oligarchy. Most of them opposed extending the vote in 1867, which Disraeli and the Tories supported, and resigned from the old Whig party in the 1880s after it accepted democracy.

In perhaps the most famous of all books about democracy, Alexis de Tocquevllle dwelt on the "tyranny of the majority," and the greatest of nineteenth-century British political philosophers, John Stuart Mill, followed Tocqueville here. The majority obviously *may* suppress individual or minority rights; many feared that it would frequently do so. ("Absolutist democracy" has been traced to Thomas Hobbes, author of the classical argument for a government of total powers, whose opponent John Locke, often called the father of modern liberalism, stressed personal liberty and individual rights but did not favor democracy.)

Hitler's Nazi state, in our time almost by definition the ultimate negation of democracy, in fact was in some respects "violently democratic," as Keith Robbins calls Hitler's ideas (see further in chapter 6). The Nazi ideal was a brotherhood of all the racial comrades, which much resembles the Jacobin democracy of the French Revolution, or Rousseau's participatory village democracy. While producing monstrous injustice, Nazism also overthrew established elites to make a place for new men. Hitler, who brought many new voters into the process, was at one time probably the most popular leader of a great nation in this century. Is it democracy if a large majority chooses to reject parliamentary government and libertarian practices? "What if your parliaments become more unpopular than kings?" Chesterton once wondered. If democracy means simply a regime, of whatever sort, that meets with the approval of a very considerable majority of the people, then Hitler's regime could claim to have been democratic, at least part of the time. The fascist/Nazi theory was a reversion to Robespierre's belief during the French Revolution, inspired by Rousseau (often called the father of modern democracy), that the will of a leader can incarnate the people's will better than a legislative assembly can.

If democratic governments can disregard human rights, undemocratic ones can respect such rights. England developed a passion for individual liberty, perhaps unique in the world and the main source of our passion in America, while governed by a hereditary monarch and a legislature one branch of which was hereditary and the other elected by a severely restricted suffrage. England's Parliament grew out of the medieval kings' feudal Council of great lords, whose consent and cooperation the monarch needed at a time when the state was weak; parliament survived almost uniquely in England, while in other major states it fell into disuse as kings grew stronger. The parliament that valiantly fought against royal domination in the great political struggles of seventeenth-century England was a thoroughly aristocratic body, the House of Commons, consisting chiefly of squires who were the masters of their own smaller domains and not easily intimidated, precisely because they had this basis of strength as petty lords themselves. They were elected by the vote of a small number of their own dependents and clients.

Initially, English parliamentary defenders of liberty, the Puritans and the Whigs, considered *demos* as much a menace to liberty as unchecked royal power. Only later was popular suffrage absorbed, gradually—and fearfully —into the English constitution. Constitutionalism—that is, the limiting of government's powers by a fundamental law—along with separation of powers, legal safeguards, and bills of rights, remained as a legacy of undemocratic times to underpin later democracy. Constitutionalism, often linked to democracy, is antidemocratic in essence, rooting law and policy in a written constitution not easily amendable and subject to interpretation by an independent, nonelective judicial authority. (The U.S. Constitution, written in a predemocratic era, can be amended by vote of two-thirds of both houses of the federal legislature, followed by the approval of three-fourths of the state legislatures. The Senate, the upper chamber of the legislature, was not directly elected until 1916.) Some treatises on democracy claimed that only the presence of such ancient checks on popular will, left over from predemocratic times, make modern democracy tolerable. "Strong institutions inherited from the Middle Ages," Bertrand Russell thought, form the basis for freedom; he saw American democracy as prone to an oppressive "tyranny of the majority" because it lacked such institutions.

However that may be, the view that local groups with an autonomy rooted in long usage are a necessary part of a healthy democratic culture is frequently found. Another case: Today the free-market revolution all over the world is often associated or identified with democracy. *The Economist* constantly sings the praises of democracy, by which it means, chiefly, freedom of business enterprise. Mario Vargas Llosa called his Peruvian free-market program a "revolution in democracy." The free-market reformers in Russia like to be called democrats (but so do their old communist foes). What is meant, however, is not so much elected parliaments as relief from statist restraints on entrepreneurial activity. If this economic liberty could be guaranteed by some authority beyond the reach of partisan politics, as did Vargas's successor, Vargas would doubtless be delighted. Boris Yeltsin dismisses the Russian Parliament in the name of "democratic reforms" and hopes to postpone elections lest these reforms be overthrown. The order of capitalism is as much an order as is socialism, if less arbitrary. Market economies and democratic politics are not the same.

Different Kinds of Democracy

Those who seek a definition of democracy usually end by distinguishing between several types. C.B. Macpherson found four (see his *Life and Times of Liberal Democracy*, 1977). Others have made a distinction between two basic clusters of meaning. Louis Rougier (*L'Erreur de la démocratie française*, 1963) thought that these two kinds of democracy were "so opposed that to confound them is to render unintelligible the political history of human societies." Joseph Schumpeter's well-known essay "Two Concepts of Democracy" distinguished between democracy as procedure and as result, roughly between majority rule via popular elections and a society marked by equality and liberty.

Rougier joined numerous others in identifying two quite antithetical types. First, what has been called "monistic democracy," or sometimes "totalitarian democracy," "organic democracy," perhaps "participatory democracy," is characteristic of small, close-knit groups. It is found in many premodern societies but also in smaller or spontaneously generated groups in modern times (e.g., the revolutionary Soviets who began the Russian Revolution only to be suppressed by the centralizing Leninist party, as the Parisian neighborhood committees were suppressed by the Jacobin state during the French Revolution), and it survives in a few Swiss cantons today. Such direct democracy was found in ancient Athenian democracy, in that all citizens (a minority, however, of the populace) participated directly in government.

The second kind of democracy is modern, "pluralist," or representative. The term *democracy*, Peter Jenkins remarked, "since the eighteenth century has been bandied between the proponents of the classical or direct version of the people's rule (what we call today participatory democracy) and the American or indirect version (what Paine called representative democracy)." In history, the two democracies have often gotten semantically as well as practically mixed up. Each has at times leveled damning criticisms at the other (see further in chapter 9). Your "representation" is not democracy at all, the monists cried, perhaps quoting Georges Sorel's withering remark that each French voter was one ten-millionth a tyrant and every bit a slave. Or they might question, as a great British newspaper did not long ago, the democratic value, other than ceremonial, of "four weeks of hectoring every five years or so." To almost anyone prior to about 1800 it would have seemed evident that government by elected representatives (at a ratio of one to every few hundred thousand at best) is not democracy at all but a form of oligarchy.

On the other hand, the pluralists have declared monist democracy intolerant, persecutory, exclusivist, "totalitarian," failing to respect minority rights and fair procedures. "Nothing could have been less egalitarian than a French village community," historian Pierre Goubert remarks. Lawrence Stone has described the village community of premodern England as "interfering and inquisitorial, riddled with malicious gossip, quarrels, spying, delation, lawsuits, and all uncharitableness, except at such times as it ganged up against a common victim" (which sounds rather like a modern office or department). Yet in such communities a pure form of participatory, consensual democracy was practiced, one that involved all the people directly. At a simpler stage of society, in small, highly integrated communities, before the large territorial state and a complexly organized society existed, a kind of democracy was possible because no question had arisen between popular belief and some other standard. In the primeval solidarity of the tribal village, where individualized consciousness scarcely yet existed, the principle of authority was consensus, a general recognition of the right leader or policy. Stern authority is not felt as tyranny in the state any more than it is in the family, the ultimate source of patriarchal authority, until alien ideas intrude to corrode the innocent integrity of the group. (Such methods of government still operate in small, cohesive communities, of course.) We have this combination of severe discipline with intense group solidarity in the athletic team today—the exaggerated popularity of sports has as one leading cause its perpetuation of a once organic human experience, now lost in the large society. Some such condition was presumably the human one through long millennia of primitive existence; its roots are deep and it continues to persist at the grassroots level of even thoroughly modernized societies. How much more so is it taken for granted in many societies around the world today that are still largely premodern in their outlook?

It was only in such humble and generally scorned precincts that one could speak of democracy. Medieval cities, though inhabited by free citizens, were usually governed by an oligarchy and marked by social hierarchy. But hierarchy was in fact very much a part of the older society even where "democratic"; so was respect for authority. The people choose a leader, by processes less mechanical than a counting of votes; they spontaneously recognize their leader and then grant him full powers to rule, until he badly fails, when he may be summarily sacked. In his study *The Authoritarian Personality*, Theodor Adorno found that acceptance of authority was more common near the bottom of the social scale than near the top—a relic, surely, of traditional society.

Both kinds of democrats seem to have been right in their criticism of the other. A muddled mixture of the two has presided over the most dynamic and materially successful society in history. There is a troubling split between democracy's classical heritage and its modern epiphany: Athenian democracy, source of the word and the idea, was totally different from what is usually understood by the word today. The great American jurist Oliver Wendell Holmes, Jr., in an introduction to an edition of Montesquieu's classic *The Spirit of the Laws*, was amazed to find that the eighteenth century understood democracy as a New England town meeting rather than as the government of a great nation like the United States.

Preparations for Pluralism

During the crucial premodern period of modern western civilization, in the sixteenth and seventeenth centuries, experience gradually taught the hard lesson that where a plurality of cultures and beliefs exists, a viable society would have to learn not to value these above social peace. It was indeed a hard lesson to learn, for it went against basic human instincts and most previous human experience. The shared values of a successful democracy on any scale but the smallest would have to be an agreement not to have (absolute) values and to accept the limited purposes of government. It took several centuries for western civilization to accede to this.

In the sixteenth and seventeenth centuries bitter warfare between Protestants and Roman Catholics forced religious toleration grudgingly; only after bloody persecutions and civil wars was toleration reluctantly accepted as the lesser evil. That "[a]greement in religion is the only social basis of the state" had long been axiomatic; how could there be the necessary unity if people differed on the very fundamentals of life? Equally undisputed was the role of the state in promoting these shared values in positive ways. To regard government as ideologically neutral, confining itself to preserving public order while allowing its subjects to practice whatever faith they prefer so long as they do not disturb the peace, would have been as incomprehensible to the ancient Greeks as it was to medieval Christians.

The Protestant revolt against the supremacy of the Roman pope in western Christendom, beginning with Martin Luther in the 1520s, led to a century of convulsion, not only because both (or all) sides in the religious dispute were intolerant, insisting on doctrinal orthodoxy, but because the issue split existing states: Lutheran, Calvinist, and Catholic churches contended in religious wars in Germany, France, and England, then in the Spanish Netherlands. The seed of religious toleration grew only slowly because in many respects it went against basic human characteristics. Toleration seemed indifference; if we really believe our religion and care for it seriously, it is hard for us to think that it may be in error and hard not to think that erroneous belief is dangerous to the community. So a revolution in basic attitudes toward government and religion had to take place. Only sheer necessity, the need to end bloody civil conflict, drove people gradually to accept the limited state and the intellectually divided community. Imposing arguments for toleration eventually came forth, of course—great monuments of early liberalism, from Castellio, Roger Williams, John Milton, and others. Most of them struck at the belief in absolute truth: how can we be so sure? It is valuing one's opinions rather highly, Montaigne commented drily, to put another person to death because of them. And so were planted the seeds of a skepticism necessary to pluralist democracy.

The 1689 Act of Toleration in England, imperfect as it was, set the stage for substantial acceptance of religious diversity in the political order. The great scientist Isaac Newton, in 1687, just before England's Glorious Revolution against the Roman Catholic king James II, thought that "a mixture of Papists and Protestants in the same University can neither subsist happily nor long together." That an overwhelming percentage of Englishmen agreed with him is a measure of how much things were to change; it would certainly amaze us today if a leading scientist were to claim that Catholics and Protestants could not work together. Religious toleration was the first step toward the modernization, or pluralization, of western civilization—a condition, we are inclined to forget, that in some basic ways is not common or natural to human communities.

What we in Western Europe or the United States call democracy, and assume must be good for everybody else, turns out to be a complex mixture of many things peculiar to our history and culture, built up through centuries of special experiences in the European as well as the American past. When Euro-Americans today lecture other peoples on their lapses from democracy, they usually mention a number of things in addition to universal suffrage; indeed, this is probably not high on the list. Thus, in chiding Mexico, *The Economist* (March 4, 1995) included among "the reforms that need to be in place before Mexico can be called truly democratic" the following: "the creation of an independent judiciary and civil service; an uncorrupt police force; a free press and television system; clean elections and an end to patronage." Such institutions as these took shape in Great Britain and Europe over a long period of time, at least from the early seventeenth to the late nineteenth century. Nor did some of them have much to do with democracy in the sense of majority rule and parliamentary elections. In England the judiciary vindicated its independence in the long struggle between Common Law and Royal Prerogative that was a part of the civil wars of the seventeenth century.

Civil service reform came two centuries later, after long ages in which patronage was the normal lubricant of government. The most democratic of nations, the United States, conceived its democracy in the image of the motto of Andrew Jackson, first of the fully democratic American presidents: "to the victor belong the spoils." The bare beginnings of a system of selecting government officials on the basis of merit, via examinations, came to the United States only in 1883, after a disappointed office seeker assassinated a president. Jacksonians regarded such a Chinese mandarin–like custom as highly undemocratic, as indeed it is if we think of democracy as the selection of officials by popular vote or as the people's entitlement to a chance at public office without regard to birth or fortune. The qualification for office under a merit system rests primarily on education. The pioneer in Europe of a merit system was the king of Prussia, not usually regarded as a democrat, and his autocratic government long maintained its reputation for having the most honest and efficient bureaucracy in the world.

Before elections could be "clean," a whole social order had to be changed, one in which tenants and laborers were so dependent on their landlord or their employer they could not dream of opposing his wishes at election time. (This gradual decline of deference was not completed in Britain until the twentieth century.) Of course, decidedly unclean elections had long been almost institutionalized in American cities. This ancient and honorable practice of ballot-box stuffing did not seem to disqualify the United States from being called the first of the democracies.

Freedom of the press began in Britain and the United States in the eighteenth century prior to election of governments by universal suffrage. It may be abridged by democratic governments as well as undemocratic ones, and has been, notably in time of war. And so, as we look at this list of what is characteristically thought of as democracy today, we find a number of practices that are not democratic at all, in their provenance or in their nature. Some of them are, if anything, antidemocratic in that they contravene the principle of majority rule.

In the eighteenth-century Enlightenment, Newtonian science stimulated a new kind of intellectual absolutism. "The heavenly city of the eighteenth-century philosophers," in the title of a notable essay by Carl L. Becker, replaced the Christian heavenly city; intolerant reason replaced intolerant religion and proved equally unfriendly to democracy. In Europe from roughly the fifteenth to the eighteenth centuries, there had occurred a "great divorce" between popular and elite culture, or at least a considerable estrangement. In the 1580s L. Joubert was already reproaching the populace for their "popular errors" on medicine and health (*Des Erreurs populaires touchant la médicine et le régime de santé*, 1587). This was in good part a consequence of the rise of printing and literacy, which, if they eventually aided democracy by making ideas available to all, did not do so initially, when books were scarce and expensive.

Both the Reformation and the scientific revolution made war on the old folk culture, the one regarding it as heathen, the other as ignorant. Meanwhile the state was engaged in organizing a larger territorial area and centralizing power at the expense of the old local jurisdictions, creating at the same time the large and glittering capital cities, such as Paris and London (imitated in Russia by St. Petersburg), to which the new literate elite was drawn. There, amid publishing houses and salons, learned societies and journals, they began to form an intellectual class estranged from the mass of people still settled on the land. The old universities, small, church-dominated, and mostly provincial, had never had the same impact. There had always been a stratified society, made up of classes unequal in power and status, but these had lived together, united by human, personal relations —more so, at least, than later. Above all, they had shared a common culture: the amusements, pageants, songs, and stories of squire, yeoman, and laborer were about the same. Later societies found it amazing that both bumpkins and gentlemen in Shakespeare's time could understand and enjoy those great plays. All that was to change.

Notes

1. John A. Scott, *Republican Ideas and the Liberal Tradition in France 1870–1914* (New York: Columbia University Press, 1951).

2. See, for example, William A. Galston's and Jerry Weinberger's essay "Liberal Democracy and the Problem of Technology," in Arthur M. Melzer, Jerry Weinberger, and M. Richard Zinman, eds., *Technology in the Western Political Tradition* (Ithaca, NY: Cornell University Press, 1993).

3. In R.R. Palmer, *The Improvement of Humanity* (Princeton, NJ: Princeton University Press, 1982).

2

Democracy's Classical Image

Classical Republicanism

In the premodern era, including most of the eighteenth century, *democracy* was a word with generally unfavorable overtones; *republican* was a much more honorific term. It summoned up images of the ancient "mixed" constitution, safeguard of liberty in which, as the eighteenth-century British statesman Robert Walpole explained, "the monarchical and the aristocratical and the democratical forms of government are mixed and interwoven so as to give us all the advantages of each without subjecting us to the dangers of either." An unadulterated democracy was perhaps the most dangerous form of all.

The wisdom that so orders a state that no one element in it can seize total power, and that classifies pure or simple democracy as just one element in the state, led back to the ancient sages Aristotle, Cicero, Polybius, Tacitus; classical republicanism came close to being the political consensus, especially (but not exclusively) in Anglo-Saxon political thought and usage (Venice was almost the model for the type). It was as much an article of faith with American president John Adams as with Charles James Fox, radical British politician of the era of the American and French Revolutions, who considered "any of the simple, unbalanced governments bad: simple monarchy, simple aristocracy, simple democracy" (House of Commons, February 9, 1790). In the eighteenth century the great authority of Montesquieu's *Spirit of the Laws*, with its stress on separation of powers and checks and balances, reenforced classical republicanism and strongly influenced the authors of the U.S. Constitution in 1789.

Among the revered ancients whose authority dominated European thought for many centuries, Aristotle had disapproved of democracy, not without some ambivalence. He thought some element of popular participation was practically, if not theoretically, wise; but a pure democracy, such as Athens at one time had, he and most other thoughtful Greeks believed to be about as bad as government could get. The majority can act tyrannically unless a fundamental law sets limits to its powers. Here were the foundations of western liberal constitutionalism, but not of majority rule. The majority is not the people; that is to say, the entire community has an ideal existence that the vote of a majority on any particular day does not fully represent.

Plato added a more severe indictment, based on the principle that the true and the good do not stem from the majority but from the few who are wise and expertly trained. A subtle and difficult art, politics is as little suited to ordinary people as is physics or philosophy. If, as Walter Agard maintained in his *What Democracy Meant to the Greeks* (1942), Plato "was much more of a democrat than is usually admitted" in conceding that the people should have *some* share in government, clearly he was not a very good one. We must remember that the Athenian democracy so repugnant to Plato was indeed a pure one, in which officials were chosen by lot and all citizens participated in both legislative and judicial decisions; by Athenian standards our elected representatives and appointed officers would not constitute a democracy at all.

Enlightenment Rationalism as Antidemocratic

As we have already observed, the eighteenth-century Enlightenment, that powerful improvement of the human spirit that deeply affected virtually every country in Europe (and America) from about the 1740s down to the French Revolution of 1789, was in most respects hostile to democracy. In an influential essay Alfred O. Lovejoy (see his *Essays in the History of Ideas*) did indeed once argue that "intellectual equalitarianism" was one of the key ideas of the Enlightenment; he described it as "a democratic temperament in matters of religion and morals and taste, even in persons not democratic in their political views." Possibly so, but the French eighteenth-century philosophes, self-styled bringers to the human race of a new Enlightenment based on reason, deeply mistrusted the multitude. The common man appeared to them almost the gravest danger to enlightenment. These famous leaders of thought, influenced by the scientific breakthrough of the seventeenth century, placed their hopes for the triumph of reason chiefly in a kind of enlightened despotism, whether working through kings (instructed by the philosophes, of course) or some sort of new priesthood of the Enlightened. The reasons for this were simple. The Enlightened were few, and, as John Locke—a prime source of the Enlightenment, as well as of the American Revolution—confided in his journal, the great bulk of mankind wallows in "passion and superstition."

Another great forerunner of the Enlightenment, Pierre Bayle, found "no counsel, no reason, no discrimination, no study or exactitude" in the common herd. The irrationality of the masses is a refrain of the literate, from Milton to Voltaire, who called them cattle and held they would always remain such. "The greater part of men, and still more of women [!] judge without reflecting and speak without thinking," the great iconoclast remarked. Voltaire doubted that the multitude should even be educated. It was a later Voltairean who observed that attempting to instruct the masses was like building a huge fire under an empty pot.

Most of the philosophes thought the great majority uneducable, not necessarily as a class—many of the Enlightenment intellectuals sprang from humble lineage (D'Alembert was a foundling) and the universities admitted some poor students—but because they thought the spirits are naturally unequal, implying that only a few can aspire to reason and knowledge. Lord Bolingbroke, the eighteenth-century English deist and freethinker, is the most frequently cited source of the description of the people as a "monstrous beast," but it was a familiar refrain. (Plato seems to have said it first.) Smollett's Squire Bramble (in *Humphrey Clinker*, 1771), in calling the mob "a mass of ignorance, presumption, malice and brutality," only expressed the conventional wisdom.

Certainly none of the leading eighteenth-century minds, who were critics of the established order, eager prophets of a new and better age to come, thought it other than preposterous to suppose the majority capable of government. "What operation capable of producing any durable good can be understood by the people?" wondered Voltaire's disciple Condorcet, a notable participant in politics down to and including the Revolution. One of the most radical of the philosophes, the atheistic Baron d'Holbach ("personal enemy of God"), condemned democracy. David Hume is only one more of the bold and brilliant eighteenth-century spirits who thanked God (if such existed) that he did not live in a democracy.

Enlightenment writers like Voltaire, D'Alembert, and Denis Diderot felt strongly that the future of the race must be kept out of the hands of the majority and firmly in their own. Humankind had heretofore dwelt in a far from happy condition, they believed. They blamed this sad state partly on the dominance of priests, who kept people in a state of "superstition." The main ideological offensive of the philosophes was not so much against the church as against its obsolete credo and its uninformed clerics. Clericalism: *voilà l'ennemi*. They set out to destroy it with ridicule. The new clergy, i.e.

themselves, were enlisted in the cause of science; Bacon, Descartes, and Newton were their gods. And here these two antidemocratic strains came together. Thinking of Newton's mathematical physics, with its exact and simple law of universal gravitation, the philosophes considered science clear, certain, geometric. With a certain intolerance they banished all previous modes of knowledge as irrelevant and outmoded, whether coming from the long-idolized ancient Greek philosophers (now proved wrong) or from the church. The future hope for humanity, so much in need of rescue from centuries-long stagnation, lay in modern science. But the ignorant masses did not understand it. They tore down Franklin's lightning rods and still believed in witches; they approved the silencing of Galileo and let their priests guide them. Toil-ridden as they had to be, the masses could never grasp the complex truths on which human progress depended. Far better to penetrate the royal palace and install a dictatorship of reason than to rouse up the multitude. Francis Bacon, the pioneer ideologist of modern science, had in its infancy already sketched the model of a scientific elite able to attain wisdom and then impose it on the majority.

So the educated people, most of them closely associated with the ruling elite, tried to conceal their atheism from the servants and hoped to control the necessary revolution from above. Of course, they were unsuccessful. They wrote books the second editions of which, someone has remarked, were bound with their own skins.

Such ambivalence lay at the dawn of modern politics: because of its powerful scientific knowledge, an educated elite that was largely alienated both from the people and from the established government thought it could prevail over both to install a brave new world of enlightenment and progress, immeasurably good in the long run for everybody.

In the eyes of the Enlightenment rationalists there was a fundamental opposition between reason and democracy. William Godwin, in his well-known *Political Justice* (1793), referred indignantly to "that intolerable insult upon all reason and justice," the deciding of truth by the counting up of numbers, adding that truth "cannot be made more true by the number of its votaries." If we are as confident as the Enlightenment thinkers were that reason exists, then it is absurd to suggest arriving at decisions by any other method than the application of reason. The test of truth cannot be popularity. Two plus two does not equal five (except in George Orwell's *1984* nightmare state) though an army be found to affirm it. Schiller had this in mind when his character Demetrius declares that "Mehrheit ist der Unsinn"—it is irrational to suppose that truth depends on a majority. The greatest of eighteenth-century thinkers, Immanuel Kant, regarded democracy as the one illegitimate form of government because it is based not upon reason and right as found in the eternal order of things, but upon the caprice of majorities. A man can be in the majority for truth though he be in a minority of one, Henry David Thoreau pointed out.

We may even feel that we have a right to coerce a populace that lacks the ability to attain a truth that is certainly available to us. John Milton held that it was better that an enlightened minority compel the majority to be free "than that a greater number, for the pleasure of their baseness, compel a less most injuriously to be their fellow slaves." The French Revolution's often savage course cannot be understood unless we realize how much the major Enlightenment thinkers, who had enthralled the literate world in the 1760s and 1770s when future leaders of the Revolution were in their formative years, had absolutized political theory. They greatly reenforced the idea that a single, exact, universally valid political standard exists and needs only to be applied. They did not, incidentally, expect or want a revolution but looked forward to an ordering of society according to rational principles, followed perhaps by the gradual enlightenment of the masses, which would take a long time. Not by "angry revolt," as Alan Kors remarks in his scholarly study of Holbach's influential salon, but by "gradual, controlled, and maximally predictable reform" did the philosophes want to achieve the necessary progressive change.

In his biography of Edmund Burke, Philip Magnus remarks that "[t]he venality and appalling ignorance of the eighteenth century voter made democracy inconceivable" to cultivated Europeans in the eighteenth century. One might reply that voters have remained appallingly ignorant even to the present, if we are to believe numerous public opinion polls, and not necessarily incorruptible, which has not prevented the coming of universal suffrage and popular political power. But the common people, especially in England, were much more dependent on their masters. Complete democracy was long considered a reactionary idea because a rabble would vote as their landlords or employers told them. This was true until the Secret Ballot Act of 1872 helped change the pattern of dependence. It was understood early that political democracy requires economic independence. James Harrington, the important seventeenth-century political theorist, had stressed this point. "The basis of a democratic and a republican form of government is a fundamental law favoring an equal or rather a general distribution of property," said the American Noah Webster. As Poor Richard put it, an empty bag cannot stand upright.

Alfred Cobban wrote that "the revolutionary idea of popular sovereignty is not easily to be found in the writings of the philosophes." The school of Locke wished to limit all sovereignty, equally unacceptable where it derived from people or king. "Holy people" is as bad as holy king, Kipling later wrote. "To Rousseau alone is it even plausible to attribute any conception of the sovereignty of the people; and . . . even in his case the attribution rests on an elementary, though common, misunderstanding of his thought." Rousseau's sovereign is the general will, and this is an ideal will: that which would be willed by the people if they were able to conceive of the common interest in an enlightened and disinterested way. "Even so, the General Will is restricted by him to the function of making general laws [a Constitution]. Government, involving individual acts, does not enter into its scope." "Indeed, any theory of absolute sovereignty is incompatible with the political liberalism of the Enlightenment."

Still, in a certain loose sense people spoke of popular sovereignty. The Enlightenment thinkers tended to hold that the interest of the people, conceived in utilitarian terms as happiness, was the proper goal of government. The belief that government should be in the interest of the people fused with the old principle of sovereignty to create popular sovereignty: power was simply transferred from the monarchy to the people. Then, during the Revolution, Rousseau's idea of general will was employed to validate a dictatorship in the name of the people.

It is wrong to call Rousseau a democrat, his modern interpreters insist. Or at any rate, "He believed that democracy was suited only to very superior people, who were also very simple people." They were virtuous because they were uncorrupted by civilization: Rousseau opposed educating or otherwise enlightening the masses (they should remain poor) because this would entail all the corruptions of civilization. There is no doubt that Rousseau, a "dictatorial libertine," as he has been called, betrayed his own alienated intellectual soul in deeply mistrusting ordinary people, though his political theory glorified them in the abstract.

The French Revolution

No wonder Robespierre, in the heat of the French Revolution of whose terrorist phase he became the chief executioner, denounced the philosophes as elitists, snobs, traitors to the people's general will. The only exception was Rousseau, who was an enemy of the mainline philosophes in his stress on feeling rather than intellect, nature rather than learning. Rationalism, together with its brother atheism, Robespierre said, are aristocratic. During the French Revolution, both the bitterly warring factions, loosely designated as Girondist and Jacobin, appealed to Rousseau, taking different ideas from him. The Jacobins, as represented by Robespierre's Montagnards, who mounted the Reign of Terror, claimed him most vociferously. They identified the philosophes with a cold intellectualism, including atheism (the enemy of democracy), which leads to elitism and thus to treason against the people. Rousseau, they said, had called for a moral restoration based on group solidarity. Robespierre and Saint-Just constantly used this Rousseau-istic "virtue" as an excuse for suspension of individual rights, invoking Rousseau's idea of general will, which they claimed could be expressed by a small, revolutionary priesthood.

Thus it was to the democracy of primitive solidarity that its only defenders during the Revolution appealed. But Rousseau had said that this rather ideal democratic community could exist only at the local level. Rousseau was not alone among the eighteenth-century political writers in thinking democracy feasible only in a small community. Voltaire gave as one reason for doubting that democracy could exist beyond the local level, "It is impossible to love tenderly an overly large family that one scarcely knows." Rousseau's kind of democracy, if such it was, was utterly inconsistent with the large state. To extend its mandate of totalism to all France was a manifest misreading of Rousseau, whose democracy had to be communal, static, like-minded. The Gironde also claimed Rousseau's mantle, assailing Robespierre as an ignoramus (until he had the last word at the guillotine). Even the defender of King Louis XVI cited *Du Contrat Social* against the regicides—which did not, of course, save the royal neck.

Robespierre found himself impaled on the horns of this dilemma; for he did not want a France made up of innumerable small governments but rather (like most of the revolutionaries) a large, united country. The urge to national integration, which was a potent force in the Revolution, sprang from more than desire for national power. Expressed during the Revolution by a drive to standardize the language and to create via education and publicity a single French culture, such integration reflected the Enlightenment's typical thirst for order and clarity on a cosmopolitan basis. Robespierre shared it with his foes, the more moderate and rational Girondists.

Thus nationalism contradicted democracy, unless subject to those tortuous constructions the Jacobin dictatorship was forced into: "The people will the good but left to themselves they do not see it," Robespierre explained. A few inspired leaders must speak for them. He held the Reign of Terror to be "an application of democracy." The real people, in brief, are not the same as an ideal people; we may have to liquidate most of the former. In order to attain those goals we desire, which we may designate as democratic because we think in the long run they are good for the people, we must coerce the existing grubby mass of humanity, which is too stupid to know what is good for it. We must, in brief, have a dictatorship. Democracy did not signify the compromises arrived at by a motley amalgam of diverse individuals and groups, but rather the one pure will of a truly virtuous people. The incarnation of that will could be one person. "Je suis peuple moi-même," Robespierre declared. I myself am the people.

We find here, of course, a conflict and a contradiction between the two different kinds of democracy noted in chapter 1, the democracy of organic solidarity in a small community and the democracy of elected legislators in a large one. In fact, the word *democracy* was not a common one in the rhetoric of the Revolution; unhappily one of its few notable uses was in Robespierre's speech of February 5, 1794, which virtually launched the Reign of Terror.

A representative thinker of the Revolution, the Abbé Sieyes, whose 1789 pamphlet demanding a place for the "Third Estate" virtually started the revolution and who survived to end it a decade later by conniving at Napoleon Bonaparte's installation as First Consul, favored confining the vote to those who paid taxes, approved highly indirect methods of election, and opposed the *mandat imperatif*, or instruction of delegates by their constituents. A furious debate broke out about this point: should delegates follow the instructions of their constituents or exercise their own judgment? But any sort of representation was anathema to the Rousseauistic democrats. That representation was not really democratic was perhaps less important to them than that it was not truly communitarian. Representative democracy divides up the general will into selfish particular interests. A mere collection of individual wills amounts only to the old illegitimate rule of force and injustice.

In the sections of revolutionary Paris, among the sansculottes, at a very common-man and precinct-politics level, direct democracy did spring up. But the Robespierrian dictatorship assailed and suppressed it; because the sansculottes opposed central government, they were what later would be called (Proudhonian) anarchists. To democratize was evidently to fragmentize and thus to destroy the nation, the now revered *patrie*, at a time when it was becoming embroiled in war with much of the rest of Europe.

Robespierre's attempt to square the circle of democracy and nationalism, or Rousseauism and reality, led him to fantasize about a kind of representative legislature that would sit surrounded by the masses in a large stadium, feeling their hot breath at every moment—rather like a boxing match or a football game. Actual mob intervention into the legislative chamber, which happened in 1793, led him to break with the radically democratic sansculottes. That "[d]emocracy is a state in which the people, guided by laws of their own making, do for themselves what they can do well, while their delegates do that which the people cannot do" was a precarious compromise. That the great regicide in the end found himself at war with both left-wing and right-wing revolutionaries was in good part responsible for his downfall.

The choice thus seemed to be between a democracy of poverty, weakness, and backwardness, and a power state of vice and corruption, with the only other possibility mob rule and reigns of terror. The kind of democracy that appeared in the writings of Rousseau and briefly in the neighborhoods of revolutionary Paris might or might not be attractive, but it bore no relationship to the realities of the modern state and society. Robespierre's attempts to transplant this rural species to the national level led to monstrosities: a tyrant-dictator claiming that the general will somehow dwelt within him, or mobs looking over the shoulders of legislators.

Robespierrian democracy, associated with the Reign of Terror, came crashing down in July 1794, when the short-lived dictatorship of his faction fell victim to its own machinery of purification by persecution. As Robespierre and his colleague (and fellow Rousseauist) Saint-Just were dragged to the same guillotines to which they had sent others for the past year and a half, reaction set in and democracy, the only kind identified during the Revolution, came badly out of the whole experience. No effective procedures of elective government had been established. The several legislative assemblies seen in France between 1789 and 1799 (elected by a highly restricted body of voters) had never functioned effectively. The 1793 constitution, providing for universal (men's) suffrage, never went into effect. The only government that had emerged was a tyranny more monstrous than the old one, claiming to rule in the name of the people.

General Napoleon Bonaparte's coup d'état of 1799 overthrew the revolutionary republic and reduced the legislative assemblies to no more than fig leaves for autocracy. Though he soon proclaimed himself emperor, the Corsican usurper's despotism rested on the masses. It was a Caesarism with popular roots and a commitment to carrying out (by undemocratic means) the socially democratic (egalitarian) goals of the Revolution. What Napoleon meant by democracy was more nearly what the nineteenth century would know as liberalism. "Democracy, if it is reasonable," he said, "limits itself to giving everyone an equal opportunity to compete and to obtain." John Stuart Mill would add equal access to the podium. Democracy as a government by popularly elected representatives, needless to say, had no place in the Napoleonic order. He did not think it reasonable to consider every man's opinion of the same weight: "The presidents of the cantons and the presidents of the electoral colleges, the army—these are the true people of France, not 20,000 or 30,000 fishmongers and people of that ilk . . . they are only the corrupt and ignorant dregs of society."

Nevertheless the upstart Corsican, even though he had crowned himself emperor, could claim no legitimacy except popular support, which he undoubtedly had for most of his sixteen-year reign. He dethroned monarchs and old nobility as he offered to all of Europe a regime based on equal (male) rights under the law. "To secure the dignity of man" by just and impartial laws had been his mission, Bonaparte declared on his deathbed in exile; to open opportunities to the common man via the "career open to talents" principle; further, to destroy "feudalism" and unite the continent of Europe around general liberal principles. The man whom much of Europe finally came to hate as a tyrant and military conqueror had on anyone's reckoning so thoroughly shaken up the old order that it could never be restored. Something like total political and social reconstruction would have to be undertaken after his fall.

Democracy in the sense of government by popular majorities or elected representatives was never a part of Bonapartism. Yet one may say that after Napoleon every French regime had to be based in a broad sense on public approval. Jean Lhomme remarked that no government in nineteenth-century France was undemocratic in the sense of not resting on a popular mandate. But this might include a number of different forms, among them despotism. Another Bonaparte, Napoleon III, became an emperor confirmed by plebiscite; his rule, from 1851 to 1870, which did in fact seem to meet with the approval of most French people through most of its term, was called a democratic despotism and a liberal empire. Such was the confusion of categories.

When the young Romantic poets Coleridge and Wordsworth, in the 1790s, earned the mistrust of their neighbors in rural England, the latter could find no worse thing to say about them than that they were "a set of violent democrats." Reaction against the French Revolution helped provoke such epithets; the long war against Napoleon further confirmed the British in their dislike of anything that smacked of French political innovations.

A somewhat similar reaction occurred in the United States. Though destined soon to be the greatest force working toward acceptance of democracy, the states of the new American republic did not establish universal suffrage until a generation after 1789; few of the Founding Fathers wanted to be called democrats. Thomas Jefferson, often viewed as the fountainhead of American democracy, according to historian Charles A. Beard, never used the word in any of his public papers or called himself a democrat in public; the opposition party dubbed the Jeffersonians "Democrats" in derogation, and they preferred to call themselves Republicans, a term with more honorable but distinctly oligarchical connotations. Eventually they settled for the equivocal Democratic Republicans. But it is well known that the

1789 Constitution, creating a federal union, probably had as its chief stimulus a fear of overly popular state governments that were sometimes inclined to impair property rights and encourage violent uprisings.

The Skeptical Basis of Democracy

From the Age of Reason to the Reign of Terror and dictatorship, the lesson that emerged was that any effort to impose uniformity on a great state, even a democratic uniformity, would end in tyranny. Pure democracy is inconsistent with any belief in objective standards of truth. Modern democracy rests on a basis of skepticism or multiple truths; "polytheism," in the term of one commentator (Georges Guy-Grand), or "the regime of social relativism." (American philosopher John Dewey later thought that his version of pragmatism was the only reputable philosophy compatible with democracy.) If an absolute standard of truth exists, however one obtains it (by reason or by revelation), one does not leave its determination to a show of hands. If, as T.C. Hall once wrote in discussing the Puritans, "the sovereignty of God does not wait upon a majority vote," neither does the sovereignty of reason. Vox populi, Coleridge remarked, must be tried "by the prescript of reason and God's will." The people's voice is valid only if it agrees with these, and they are valid whether or not the mass of men, or a majority, does so. "A strange theology, which believes that God speaks only to 51% but not to 49%," an old-fashioned Christian of the present century (Lord Percy of Newcastle) exclaimed. (Or, as Dean Inge put it, a belief in "the plenary inspiration of the odd man.") Dogmatic religionists, of whatever sort, must hold that no form of government in itself is superior to another; a Christian (or an Islamic) monarchy would be preferable to a pagan democracy. The eighteenth-century philosophers, as dogmatic rationalists, only transferred this absolute standard from revelation to reason; they had not abjured all standards in favor of what a later Frenchman, the Christian Democrat Marc Sangnier, called "the stupid tyranny of blind majorities."

Vox populi becomes acceptable, indeed necessary as the mode of decision making, when we have given up faith in absolute standards of truth and have come to think either that there are no such standards, that there are many incommensurable ones, or that we cannot be sufficiently sure that they exist. Nobody who is sure of the truth will think it sensible to leave it to an election. That would be letting uninstructed pupils determine the right arithmetic or spelling answers. We do not leave decisions up to the majority in the classroom, the laboratory, or the business office. If we do so in society as a whole, it is because people have become gradually and painfully aware that there is no exact political truth on which everyone can agree.

The eighteenth century swarmed with hopeful illusions that there is such a science of politics or social relations. By no means did all of them die with that century. The so-called sciences of economics and then sociology, after all, flourished in the nineteenth century and still more or less survive, though they suffered some setbacks after the mid–nineteenth century. In the earlier part of that century John Stuart Mill moved away from the Benthamite democracy of his youth to place his main hope in a general science of politics on which "all thinking and instructed persons" might agree, while his rival in the field of nineteenth-century English political thought, Samuel Taylor Coleridge, yearned for a "clerisy" of enlightened leaders who would steer the ship of state by the stars of science and reason. For his part Lord Acton, the famous liberal Roman Catholic historian, was still dreaming in the 1860s of a science that would "establish the policy of the State on a sure foundation, beyond the antagonism of classes and the tumult of fluctuating opinion," triumphing over "ignorance and error, over passion and interest, over the irresponsible authority of tradition, and the blind force of numbers."

"[T]he blind force of numbers" was as irrational a principle of government also to Herbert Spencer, the Victorian sociologist, as it had been to Bayle or Condorcet. Spencer called "the divine right of parliaments" "the greatest political superstition of the present." Social reformers of the doctrinaire variety held similar views; Robert Owen, from whom Karl Marx learned socialism, thought government by a democratically elected parliament about the most absurd notion conceivable, likely to be as inefficient as it was turbulent. But any sort of moral absolutist must think the same. Thomas Carlyle, the great Romantic social critic, was staggered by the heresy of ballot-box rule: "Alas, that there should be human beings requiring to have these things argued of, at this late time of day!" To him it meant an abjuration of the sacred quest for the noble and the true. And to this day there are many who yearn for some sure standard of truth by which to steer the state, whether it comes from religious text or the social science laboratory, and who are uncomfortable with democracy because it seems to be a kind of denial of such a standard, a cheerful willingness to accept that one man's opinion is as good as another's because none is more than an opinion.

Ends and means: a political process such as elections, or a condition such as liberty for all, can hardly be a supreme value, an end in itself. If one holds to any such value, these procedures or conditions can only be approved if they are the best means to the valued end. In the nineteenth century a number of different causes accepted democracy as a means to the end they valued: nationalists, capitalists, socialists, all saw democracy as on their side, so long as a majority of people approved their values. If they failed to gain a mass following, they could quickly turn against democracy.

Thus socialists, originally believing fervently that they represented the toiling masses who were the great majority, could turn against democracy when the masses seemed unreceptive to their message.

Large numbers of people voting, or being free, is in itself quite meaningless, or pernicious if they are in error. In this regard we might note that any study of democratic ideas quickly discovers that virtually all those who dealt in ideas, the thinkers and intellectuals, were antidemocratic. Not theory but experience, on the whole, produced democratic regimes. In the mid–nineteenth century (1859), John Stuart Mill observed that the changes made in the direction of democracy "are not the work of philosophers but of the interests and instincts of large portions of society recently grown into strength." It could be said of democracy that all theory was against it and all experience for it.

3

Democracy's Nineteenth-Century Advance

The Feeling of Inevitability

One of the most remarkable themes in the history of nineteenth-century writing about democracy in Europe is the sense of fatalism about the coming of democracy. It was regarded, for the most part gloomily, as an inevitable trend, making its irresistible way as a movement of the social tide that nothing could hold back. No one really wanted it; it just came. A host of observers noted, joyfully or regretfully, that it was the wave of the future. Democracy is "the inexorable demand of these ages," Thomas Carlyle said; to Italy's Count Cavour at about the same time, in the 1830s, it seemed a "predestined evolution." (Neither of them liked it.) As early as 1821 the Frenchman Royer-Collard had—unhappily—found "democracy everywhere, in industry, in property, the laws, memories, things, men."

In 1837 Cardinal Manning reflected that "[t]he course of Europe seems to be toward a development of national life and action by calling into political power large numbers of people." To this same moment belongs Tocqueville's magisterial inquiry into democracy in America, which had resulted from his conviction that it was futile to deplore the spread of democracy (as his French colleague La Mennais, for example, had done in 1825); it only remained to examine the consequences in order to prepare for the inevitable coming.

Such curiosity about what seemed a strange new visitor, uninvited and perhaps unwelcome, but clearly here to stay, was a major undercurrent of thought and expression in Europe, especially in the 1820s and 1830s. It was like those disturbing physical novelties, such as the steam engine, that were also intruding on life. "It is too bad," Chateaubriand wrote, "but that is the way it is; what can we do?" The analogy between democracy and the Industrial Revolution often occurred to people; French political leader Leon Gambetta said that "the locomotive is republican."

In 1847 Mazzini, the famous Italian nationalist and political orator of social romanticism, declared that "[b]y decree of providence, gloriously revealed in the progressive spirit of humanity, Europe is fast advancing towards democracy." Despite a check stemming from the failed revolutions of 1848, this sense of an irresistible tide continued. We find Etienne Vacherot, in his *La Démocratie* (1860), writing of a "law of progress" that "scarcely permits us to doubt that the next century will see, at its beginning, the United States of European Democracy." In 1867, at the time of the extension of the vote in Britain (the Second Reform Act), Sir Wilfred Lawson affirmed that "[t]he great tide of democracy is flowing on, and no hand can stay its majestic force." A few years later James Fitzjames Stephen, to whom the tide was not majestic, nevertheless conceded, in his ironically titled *Liberty, Equality, Fraternity* (1873), that "[t]he whole current of thought and feeling, the whole stream of human affairs, is setting with irresistible force in that direction." In his notable essay on democracy, Victorian sage Matthew Arnold (1879) had, like Vico, seen it as a kind of "principle of human nature" at a certain stage of social development.

And a half century later, by then thoroughly disillusioned with the creature, Gustave Le Bon observed that while the parliamentary regime is universally despised, it endures and will probably continue to endure "because it is just about the only government possible among civilized people" (*La Psychologie politique*, 1912). He did not say why; it was just that way, inevitably. James Bryce's widely heralded work *The American Commonwealth* (1888), written to commemorate the 100th birthday of the new Republic, had meanwhile found democracy destined to worldwide triumph "as by a law of fate."

What was the source of this sense of an inevitable democratizing trend? Though Matthew Arnold thought it was related to improvement in the material condition of the common folk, a perception of greater well-being among the masses of people hardly existed in the 1830s, when the feeling of democracy's inevitability was especially strong. Quite the opposite opinion about economic welfare flourished in that era; the 1830s rang with laments about poverty and class war. It was the decade of the great uprising at Lyon that sent shock waves through France and of Carlyle's laments about an ugly estrangement between rulers and the ruled. Carlyle, the same perceptive observer of the social scene who remarked on democracy's inevitable advance, announced a great crisis growing out of widespread popular suffering and the indifference to it of leaders captivated by the gospel of mammon. Benjamin Disraeli joined Carlyle in deploring the division of society into two nations of rich and poor. There followed Friedrich Engels's report on the terrible plight of Manchester workers (itself based on a parliamentary investigation). Indeed, the 1830s and 1840s brought the real birth of modern socialism, as the ideas of Fourier, Saint-Simon, Cabet, and Owen circulated widely. It was also the time of the discovery of the urban poor, especially in the journalism of Eugene Sue (*The Mysteries of Paris*) and, in London, Jonathan Mayhew. The feeling that the people were relentlessly marching toward power paradoxically accompanied a conviction that they were growing ever more miserable (as Marx was to argue) and, presumably, powerless.

Perhaps the two ideas were connected, in that they both reflected a rising social consciousness, a growing compassion about the condition of lower orders once considered almost outside the bounds of humanity. Strikingly, the era also featured attempts at reform of prisons and criminal law; complaints resounded about such expressions of a callous attitude toward life at the lower levels as public execution of criminals for petty crimes, which was to be substantially abolished in England in the first half of the nineteenth century.

More likely, the concern about encroaching democracy was based on a fear that the dikes that had long held back a great black tide welling up from the lower depths were beginning to weaken. The "dangerous classes," as the French called them, threatened bourgeois households. The French Revolution had severely damaged the old unquestioning acceptance of authority and hierarchy. Attempts in 1815 to turn back the clock and restore monarchical legitimacy as the foundation of government obviously had not succeeded; revolutions against the Vienna settlement broke out all over Europe between 1820 and 1830. France overthrew another Bourbon in 1830; England drastically tampered with its ancient constitution in 1832. Efforts to censor the press no longer had a chance against the growing ease and affordability of publishing books, newspapers, and magazines. To dismiss liberal professors, as happened in Germany on one famous occasion, only created martyrs who fed the flames of unrest. Prince Metternich, trying to govern Europe from Vienna, had a sense of being the last barrier vainly trying to stem the tide of anarchy. "For thirty-nine years I played the role of rock, from which the waves recoil . . . until finally they succeeded in engulfing it."

"The world," Europe's foremost conservative reflected, "is subject to two influences, the social and the political." The latter, Metternich said, can be "manipulated," which was his supreme talent. Political forces can be managed; "[n]ot so the social element." As a conservative, Metternich held that order is the foundation of freedom; and order is something that either does or does not exist. Despotism is not the answer; if despotism is needed, it is already too late. Social order, as Edmund Burke had argued, is an organic growth, ripening in a people's consciousness over the centuries. When it decays or changes, there is little the statesman can do about it, since the change does not depend on the will of any one person but on a vast social process. Something like this was the feeling about democracy that began to spread in Europe. It was happening; it couldn't be stopped. What it portended couldn't be foretold, though there were dire fears.

At work in the inevitable tide of democratization was a social version of the famous physical law of entropy, much discussed in this era (beginning with Sadi Carnot's formulation of the principle in 1824). Power once dispersed can never be drawn in again. With time, power passes gradually downward, as the plebs win small victories time after time. It is almost impossible for the elite to take these privileges back. Let the vote be given to some, as in 1832, and then it must be given to more and more, as happened in England in 1867 and 1884. To reverse this process by getting legislation enacted to take away the vote from those who had gained it was out of the question; a vested interest had been created, a habit formed, a privilege entrenched.

To maintain aristocracy, the great eighteenth-century Italian philosopher and historian Giambattista Vico had theorized, requires great moral effort, and it decays like any structure. Time, which corrupts all, is the enemy of aristocracy. The growth of wealth, economic differentiation, and knowledge all corrode the authority of a governing elite. Democracy must run its course, Vico had thought, down to the last removal of inequality, until some mighty catastrophe inaugurates a whole new cycle of history. Vico was rediscovered and much discussed in the late nineteenth century; those he deeply influenced included Georges Sorel and James Joyce.

In the last analysis the great growth of wealth over the nineteenth century was the most obviously important factor in the spread of democracy despite all who denied it. As England's population multiplied, the average standard of living, however measured, rose. "There is not a poor man in England who is not conscious that he is vastly better off ... than his grandfather was," the American editor E.L. Godkin observed in 1888. The hungry 1840s had been left far behind, even if large inequalities remained. British author Arnold Bennett in 1909 thought that only about 1 million out of 40 in his country could be called prosperous. In his famous study of poverty in England, Seebohm Rowntree (1900) estimated that nearly 30 percent lived below a tolerable standard of existence. There were still plain evidences of

social and economic inequality. But a huge movement of popular ameliora-
tion had been set on foot, and with material improvement were bound to
come demands for equality.

Continuing Criticism of Democracy

Looking further ahead, we see that in fact democracy still had few friends
among the literate. John Stuart Mill's remark that democracy had come
without anyone among the intellectual classes wanting it was very nearly
true, for Europe at least. Major intellects continued to think of democracy as the deplorable habit of settling matters of importance by majority
vote. This view of democracy as an irrational principle, opposed to reason, was never made clearer than in a passage from Ernest Renan, prominent French essayist of the 1848–71 era, often associated with scientific
positivism.

> It is clear that the absolute reign of one portion of humanity over another is
> odious, if we suppose the governing body to be swayed only by personal or
> class egoism; but the aristocracy of which I dream would be the incarnation
> of reason: a papacy of true infallibility. Power, in its hands, could not but be
> beneficial.[1]

Renan, or his spokesperson in this dialogue, even suggests "unlimited terror
in the service of truth." The antidemocratic spokesman goes on to excoriate
democracy for tending to "lower the race" and for its hostility to genius.

The century's leading philosopher, Hegel, was no democrat, retaining the
Enlightenment's belief in reason as "trained intelligence" rather than simply
"a matter of people." He tended to locate reason—the Absolute Spirit
whose self-unfolding was the essence of history—in the thinking portion of
humankind, an intellectual elite whose wisdom stood in contrast to the
hopeless ignorance and misjudgment of the toiling masses. Democracy was,
to him, a form that had become obsolete in the modern state; it belonged to
a bygone era of small communities. In the last year of his life the greatest
thinker of his age opposed the British Reform Bill, enacted in 1832 to
extend the right to vote somewhat (but by no means to all) and to make
representation fairer.

Hegel's fellow historian, the versatile British writer and statesman
Thomas Macaulay, agreed that universal suffrage could only mean a new
despotism, "fatal to all the purposes for which government exists; utterly
incompatible with the very existence of civilization." This was largely because only a few can understand the intricate science of political economy,
which is essential to human well-being. It is "the most difficult of all the

sciences," leading economist Nassau Senior thought. Ignorant voters were tempted to tamper with political economy's often unpleasant prescriptions, in the interest of some apparent short-term advantage. If, indeed, the world is ruled by such laws as the economists had discovered, then the concept of government as the willed action of any ruling group becomes almost irrelevant; for what controls our destiny is not deliberate decisions, based on our hopes, our ambitions, our interests, but great forces that operate impersonally on large units, perhaps global ones, via the marketplace.

Though a leader in Britain of the fight against privilege and aristocracy, the manufacturer, Quaker, and member of Parliament John Bright said, "I do not pretend to be a democrat." An enthusiastic liberal believer in laissez-faire or negative government, Bright held that if we must have government, the sort guided by adepts in the high art of economic theory is far better than the kind subject to the whims of an unenlightened populace stirred by demagogues. Again, we see a faith in absolute standards of truth against which an appeal to electoral majorities seemed simply obscurantist.

Political economy, the sensational new study that grew from eighteenth-century beginnings to flourish in the nineteenth century, may be regarded as the chief perpetuator of the Enlightenment faith in a science of society. Its antidemocratic bias existed despite a leveling element in the creed of the marketplace, whereby everybody is equal, "each counts as one." This ultimate liberalism pared away every kind of social distinction to establish cash as the great equalizer; each one of us has the right to bring his produce and his wants to the market and let the outcome of this trucking and bartering determine what is produced at what price, and what income each derives from this process. But because few people can understand and adhere to this austere order, its rules have to be upheld by the government of an enlightened minority. Recent liberal economists such as Ludwig von Mises, F.A. Hayek, and Walter Eucken, who stress the close connection between democracy and free-market capitalism, concede that the market requires a long and difficult preparation before it can function effectively.

Close to the economists, and virtually their philosophical underpinning, was the Utilitarianism of Jeremy Bentham. Benthamism has been claimed as modern democracy's intellectual ancestor. According to E.H. Carr (*The New Society*, 1951), it "laid the theoretical foundations of mass democracy in Britain." Though Bentham did come to believe in political equality, his final inclination evidently was to restrict the vote to literate adult males. His principle of maximizing pleasure and minimizing pain leaves no room for qualitative distinctions: one person's happiness is as good as another's. Bentham was briefly a convert to democracy in 1790 but slid back under the impact of the French Revolution and did not return to it until 1809, when he was sixty-one. He was inconsistent on the details but at one time even favored the vote for women, as his partial disciple John Stuart Mill did (unsuccessfully) later.

But the followers of Bentham did not in fact mount any great campaign for political democracy. They showed a greater inclination to revert to his original preference for enlightened despotism or elitism. They wished to reform institutions and maximize efficiency via administrative leadership. Clearly for Bentham democracy was a means, not an end. The utilitarian impulse did attack all manner of ancient privileges and institutions, in the interest of equality for all under the law. With an admiration for the United States, Bentham and his followers opposed the monarchy, the established church, the titled aristocracy. But, essentially a figure of the Enlightenment, Bentham could not escape its preference for a rule of reason via the intellectual class.

Other nineteenth-century liberals agreed in disliking the democratic principle of majority power or popular control of government. Classical liberalism presented itself as the triumph of individualism over despotism *and democracy*. Benjamin Constant, the leading theoretician of early nineteenth-century French liberalism, saw "unlimited popular sovereignty" as "an evil no matter in whose hands it is placed." Likewise, Tocqueville, perhaps the greatest liberal of this liberal era between circa 1815 and 1848, when the in-word was *liberty*, made the contradiction between liberty and democracy the guiding theme of his memorable *Democracy in America* (1835–40). The masses, Tocqueville thought, produce a culture that blights individual creativity by imposing a "tyranny of the majority." Majority rule, whether of the mind or the body, oppresses the free individual, especially anyone not cut from the standard mold. John Stuart Mill, influenced by Tocqueville, qualified his support for democracy by warning against its insidious leveling effect, its intimidation of free spirits and nonconformists. "It will no longer be a despot that oppresses the individual," Gustave Flaubert thought, "but the masses."

Classical liberalism and political economy found a mortal foe during the early nineteenth century, to be sure, in Romanticism. Poets intoxicated by this new mode of expression were in a state of rebellion against the low materialism of the eighteenth century, when "soul was extinct and stomach well alive," as Thomas Carlyle exclaimed. This included above all the economists' hedonistic calculus. Nothing infuriated Coleridge so much as the "pig philosophy" of Bentham; Carlyle raved against the gospel of mammon. But this scarcely made them democrats. Coleridge opposed extending the vote in 1832; Carlyle called for heroes and hero worship.

Romanticism was far from a single thing, and some basic versions of it contain a sort of democratic impulse. Literature was to be sought among the plain people, even if Wordsworth's peasants and Herder's "folk" existed more in their imagination than in reality. Classicism, against whose aesthetic canons the Romantics revolted, is "rational, aloof, and aristocratic," Wyndham Lewis once pointed out, while Romanticism is "popular, sensational, and cosmically confused" (*Time and Western Man*, 1927). A confirmed classicist himself, Lewis added that "no artist can ever love democracy." Metternich, the 1815–48 era's prime conservative, was an Enlightenment rationalist (and a keen student of the sciences) who disliked Romanticism, which he tended to call "mysticism"; the European "order" that he defended he thought was founded on reason. Romanticism, to him, stood for unchecked freedom, the uncontrollable powers of the imagination, the destruction of authority; as such it might lead almost anywhere but almost certainly subverted any kind of order.

"Herder taught to the young Goethe," Walt Whitman recalled, "that really great poetry is always . . . the result of a national spirit, and not the privilege of a polished and select few." What interested these poets, of course, was poetry. They found a new source of it, a great renewal of language, in popular traditions and in what they thought was the speech of the people. (It is difficult to believe that Wordsworth really had much in common with English plowmen.) This was associated with nationalism and with democracy as an aspect of nationalism. All these ideas blended in an intoxicating mixture.

Whatever attraction existed between some Romantics and an idealized people, their dominant interest hovered around the self, the unusual self— usually their own unusual, unhappy consciousness. The misanthropic Byronic hero despising the crowd, full of *Menschenhass;* the soaring individual genius rising far above the "unforeseeing multitudes"—these were the Romantic exemplars. The individual self, lonely or creative, narcissist or proud, if it did not exactly make its debut here, assumed a significance not hitherto known in the course of European history. Beginning with the Swiss-born Jean-Jacques Rousseau, the unique human self received endorsement in the most profound philosophical thought of the era, that of Immanuel Kant and German Romanticism. Such basic individualism clashes with democracy; for the autonomous individual requires protection against any external authority, and a democratic one can be as oppressive, indeed more oppressive, than a monarchical one. One wants to be oneself against the crowd, perhaps a rebel, a minority of one for truth. Like Henry David Thoreau, one does not relish being pursued by those "who paw him with their dirty institutions, and, if they can, constrain him to belong to their desperate odd-fellow society."

Romanticism was dubiously democratic; if it overthrew the grounds on which an undemocratic authority rested, it transferred authority not to the masses but to the creative imagination of the rare poetic soul. The great Romantic poets tended to be of humble birth. Not always, of course, for Byron was of a noble family, Hugo the son of a general, George Sand the illegitimate daughter of an aristocrat. But most of them came from much lower in the social scale. John Clare was a farm laborer, John Keats the son of a livery stable manager, William Blake the son of a haberdasher, Tom Moore the son of a grocer. They did not for that reason care much for the hoi polloi.

Democracy and Progress

Absolutist rationalism continued throughout the century to be a foe of democracy in that it put the truths discovered by scientific reason above the opinions of the multitude and looked to a ruling priesthood of seers or scientists. As a legitimizer of causes, however, it was joined, if not superseded, after 1815 by history. (Reason and history are the same, Hegel argued, in the age's leading philosophical idea, but most practicing historians were inclined to doubt it.) In politics at least, reason had proved a fallible and even dangerous guide. In his important and influential critique of the French revolutionaries, Edmund Burke had referred to the "fallible and feeble contrivances of human reason." So far as concerns politics, there are no general rules and principles, no formal logic; we must lean on the fabric of custom and tradition, built into our culture as precedents, that represents the collective wisdom of many centuries. Compared to this body of complex understandings, the ideas of some simple-minded reformer with a plan for the redemption of the race are indeed laughable. "Abbé Sieyes," Burke wrote scornfully, "has whole nests of pigeon-holes full of constitutions ready made." But constitutions are not to be selected from the wares of political theorists. They have to grow like a great tree from the soil of a country over many centuries.

The eighteenth-century philosophers had tended to reject history (i.e., tradition) because the customs of the past seemed to support the authority of kings rather than the liberty of subjects. John Locke at the time of the Glorious Revolution of 1688, like the Fifth Monarchy men earlier, appealed rather to nature, or to an ideal past rather than the actual past. In hypothesizing an original human "state of nature" followed by a "social compact," the natural rights theorists did not pretend that any such things had actually happened, nor did they much care; this was what should have happened, and in some ideal sense did happen.

But reason and nature had fallen into disrepute, while the dynamic French Revolutionary era had engendered a sense of change. Everyone in the years from 1789 to 1815 became aware of the instability and inconstancy of human society, perhaps for the first time in European history; this was literally the discovery of change. The Revolution had swept away ten centuries of long uncontested institutions, only to fail and fall itself and to be replaced by a new kind of monarch (Napoleon), who himself went down in flames, leaving open the question of what the future held for Europe. It was as impossible to go back to the old pre-1789 order, though a few tried, as it was to find any certain new principles of stability. "The people who have gone through 1789 and 1814 bear two wounds in their hearts," Alfred de Musset wrote, ascribing to these wounds "all the sickness of the present century."

"The times are pregnant with change," young John Stuart Mill wrote in his 1831 essay "The Spirit of the Age." "The nineteenth century will be known to posterity as the era of one of the greatest revolutions of which history has preserved the remembrance, in the human mind, and in the whole constitution of human society." Historical systems, plans of human evolution through various stages, appeared on all sides. Auguste Comte, the French Positivist and founder of sociology, offered a stage theory, as did Hegel; Karl Marx was to improve upon them. Meanwhile more earthbound historians began the systematic, professional discipline of history, ransacking the archives and examining the sources with a new critical rigor.

Reason itself was converted into a progression, truth being developed via a series of events spread across time, not by a static analysis. Endowed with teleology, the forward movement of history appealed to all sorts of people as a substitute for nondialectical reason. Kant and Hegel were only the loftier peaks in this new landscape. Historicizing political ideologies sprang up everywhere, among liberals such as Benjamin Constant and socialists in the era of Saint-Simon, Leroux, and others. With pretensions more or less to real scholarship, they wrote histories showing how the path of human development was marked by the birth, growth, and eventual fulfillment of liberty, the nation, or socialism. History was the story of progress toward some definite goal, which varied according to the author's outlook.

It may be noted that a simple idea of progress logically entails democracy. If we are to attain a perfect condition, obviously it is more perfect if all attain it; this is rather like the medieval ontological argument for God's existence, that there is a greater perfection in something that actually exists. As the idea of secular progress seized hold of the nineteenth-century popular mind and became its chief principle of faith, it inevitably carried democracy with it. Writing about that celebration of progress, the great 1851

Crystal Palace industrial exhibition, Dr. Whewell, master of Trinity College, Oxford, and schoolmaster to Victorian England, defined progress in the arts and sciences as their extension from the service of the few to the service of the many.

In any case the discovery of change and the passion for history tended to endow whatever happened with value. Hegel was accused of teaching that "[w]hatever is, is right." If it is not right, then it is certainly entitled to respect, as a possible direction signal on the uncharted sea on which people felt themselves to be. "Can we never drop anchor for a single day/On the ocean of the ages?" Lamartine wondered. Thomas Arnold felt around 1825 that "[w]e have been living the life of 300 years in 30." This sense of being adrift, borne on powerful currents toward some unknown destination, was common for some time after 1815. One possible answer supposed that the course of human history has its own immanent logic, which will eventually reveal the divine purpose, and that one must therefore surrender to whatever seems to be the manifest spirit of the age. So the evident actual spread of democracy gave it credibility.

The Revolutions of 1848

The explosions of rebellion in one European city after another in 1848—in Paris, in the cities of both southern and northern Italy, in German cities, and in the imperial capital of Vienna where Prince Metternich presided over the attempt to stabilize Europe around legitimate monarchs—resulted from the widespread feeling that some denouement had to take place, something that would make the future of Europe at last clear.

Democracy was involved in it; the 1840s saw a surge of rhetorical passion for the people, of which the oratory of Giuseppe Mazzini was only one example. Guizot, historian and classical liberal, trying to govern France as chief minister of King Louis Philippe, declared that "every party invokes democracy and wishes to appropriate it as a talisman." Who wanted to be known as an enemy of the people? But we must again notice that democracy was seldom regarded as an end in itself but rather as the means to some end. Just to have a lot of people acting and voting was of no importance; it was what they were trying to bring about that counted. In 1848 the positive goals, the leading causes, were liberalism, socialism, and nationalism.

Liberals wanted equal rights under the law, "a fair field and no favors," the career open to talents; they wanted legal protection for property, law and order, free commerce; they wanted to do away with all manner of government restrictions on free trade and in general severely restrict the powers of the state to interfere in private affairs. Government should content itself with "preventing crime and enforcing contracts." Led by the new manufacturing class of owners and employers, this classical liberalism wanted democracy only insofar as it gave equal rights and prestige to the new bourgeois class of commoners, against the aristocracy. Its adherents held serious reservations about giving the vote to everybody. They were not the less committed and sincere in their push for drastic political change.

Socialists, of whom the period 1815–48 produced a bumper crop, replied that this liberty was a fraud, because it helped only the wealthier owners of property, the employers and the merchants, while leaving the poor worse off than before, deprived of what protection they might have had under the old feudal or patrimonial society. As Harold Laski wrote, socialism arose from the realization that "the liberal ideal secured to the middle class its full share of privilege, while it left the proletariat in its chains." Socialists wanted an end to private property or its sweeping regulation; most of them wanted a strong state. The leading socialist theoretician Henri Saint-Simon, like his mentor Auguste Comte, conceived of an authoritarian government run by engineers and other experts planning the economy and running it like one huge factory in the interest of greater efficiency. They had little interest in elections, none in government by the masses. (See chapter 4 for a discussion of socialism and democracy.)

Lord Shaftesbury, the leading English humanitarian of his time in Parliament, admiring the achievements of Napoleon III in the 1850s, said that any working man who saw them and compared France to England would cry, "Long live despotism! Down with free governments!" Utilitarian reformers like the engineer Edwin Chadwick, struggling to save London from dying of typhus and cholera, found it hard to wait on the slow processes of parliamentary government. All those interested in getting something done preferred an enlightened despotism.

Louis Blanc, leading French socialist of the 1840s, seemed to have believed that, given the vote, the people would choose socialism. In 1848 the vote was extended to all Frenchmen, a huge expansion overnight of the extremely restricted suffrage established in 1830. But the voters, countryfolk in the large majority, did not vote for the Parisian socialist intellectuals. They gave their preference for president to another Bonaparte, who proceeded within three years to overthrow the 1848 Republic and establish himself as emperor.

Nationalism, represented above all by the eloquent Italian Romanticist and revolutionary Mazzini, paid its respects to democracy in seeing everyone as equal citizens of the national state, *enfants de la patrie*. All other claims to special status must be swept aside to make way for this mystical community of all the (national) people. Nationalism to Mazzini was a religion, its main function to provide humanity with something viable to believe in thus inspiring people to heroic action. With his friend Thomas Carlyle, Mazzini shared a yearning for new heroes along with a new, secular religion—a *nouveau Christianisme* perhaps, as Saint-Simon wished. There was a socialist strain here (Mazzini called it "association") in that the people of a nation must sacrifice and abjure all other loyalties to stand together as brothers under the flag. The democratic element is obvious, but it was subordinate to nationalism; the people exist to form the nation, to be Italians first and foremost. As such they are equal in all respects.

Like the other ideologists, nationalists could turn antidemocratic if the people deserted them; they would seek the desired national unification and expulsion of foreign domination by other means. In the failed revolutions of 1848, contradictions appeared all over the place: between democracy and liberalism, democracy and socialism, democracy and nationalism, as well as between liberalism, socialism, and nationalism. The revolutionary movement stumbled and fell over these contradictions, and within a year or two the old authorities had returned. In 1848 the people of Rome forced the pope to flee from the city in disguise, and Mazzini headed a short-lived Roman republic; French soldiers under the command of Bonaparte, elected by universal suffrage, overthrew the Roman republic and restored the pope to power.

In general, the ideologists of 1848 emerged with their faith in the people badly shaken. The more I see of people the more I love my dogs, said the poet Lamartine, who had briefly headed the 1848 French Republic. George Sand discovered that the people she had idealized were really "blind, credulous, ignorant, ungrateful, wicked, and bestial" (some of their finer points). Countless disavowals of this sort may be illustrated by one from the English Chartist George Julian Harney, who had fought for universal manhood suffrage as one of the basic demands of the People's Charter: "I have not the slightest confidence or belief in the class towards whose political and social emancipation I gave the best years of my life," he wrote in his old age. Conservatives found fresh reasons to mistrust the mob, of course. As in 1789–94, democracy came badly out of the whole experience, and once again the search for a new order seemed sadly frustrated.

Nevertheless it is often noted that the universal suffrage so abruptly introduced into France in 1848 has never since ceased to exist. The next dictator, Napoleon III, had himself confirmed by a vote of the people. France, someone said, was less the victim than the accomplice of his 1851 coup d'état, which converted the Second Republic into the Second Empire. After that there would be a Third Republic, then a Fourth, then a Fifth, none of them much liked, interspersed with threats of another plebiscitary Caesarism. But all of these regimes rested in some sense on majority public opinion. Is it democracy if the masses do not want democracy?

Note

1. *Philosophical Dialogues and Fragments* (1871), trans. London, 1883; reprinted in Frank E. Manuel and Fritzie P. Manuel, eds., *French Utopias: An Anthology of Ideal Societies* (New York: Free Press, 1966).

4

The Late Nineteenth-Century Crisis of Democracy

Practical Successes

In roughly the last half of the nineteenth century, the overall climate of opinion changed greatly, from the soaring hopes and dreams of the Romantic age that culminated in the revolutions of 1848 to a soberer time of industrial progress and scientific success. During this crucial period democracy both gained and lost. It lost much of its earlier aura of romantic radicalism as it underwent embourgeoisement and became respectable. As democracy of the second kind, not wild and French but British and pragmatic, even conservative, it made slow but steady progress, finally to become accepted, almost faute de mieux, as the least intolerable form of government. At the same time, and by the same token, it ceased to interest, even disgusted, a crowd of increasingly alienated artists and intellectuals. Opposition to democracy from the Left was something quite new.

This practical progress amid growing disenchantment was characteristic of the age in general, of course. Mazzini lived to see Italy united, but this outcome, which one would have thought fulfilled all his dreams, left him crushed, "all my Italian pride gone," because of the quite un-Romantic way it was accomplished: by cunning diplomacy and power politics, by people whom the great romantic-nationalist-democrat called "opportunists and cowards and little Machiavellis," not by a popular uprising led by heroes. Comparable was the postwar dismay of American Civil War radicals who saw slavery end only to usher in the Gilded Age of booming capitalism and corrupt politics. A novel like Trollope's *The Way We Live Now* reveals a similar disgust at greed, corruption, the decay of gentility in England, something even more characteristic of Louis Napoleon's Second Empire. The idealism of the German 48-ers faded into Realpolitik; numbers of them migrated to the United States, others as National Liberals accepted Bismarck's authoritarian regime as the price of political and material success.

Yet it was exactly at this time that democracy advanced, along with technology and increasing material wealth, most unevenly distributed. The respectable classes lost their fear of what would happen if the masses gained power. In 1858 Lord Greville, recording in his celebrated diary an enormously enthusiastic reception given to Queen Victoria in Birmingham, commented that such increasingly frequent demonstrations "evince a disposition in those masses of the population in which, if anywhere, the seeds of Radicalism are supposed to lurk, most favorable to the Conservative cause. . . . There is so little [danger] to be apprehended from the extension of the suffrage, that universal suffrage itself would be innocuous." And indeed in 1867 Britain widened suffrage in a move furiously opposed by a small number of embattled reactionaries but now supported by both major political parties; the astute Disraeli, chief of the Conservatives, had also discovered that the working class is in fact conservative. "Shooting Niagara," as the old Carlyle called the 1867 gamble, turned out to be easy. The British masses dropped their pre-1848 radicalism to spend the next decades cheering for the patrician Oxford scholar turned democratic leader William Ewart Gladstone.

Converts to democracy included the authors of the prodemocratic *Essays on Reform* (1867), A.V. Dicey, Leslie Stephen, Goldwin Smith, and James Bryce; the latter was soon to write the classic late nineteenth-century study of American democracy. Lord Acton came to believe that "democracy is what divides us least." It is remarkable that Matthew Arnold's famous essays on democracy are so relatively sympathetic; a few years later such a fastidiously aesthetic and tradition-conscious humanist almost certainly would have screamed his disgust at democracy for ruining civilization, but Arnold, writing in 1869 (*Culture and Anarchy*), tended to blame the impoverished state of culture on the masses less than on the classes, who provide no worthy example. Meanwhile in the great stream of Victorian literature "the setting of tragedy moves to the abodes of the humble," Mario Praz wrote in his study *The Hero in Eclipse* (1956). Though by 1857 Charles Dickens had given up on parliamentary democracy, his fundamental influence, as Chesterton recognized in an eloquent tribute, was democratic in showing that every human being, even the humblest, is interesting. And perhaps it is to Dickens that all those paeans to the common man, from Walt Whitman, Edward Carpenter, and others, ultimately derived:

> Crowds of men and women attired in the usual costumes! how curious you
> are to me!
>
> —Whitman

This change toward democracy was related to a more general shift in attitudes that was taking place in roughly the first half of the nineteenth century. Writing in 1861, Thackeray exclaimed: "In this [last] quarter of a century, what a silent revolution has been working! how it has separated us from the old times and manners!" Thackeray associated it with the decline of gambling, drunkenness, and dueling among the English upper classes. William Wilberforce, upon his retirement from the House of Commons in 1825 after forty-five years of service, spoke of that body's transformation in this period from an assemblage of alcoholic and brawling rakes to a sober deliberative chamber. This silent revolution is frequently associated with Wilberforce's own cause, that of the Evangelical movement within the Church of England, which had begun as a reaction against the infidel French during the era of the French Revolution and Napoleon. Others would point to the ascendancy of the middle class. Queen Victoria made herself a symbol of the new respectability in England but was hardly its cause. A general softening of manners and tastes affected criminal law, ending executions for minor offenses, for example, and, by 1867, public hangings. Prison reform, the temperance movement, outlawing of brutal sports were other aspects of this greater sensitivity to human life and suffering.

"Both the political and social state of the country have greatly changed, and are changing every day," John Stuart Mill observed in 1859, with special regard to freeing the voter from intimidation by "the higher and richer classes" (*Thoughts on Parliamentary Reform*). As he noted, in former times such was their power that "the habit of voting at the bidding of an employer, or of a landlord, was so firmly established that hardly anything was capable of shaking it." But he thought this was no longer true. "The higher classes are not now masters of the country." Both the middle and the working classes had become less subservient. This was "the temper of the times," which Mill could only attribute to "the events of the past quarter of a century."

Of these events it is clear that to him the most important were connected with the rise to dominance in society of a "commercial class," the middle class, Marx's bourgeoisie or capitalist class, and, even more important, of a utilitarian or practical mentality. "What grows on the world is a certain matter-of-factness," Walter Bagehot observed. Mill spoke of "a positive, matter-of-fact spirit" and of "the dogmatism of common sense." (See his essay on Tocqueville's *Democracy in America*.) The reigning school of philosophy in France at midcentury was positivism, in Britain utilitarianism. This was a respect for practical things, of science insofar as it meant useful results, of the experimentally verifiable as the only kind of knowledge worth bothering with. The new mentality disdained art, religion (except as practical rules of conduct), and the past in general. In brief, it bordered on philistinism. In *Hard Times* Dickens flayed it as inhuman, and it is not coincidental that the great writer disliked democracy almost as much as utilitarianism. Mill accused Tocqueville of confusing the democratic and the commercial spirit, but in fact the two things were closely bound up together. And they jointly declared war on culture, driving sensitive souls into embittered opposition. They were both egalitarian, and whenever there is equality, it was noted, quality ceases to exist.[1]

The success of the United States of America played a notable part in the acceptance of democracy, of course. It was the great test case, especially after 1830 (though it had been important earlier among the Benthamites, who praised the Americans for abolishing monarchs and lords and, as they thought, all old institutions), and it passed the test. Tocqueville's notable inquest gave American democracy credit for proving that popular rule need not imperil property rights or destroy morals and religion. The United States was in general a conservative society in these respects (and, indeed, in others: an English visitor in 1832, G.T. Vigne, claimed that "[t]here is an aristocracy in every city of the Union"). Given their head, the people will not run amok to burn and pillage; they will preserve what is now their own, they will create an orderly and law-abiding society. Europeans continued to deplore American manners and sometimes doubt American capacity for high intellectual achievement—a criticism that was harder to assert after the great generation of Emerson—but it became impossible to claim, as formerly, that no example of a successful democratic state existed. The American Civil War, which stirred British opinion deeply, seemed to vindicate the democratic principle (though opinion was divided, some claiming the Confederate States stood for democracy in the sense of minority rights).

The debate about America at all times played a key role in European thinking about democracy. Antidemocrats and anti-Americans argued that such success as the United States had achieved was due to unusually favorable circumstances; democracy is a system so expensive and wasteful it can survive only where a sparse population lives amid a wealth of natural resources. In return, pro-Americans and prodemocrats such as the historian George Grote blamed bad American traits on this dispersal of population and lack of settled life, which in time would be overcome.

Erskine May's *Democracy in Europe* (1878) supplies a good example of the altered, friendlier perception of democracy. If the masses had given their votes to conservatives in France in 1848 and 1849, so also the conservative vote of 1867 in Germany helped soften bourgeois fears of democracy there; after Bismarck's spectacular success in diplomacy and war led to the unification of Germany, there was no question of popular discontent.

"The conversion of the mass of French peasants to faith in a democratic republic" came in 1871–76, asserts David Thomson. Partly this was because the Empire had failed so badly; as Edmond About declared in 1872, "[N]o folly or instability of democracy could exceed the caprices of princes." But the new constitutional arrangements introduced after the 1871 debacle reflected a strain of French liberal conservatism, represented by Charles Renouvier and Jacques Prévost-Paradol, who turned toward what they called liberal democracy as an alternative to the revolutionary or Jacobin type, which had made such a disturbing appearance in 1871 in the Commune of Paris. A liberal democracy contained safeguards against too much popular control, such as an upper legislative chamber with longer terms and stricter qualifications for office, indirectly elected, like the American Senate. The French Senate did to some extent live up to conservative expectations, serving as a brake on the Chamber of Deputies and, though revised in 1884, not losing all its powers as the British House of Lords did twenty-five years later. It provided representation for the generally conservative French countryside against the radical Left and thus sustained a workable balance in much-divided France, at the cost of an *immobilisme* that inhibited adjustments in a rapidly changing technological era. (France was woefully late, for example, in establishing a social security system.) To the extent that it achieved immobility, Third Republic France supported a theory about democracy sometimes proposed, that a perfect democracy would result in a totally static society, since it perfectly represented all the groups and interests within that society.

The old animosity between democracy and liberalism vanished almost overnight, as a democratic suffrage proved to be no prelude to a seizure of property as had so often been predicted. This new alliance or détente between democracy and liberalism cast the democratic electorate as part of a pluralistic society in which such checks on popular sovereignty as an independent judiciary, local governments, an upper chamber of the legislature, and constitutional guarantees of property and free speech stand guard against majority despotism, while permitting a measure of popular influence.

By the end of the century French industrialists and bishops alike had rallied to the Republic they had once reviled. France's shattering defeat by Prussia in 1870 forced Emperor Napoleon III to abdicate, and after an interlude of civil war a bewildered France came out with a republic no one wanted. It survived for want of an alternative, because "it divides us least." Initially monarchists and other conservatives despised it, while the socialist-anarchist Left hated it for having bloodily repressed the attempted secession of Paris in 1871. It was supposed to be temporary. But as the French came to say, "Nothing lasts like the provisional."

John Stuart Mill defined such a democracy as the open society in which everyone has access to the podium but none may impose his views by the sword, and in which the people do not govern but are able to call their governors to account when necessary. Historian John Vincent complained that Mill could find nothing better to say of the people than that their superiors are even worse. But this was, after all, a considerable concession. Some thought a further extension of the right to vote in 1884 in Great Britain, to embrace just about all male heads of households, would spell doom for the Tories, already doing poorly in Gladstone's era. But in 1886 they began twenty years of almost unbroken power. After an interlude they returned to continue doing well; the Conservatives held office between 1918 and 1929, save one year; also 1931–45, 1951–64, 1970–74, 1979–96—besting their Liberal and Labour rivals in the twentieth century by a margin of about 2 to 1. This in the land of advanced industrialism and the proletariat was dramatic proof either of popular maturity or popular gullibility, depending on your point of view.

Far from being a utopia, democracy came to be looked upon as almost the exact opposite—a remedy for utopias. Georges Clemenceau cynically explained that democracy is "the least intolerable of the various frightful evils." This was much the same answer given by Lord James Bryce in his book *Modern Democracies* (1921): "However grave the indictment that may be brought against democracy, its friends can answer, 'What better alternative do you offer?' " Democracy had become not the glorious cause of radical reform but a rather tame, perhaps even sinister, consensus of professional politicians mediating the claims of various interests. But it seemed to work better than any Caesarism. Who could agree on the Caesar?

With its gradual acceptance by the bourgeoisie, rebels and radicals lost interest in the democratic or republican principle per se and turned to socialism or some other radical plan of social reconstruction. They began to find grave flaws in bourgeois democracy. They would even look upon it, as Georges Sorel did, as "the greatest error of the past century."

The Secession of the Intellectuals

It is a well-known fact that the gulf between the populace and an intellectual and artistic elite grew much greater in the latter half of the nineteenth century. The separation had tended, earlier, to exist but to be less of a chasm. Christopher Kent, in *Brains and Numbers: Elitism, Comtism, and Democracy in Mid-Victorian England* (1978), deals with a group including such worthies as John Morley, James Bryce, A.V. Dicey, and Leslie Stephen, who worried about high culture in a low democratic age but "were in no sense alienated intellectuals" and in fact hesitantly cast their lot with democracy in 1867. Most of the Victorian worthies, the great men of letters led by Mill, Arnold, and Ruskin, were often scathing critics of the dominant society, especially of the taste and morals of the reigning middle class, but they also had an almost official standing in that society, as licensed preachers whose function was to scold the established order but who never dreamed of overthrowing it.

After 1848 on the Continent many disillusioned intellectuals totally lost faith in the populace. The civilized minority turned toward art or science, widening the gulf between them and the masses so that it became a pronounced feature of fin de siècle Europe. To Arthur Schopenhauer, a spokesman for this aesthetic-aristocratic reaction, the mass was simply "the stupid, the weak, and the commonplace." As early as 1844 Karl Marx's teacher Bruno Bauer came to believe that "the mass is the true enemy of the spirit." This secession of the intellectuals and artists continued with mounting intensity toward the end of the century in Nietzsche and the Symbolist poets, who totally rejected a social milieu marked as much by vulgar democracy as by bourgeois greed; the two things had joined to create a sickening philistinism from which the sensitives, Nietzsche's homeless ones, fled in horror. Art, proclaimed the leading Symbolist poet Mallarmé, can never be democratic: "Man can be democratic, but the artist goes his own way and ought to remain an aristocrat."

That state of "permanent opposition to society at large which has come to characterize the modern avant-garde," as Peter Jelavich calls it, may well have begun earlier, with the "unhappy consciousness" of post-Revolution Romantics. Rousseau himself in his last, half-mad years felt himself completely cut off from the human race as he wrote his "Reveries of a Solitary Walker." "I see no other salvation for the poetic genius than to withdraw from the real world," Schiller declared. Richard Terdiman wrote in 1976 of "a hundred-year old tradition of attempts to understand why living has become unlivable." It went on from Stendahl to Sartre, through a variety of strategies. Romantic nostalgia was followed by Realistic irony, Symbolist withdrawal, Modernist perversity. The sense of alienation gained in intensity with each abandoned strategy, as the pain became ever more unendurable. By the end of the century the outcry against what one character in a Decadent novel called "a hideous society" had swelled to "a scream of horror."

In an essay titled "The England of Marx and Mill as Reflected in Fiction," historian William O. Aydelotte noted that critics of social conditions in the 1840s—Dickens, Charles Kingsley, Gaskell—all "showed little sympathy for democracy." They saw the social problem essentially in moral terms, calling for a spiritual revolution against selfishness. Like their master Thomas Carlyle, they brushed aside any mere matter of electing representatives to a Talking Shop, which reminded them of an abhorred utilitarianism. Dickens's contempt for parliamentary democracy and general despair of democracy is well-known. Confronted with actual examples of unreconstructed human beings, Romantic reformers were apt to call them stupid asses, as Marx did. They hoped by some means to mold these torpid masses into an ideal humanity.

In Nietzsche's generation this drastic alienation was more often expressed as hostility to democracy. A few decades earlier, Romanticists might have said the people are sound and blamed the evils on capitalism or some other force of corruption that might be overcome. That illusion vanished. For one thing, the people was so obviously an abstract idea, a myth: "This 'People' is nothing but the great soul of Mazzini," Benedetto Croce observed of one democratic ideologue (who in practice, long before Lenin, strove to create an elitist vanguard revolutionary party to seize power and *install* democracy).

Severely doused at midcentury, democratic hopes survived but dimly among the civilized minority, who in turning away in disgust from politics cultivated their aesthetic sensibilities the more. They now took up a position high in the ivory tower and affected scorn for the disgraceful scenes in the marketplace and city streets. The hero of Joris Huysmans's significant novel *Against Nature* (1884) quite literally cuts his ties to the world and goes to live on a remote hill among his treasures of art. Joyce's persona Stephen Dedalus dreams of flying up from Dublin's dirty streets to join Shakespeare and Dante in the empyrean. "But this I know, I hate the crowd!"—Walter Savage Landor's credo was a motto for almost the entire late nineteenth-century intelligentsia. (It has been argued that the term *intellectual* in its peculiarly modern denotation was first used at this time.)

This new class was not defined by wealth or rank, but by its shared values. "Every instinct of my body is antidemocratic, and I dread to think of what our England may become when Demos rules absolutely." Writing this at the end of the century, George Gissing (*The Private Papers of Henry Ryecroft*) added that it was not a matter of class; upper and lower are alike in being "blatant creatures" when they are en masse. This blatancy of the mass-men, the noisy dwarves as Nietzsche called them, the newspaper-reading "last men" of a sterile, trivializing culture, grated on the sensibility of the few whose intelligence, they thought, marked them off from the masses. Such people, defined by their sensibility, might come from almost any class. Gissing was a typical literary outcast leading a disreputable life in bohemia or grub street. H.G. Wells, who felt such disgust at the futility of "those clipped and limited lives" around him, was from the lower classes. Georges Sorel, who despised the *universitaires* as much as he did the parliamentarians, was a retired civil servant. The aristocrat Bertrand Russell, though in most moods a radical and a socialist, exclaimed in 1902 that "[t]his respect for the filthy multitude is ruining civilization!" He wished he had been a French aristocrat in the old regime, and according to his daughter, "He never did believe that men are born equal in ability, and he never felt at ease with stupid, ignorant or prejudiced people. . . . He was so used to considering the majority wrong that he felt comfortable only in opposition" (Katherine Tait, *My Father Bertrand Russell*).

In fact it was the consciousness of the literate minority as much as the "stupidity" of the masses of ordinary people that caused this hostility. The long tradition of European culture had created a body of thought and artistic expression intoxicatingly rich; it was now organized and available, in affordable books, journals, museums, concert halls that were part of that very urban, technological society the intellectuals affected to despise; many people formerly outside the aristocratic boundaries of this high culture could now enter it. This "civilized consciousness of Europe," as D.H. Lawrence called it, constituted a separate world in which those able to unlock its doors might live surrounded by endless delights of the mind and senses. But it was not "real" and it failed to match the world of producers and consumers, buyers and sellers, engineers and workmen, barkeepers and politicians, to all of whom "We and all the Muses are things of no account" (Yeats). "Action is not the sister of the dream," wrote Dostoevsky.

This is not the place to analyze the rise of the intellectuals and their encounter with mass culture, with which so much of the modern age has been filled. At the end of the nineteenth century this confrontation was at a peak, perhaps because both phenomena had just arisen. The dynamic nineteenth century had displaced millions from the traditional village environment to the suddenly swollen great cities, where a new kind of popular culture was in the throes of creation, often most alarmingly. At any rate cries of alarm sounded in chorus.

> It is a question of knowing whether in traversing this crisis humanity will not lose everything of genius, beauty, grandeur; it is a question of knowing whether, in this sullen and terrible adventure of the peoples, there is one which will not disappear from history.

Thus wrote Edmond Scherer in 1883 (*La Démocratie et la France*). This generation's brilliant crew of writers and artists was marked above all by an almost hysterical rejection of democracy in the sense of popular culture and majoritarianism. Likewise the Italian Futurist Marinetti described popularly elected parliaments as "noisy chicken coops, cow stalls, or sewers."

Such an estrangement between art and life had not been true, or at least less true, in former times. Among the ancient Greeks and in Shakespeare's time, there was little sense (despite Diogenes) that the artist-intellectual was totally at odds with mainstream society; art was an integral part of the predominant culture, something every Athenian and every Londoner could feel was his. The split between high culture and low, each sneering at the other, is a modern phenomenon, even though one may see it gradually rising from the eighteenth century on, since the emergence of the popular press. A long debate among British literary scholars established that there had long been a trash literature of cheap broadsheets and "penny dreadfuls"; a scatological gutter-press specializing in scandal appeared in quarters of Paris before the French Revolution, as Robert Darnton has shown. But this was clandestine, underground, segregated, hardly a threat to the civilized mind that reigned over the kingdom of the arts, ensconced in the salons and courts, the museums and concert halls of Europe. By the late nineteenth century, popular culture in the form of music halls and yellow journalism, as well as spectator sports (London saw football crowds as large as 100,000 by 1910), had grown to a point where it threatened to submerge the civilized tradition, confining it into a small, self-conscious coterie of defiant aesthetes.

Of course they included in their indictment of mass culture things such as commercialism, bourgeois crassness, and often, modern science too. Such different literary personalities as Strindberg and Tolstoy were in effect charter members of the flat earth society, while Yeats and a host of others dabbled in occultism and mysticism. They rejected the whole course of modern western progress and its annihilation of tradition, its vulgar materialism, its general shallowness of soul, its "sick hurry and divided aims" (Matthew Arnold). But of this disgusting amalgamation democracy was thought to be an integral part. "What the majority of the people think is stupid" became the motto of the civilized minority; Ibsen's Enemy of the People was their hero. A saying of Bruno's, "No man can be a lover of the true and the good unless he abhors the multitude," inspired the young James Joyce. Modern European literature, Lionel Trilling remarked in *The Liberal Imagination*, has been dominated by "men who are indifferent to, or even hostile to, the traditions of democratic liberalism as we know it." John R. Harrison, in *The Reactionaries* (1966), declared that the greatest poets of this century were, in his rather primitive typology, "fascists."

It is an extraordinary contradiction in the modern world, its foremost double bind, this dynamism that simultaneously produced cultureless masses and alienated artist-intellectuals.

Science versus Democracy

The criticism of democracy, however, involved something more than bruised aesthetic sensibilities. Artist-intellectuals often perceived the scientist as their enemy, one who stood on the side of democracy, an the enemy of art, beauty, spirituality, refinement, and a pillar of the dominant, mainstream society in all its crassness. There was some truth in this, for science was a popular idol. When C.P. Snow, in his manifesto *The Two Cultures* (1959), accused the "humanists" of deserting liberal democracy while the scientists were its true friends, he repeated a claim often made before. "The interests of science and the interests of democracy are one," thought late Victorian oracle John Morley, echoing pretty much what the popular French politician of the 1880s, Leon Gambetta, had meant when he said that "the locomotive is republican." A little later the great Dutch historian Johan Huizinga, no friend of democracy, found its very essence in a "mechanization of the spirit" induced by the quantifying habits of scientists (*America*, 1918). Sidney Kaplan cites the view that "the social mobilization of science" would "initiate a new type of democracy." Traditional cultures are unsuited to democracy largely because of an ingrained sense of hierarchy; the equality upon which democracy depends (each to count as one, majority rule) is indeed a "mathematical" thing; as Yeats wrote:

> And haughtier-headed Burke that proved the State a tree,
> That this unconquerable labyrinth of the birds, century after century,
> Cast but dead leaves to mathematical equality.

Still others thought they saw in science a kind of simple, easily learned method that undercut the obfuscations of metaphysics or mysticism; it was true knowledge for the masses, a faith expressed in C.T.R. Wilson's somewhat sexist belief—destined, alas, to be shot down in the Einstein era—that science could be made comprehensible even to barmaids. "Science was seen as an utterly legal-rational, therefore impersonal and democratic activity," Zygmant Bauman remarks in his *Hermeneutics and Social Science* (1978). Anybody could do it with the right method; it was not a matter of rare genius.

But elements in the scientific ethos clashed with democracy too. As we have already noticed, scientific rationalism's propensity to insist on its monopoly of truth portended a dictatorship of reason. Michael Bakunin once wrote that the rule of "scientific intellect" would be "the most autocratic, the most despotic, the most arrogant, and the most contemptuous of all regimes." The nineteenth-century proponent of scientific philosophy, Auguste Comte, was notably antidemocratic, calling popular sovereignty an "oppressive mystification." A disciple of the famous positivist was the reactionary French antidemocrat Charles Maurras, so influential in 1900–1914, who claimed to have a "scientific conception of politics"; in which claim, Guy-Grand wrote, "the anti-democratic doctrines thought they found their weightiest argument."

Slightly earlier (1871) the important French intellectual Ernest Renan dreamed of "forming through the universities a rationalist head of society, ruling by science . . ." and not inclined to surrender this power to "an ignorant crowd." Such a "papacy of true infallibility," an aristocracy that was "the incarnation of reason," was an old Enlightenment dream, now reenforced by the mounting prestige of science in the era of Louis Pasteur and Claude Bernard. Renan repeated Tocqueville's point that democracy levels down intellect, establishing a "tyranny of the majority" hostile to all fine and lofty thought; for the scientists as much as or more than the poets and artists this was a serious reproach. Many scientists (for example, the important popularizer Emil du Bois-Reymond) could echo Lucretius's old enjoyment of "the lofty peaks of sovereign skepticism" from which one contemplates with amused disdain "the buzzings of the vulgar tumult in the hot lowlands below." There were as many scientific ivory towers as poetic ones.

Across the Channel, Henry Maine, the weighty Victorian author of *Ancient Law*, in a much-quoted passage from his attack on *Popular Government* (1885), declaimed that universal suffrage "would have prohibited the spinning jenny and the power loom, along with the threshing machine," would have preserved the Gregorian calendar and barred vaccination, in effect would have vetoed scientific progress and technological change. H.G. Wells, sci-fi pioneer and prophet of the scientifically efficient organization of society—and a voice from well down in the lower ranks of society— believed that "democracy must pass away inevitably by its own inherent contradictions," the chief of which was its being based not on "any process of intellectual conviction" but on the vagaries of a largely ignorant public opinion ("The Life History of Democracy," 1901).

George Bernard Shaw was a believer in modern science, not an antiscientific aesthete, but his antidemocratic sentiments were equally strong; like that of his fellow Edwardian man of letters H.G. Wells, his case against democracy was that it is inefficient and irrational (see further in chapter 5). In Shaw's play *Major Barbara* Undershaft remarks that "670 fools become a government. Your pious mob fills up ballot papers and imagines it is governing its masters." To which Cusins responds, "That is perhaps why, like most intelligent people, I never vote."

To the late nineteenth century, science meant, more than anything else, Darwinian evolutionary naturalism, possibly the century's leading idea. When, in his *Popular Government*, Henry Maine claimed that "the opposition between democracy and science ... does not promise much for the longevity of popular governments," he had in mind chiefly the biologists. Le Bon, in his *Psychology of Socialism* (1899), devoted a chapter to "the conflict between the natural laws of evolution and the conceptions of the democrats." L.T. Hobhouse, unlike Maine and Le Bon sympathetic to democracy, agreed that among causes for the decline of democracy "by far the most potent" was the prevalent belief that science had given its vote for violence and against social justice, against "peace and equality between nations, cooperation between classes, and mercy and tenderness for the weaker brethren."[2] The French sociologist C. Bouglé, in his book *La Démocratie devant le science* (1904), cited T.H. Huxley on the absurdity of saying men are born free and equal, noting that foes of democracy such as Charles Maurras and Paul Bourget claimed to be the true heirs of the scientific spirit. As Edmond Scherer declared, "Democracy is equalitarian and inequality is a fact, an irreducible reality." Anyone claiming to be a disinterested follower of scientific methods could not be a democrat if by that term one meant human equality.

Thus the Darwinian challenge to democracy was seen as coming from both its antiegalitarianism and its Hobbesian destruction of a general will or will to cooperate. Neither of these was, strictly speaking, a blow against democracy so much as against a social meliorism that the democratic ideology had absorbed, a faith that society was growing both more egalitarian and more humanitarian. Social Darwinists might see democracy as capable of strengthening the social organism in its competition with other groups, which for some of them was the primary consideration. Karl Pearson viewed democracy as a scarcely affordable luxury because of its "terribly cumbersome" inefficiency, yet saw its possible value too as a means of organizing the masses. Benjamin Kidd, for his part, was prodemocratic, even socialist, because he thought that to compete effectively in the international jungle a people needs social solidarity. This rather curious joining of Mazzinian democratic nationalism with aggressive foreign policy characterized this extremely popular and influential writer (and amateur scientist) who was an adviser to British political leader Joseph Chamberlain.

Friedrich Naumann was a German democrat who accepted Darwinism in international relations, a position not far from Max Weber's. His National Social party envisioned a social Kaiser, dispensing with the Reichstag and ruling by his rapport with the masses. But in France Mme. Adam's *La Nouvelle Revue*, an organ of patriotic nationalism, argued rather as did Kidd in England that the republican spirit better than the monarchical could strengthen the nation for a war against Germany. In either case the important matter was national strength and how to achieve it, and as German socialist Ludwig Quessel wrote in 1909, "it matters little, if democracy is achieved, whether the person who represents the state bears a republican or a monarchical title."

What both Kidd and Pearson, as well as Le Bon in France and Naumann in Germany, really wanted was a kind of national socialism. Its democratic component was decidedly subordinate to the goal of national strength in a world of brutal struggle for survival. In France, this strain mostly criticized *parliamentary* democracy as corrupt, weakening, divisive, incapable of effective policy, a recipe for national ruin. Their ideal was that all the people obey a strong popular leader who embodies the general will: totalitarian democracy at the national level, girded for battle.

Sociologists and Democracy

Strongly stimulated by Darwinism as well as by Comte and Marx, the science of society entered into its golden age around the end of the century. The brilliant sociologizing of the Max Weber–Emile Durkheim–Vilfredo Pareto era had a notably disenchanting effect on simple ideas or idealisms such as democracy, as will be explained further in a moment. At almost the same time there arrived the reductionism of psychology à la Freud and Jung. The tendency was to find deeper and sometimes unworthier structures lying beneath the formal, conventionally accepted classifications of politics and political ideals. Freudianism shared with both Marxian and Darwinian naturalism a well-known tendency to deflate the ideals by which men live, demoting these to the status of strategies in the power struggle of life. "Ideologies," in Marx's terminology, mask the realities of class domination, and in Darwinian thought become just a means of securing an advantage in the incessant battle for survival. Political ideas are nonrational; they are rhetoric or rationalization, appealing to instincts or popular prejudices rather than to logic (Pareto). Max Weber's modes of authority (patriarchal, bureaucratic, charismatic) undercut classifications in terms of formal structure (democratic, aristocratic, monarchical).

Those who attempted to examine in a scientific manner the ways of the popular mind when dealing with political issues could hardly avoid noting the presence of emotion, mythmaking and the lack of critical thinking. Public opinion on any issue emerges as a combination of primeval archetypes, crude self-interest, wish fulfillment, accident, rumor, hero worship, scapegoat hunting, leavened by the merest bit of factual information or misinformation and very little logical thinking. This was hardly a new insight: back in 1820 Sir Robert Peel had referred to "that great compound of folly, weakness, prejudice, wrong feeling, right feeling, obstinacy and newspaper paragraphs, which is called public opinion." But social scientists now studied political behavior with a new rigor.

Sociologist Morris Ginsberg observed, in his *Reason and Unreason in Society* (1948), that "[o]ur deeper mental processes go back to very ancient times and they offer strong resistance to the relatively recent efforts at critical reflection." These archetypal primitivisms included the tendency to reify or personify abstractions such as capitalism or nations. The public en masse tended toward hasty generalization and was easily swayed by tides of feeling, mass suggestion. Among other manifest irrationalities, partisanship, that is, the primitive practice of taking sides in a gang fight, bars the majority of people from any objective evaluation of the evidence. Studies in the formation of public opinion, in the mythologies of politics, in the rhetoric of public political address could lead the trained scientific mind to an amused disgust at the passionate scenarios of democratic politics.

One book that caught the intellectual world's fancy in the 1890s and 1900s was Gustave Le Bon's *Psychologie des foules* (The Crowd, 1895), which Freud called "a brilliantly executed picture of the group mind" and which has retained its readers through many editions from its first edition down to the present. Adolf Hitler was one of its admirers. It came from a thoroughly disillusioned hater of democracy, as also was Gabriel Tarde, another famous French social theorist. Here was the irrational mob willing to follow charismatic leaders (Max Weber's term; Le Bon's was "prestige").

But easily the most significant finding of the new political sociology relating to democracy was the paradox of democratic elitism. "Everywhere, whether within or outside democracies, politics is made *by the few*," remarked the greatest of the new sociologists, Max Weber. Democracy in actuality is only another kind of oligarchy.

Like most supposedly new ideas, this one had a fairly long lineage. Hobbes, in the seventeenth century, had suggested that democracy amounts to an oligarchy of orators. (Today we might say PR people.) In the early nineteenth century Benjamin Disraeli noticed that "[w]hatever form a government may assume, power must be exercised by a minority of numbers. . . . Self-government is a contradiction in terms" ("The Spirit of Whiggism," 1836). The principle of representation was itself an obvious demonstration of this. Some, like the socialist-anarchist Proudhon, had always argued that representative government is not democracy but the governance of some by others. And then, as Bismarck pointed out, an assembly of 350 people cannot govern Germany; serving in lieu of their constituency, the elected delegates must themselves delegate power to a prime minister or a chancellor whom they can at best hope occasionally to influence. "If everyone is to govern, it means in fact that there is no government," Durkheim noted.

Edmund Burke had argued that the elected members of Parliament ought to exercise their own judgment, not just transmit that of their constituents, and though the Benthamites urged the opposite, it was evident that legislators do in fact form a special coterie with ways of their own—a "republic of pals," Robert de Jouvenel called it in a popular book about Third Republic France. (A whole series of books along this line appeared in the 1880s and 1890s, for example, *The Republic of Dukes* and *The Republic of Bankers*). "The strongest man in some form or other will always rule," James Fitzjames Stephen had written somewhat earlier. In some form or other— the sword, the tongue, the bank account, the ability to organize—doubtless in different circumstances and epochs the essential qualification changes. The point threatens any moral superiority democracy might claim over other modes of dominance. Likewise, the point that democracy subverts itself by producing insider-controlled organizations had virtually been anticipated in the classic eighteenth-century notion that democracy is possible only in a small community.

That such ideas came forth in greater abundance at the end of the nineteenth century was due in large part to evidence at hand from the actual workings of democratic government. Pareto and his fellow Italian elitist theorist Gaetano Mosca were disillusioned *Risorgimento*-ists, who had watched the hoped-for democratic renewal degenerate after the unification of Italy under a supposedly popular banner. Pareto said of one Italian head of government that he was "the leader of a syndicate of speculators ruling the country and robbing the state." Elected elites plainly could be as bad as or worse than hereditary ones. The United States at this time discovered an "invisible government" of political bosses who controlled elections, ruled the political parties, yet were neither elected by nor accountable to the people. In Britain also, the "party system" followed closely on the broadening of suffrage, frustrating, some thought, the attempt to democratize. M.I. Ostrogorski's classic study *Democracy and the Organization of Political Parties* (1902) drew heavily on American examples but was written in

England by a student of Joseph Chamberlain's organization. "It is extremely dubious whether the mass of the people have as much practical power today as they had before the process began," Hilaire Belloc and G.K. Chesterton claimed in 1911 (*The Party System*).

The more voters, the more party organization controlled by a small minority; oligarchy advanced apace with democracy. The paradox was worthy to rank with Marx's alleged discovery that in the process of making profits capitalism destroys private property: democracy creates oligarchy through the operations of its own instrument, the mass political party. "Children of democracy," the direct product of a mass electorate, necessary in order to mediate between the voters and the electoral process, great political parties found their very size forcing them into an elitist structure.

This new phenomenon, the mass political party, had more than anything else to do with this era's discovery of "iron laws of oligarchy." Max Weber's friend Robert Michels used the great German Social Democratic party to prove his point that oligarchy is "a preordained form of the common life of great social aggregates."[3] The mass institution becomes too big for self-government and falls into the hands of insiders skilled at organization. Unforeseen and unregulated, the process was peculiarly anarchic. The invisible rulers might be those American "bosses" about one of whom President Theodore Roosevelt said that he had a gift for office mongering just as other men have a gift for picking pockets. Or they might be socialist functionaries, glad to attain bourgeois status as members of the proletarian bureaucracy. The machinery for allowing popular participation in policy making within the large political parties was in any case a sham. American political scientist A. Lawrence Lowell said that in Britain the Tories were a transparent sham, the Liberals an opaque one (*Public Opinion and Popular Government*, 1913).

In other ways too, of course, those children of democracy frustrated the popular will at the same time that they made a system based on it possible. Most workable was the two-party arrangement, established in the Anglo-Saxon lands (because of what one commentator described as a salutary stupidity). But to allow only two positions to be represented was to make a mockery of public opinion. A multiparty system, allowing for a greater number of points of view, produced unstable, ineffective government. When the parties became huge, broadly based institutions, as they did above all in the United States, offering all things to all men, "microcosms of the nation," they no longer served the purpose of offering clear alternatives; moreover they drifted into corruption. If as in Great Britain the parties developed tight structures, demanding a high degree of obedience from members, they were accused of suppressing independent judgment. No form or style of political party government was entirely satisfactory; in general, the more democracy (popular control or representation), the less workability. Emile Faguet formulated the law that "[e]very party loses in strength what it gains in size, and gains in size only by losing its strength."

It may be remembered that any political parties at all were a shocking violation of democracy to the old school of Rousseau, that is, monistic democracy. In his *Social Contract* Rousseau wrote that any dissension, even any debate, is a sign of the decay of the political order. True democracy secures a consensus of all the members of the community and results in unanimity. (This actually happens in small governing bodies, for example, a university department or a church board.) As "factions," political parties were indignantly rejected in the early years of the United States as much as they were during the French Revolution. They seemed like treason. "Jacobins" put "Girondins" to death for the crime of disagreeing with the revolutionary consensus. (Actually all the factions claimed descent from the Jacobin Society, which incarnated the will of the people.) This horror of parties had a long history, reaching back to ancient times. The notion that, in a governable body politic, one could permit violent disagreements to take place and give this dissension legal and moral justification was a startling idea. It was a feature of the new meaning of democracy, as pluralism and toleration, that left truth to fend for itself.

Socialism and Democracy

Democracy gives rise to oligarchy in other ways, it was widely noted. If defined as the competition of freely acting and legally equal individuals, it eventuates in gross inequalities of wealth. This definition trespasses of course on the boundaries of the concept, in the direction of (classical) liberalism. But virtually every critic of democracy (e.g., Maine, Faguet, Bouglé, Le Bon) made much of the fact that the United States, generally agreed to be the most democratic of nations, had the greatest inequality of wealth. In *The Limits of Pure Democracy* (1918), W.H. Mallock argued that inequality is necessary to democracy. "Democracy only knows itself through the cooperation of oligarchy." The right of all to compete freely and equally requires that there be a successful class, as the object of aspiration. There must be a top to which to rise. Once it had been a titled aristocracy; now democracy manufactured its own elites. It was Emile Faguet's thesis, in *The Dread of Responsibility*, that "[a] democracy can live only on condition of producing aristocracies or permitting aristocracies to produce themselves." This inequality of wealth creates an economic power capable of subverting democratic decisions. Some American corporations, popular books pointed out, were bigger than the government (see, for example, Ghent, *Our Benevolent Feudalism*, 1902). This may engender class hatred threatening radical protest and perhaps a socialist uprising.

Such were the paradoxes of what Mallock and other conservative critics obviously saw as an unstable order; their conclusions came close to the Marxist claim that democratic society is a disguised form of class rule by the bourgeoisie, which sooner or later must fall from the weight of its economic contradictions. But elitist theory of the new sort had a dissolvent effect on aspects of Marxism relevant to democracy. "The fatal shortcoming of all Marxist theorizing (so far) about the role of the state," Theda Skocpol has observed, "is that nowhere is the possibility admitted that state organizations and elites might in certain circumstances act *against* the long-run economic interests of a dominant class." Classical Marxism assumed that, after the revolution, under socialism or communism the leaders of the workers will exactly represent their interests, being unable to act in any other way than as the faithful spokesmen of all in a classless society, just as under capitalism the state is an exact replica of the economic interests of the capitalists. That the bureaucracy might break loose to play an independent role was a thought that occasionally bothered Marx and Engels but that they usually rejected. In *The Eighteenth Brumaire of Louis Napoleon*, Marx wrote that "this appalling parasitic body," the bureaucracy, which seemed to be the basis of Napoleon III's power, was really "only the instrument of the ruling class, however much it strove for power of its own." If elites do have a life of their own, taking on qualities pertaining to them qua elites, then the socialist or communist society is not immune from oligarchy. The automatic democracy assumed by Marxists to follow the end of (economic) class domination may be threatened by new elites who do not arise from ownership of the tools of production but from other processes. Much later, it became obvious that a new ruling class did in fact arise in postrevolutionary Russia, based not on ownership of capital but on monopoly of office.

Thus the question that Pareto, Sorel, Michels, Weber, and others addressed to the Marxists was, How can political life, which has hitherto been a power struggle, turn into happy concord merely because property is transferred from one entity to another? In *Civilization and Its Discontents* (1930), Sigmund Freud remarked that "[b]y abolishing private property one deprives the human love of aggression of one of its instruments, a strong one undoubtedly but assuredly not the strongest. It in no way alters the individual differences in power and influence which are turned by aggressiveness to its own use, nor does it change the nature of the instinct in any way. The instinct did not arise as the result of property." There can be no escape via a socialist utopia. The iron law of oligarchy applies to any large-scale organization. And the process of economic and social modern-ization creates ever larger conglomerates of people. The best we can hope for is a competition of oligarchies, which prevents totalitarian tyranny, or an alternation of elites, which keeps channels open for fresh leadership making its way up the ladder. The foxes, in Pareto's terms, may at least be set to check the lions. But the democratic utopia falls along with the socialist one.

Those who did believe in equality of condition, and who reproached the reigning liberalism for bringing about a real inequality via the doctrine of equal opportunity, that is, the socialists, were a numerous and articulate nineteenth-century breed; they were likewise very uncertain democrats. Gustave Le Bon (*The Psychology of Socialism*, 1899) referred to "the hatred of the socialists for the democratic system, a hatred far more intense than was felt by the men of the Revolution for the *ancien régime.*" Perhaps a characteristic exaggeration of a splenetic writer, the judgment yet contains its kernel of truth. Socialists of course were far from united. Yet all of the many varieties held democracy as at best a secondary good and at worst a positive evil. Perhaps Le Bon had in mind Proudhon's opinion that democ-racy was the greatest fraud of the nineteenth century. (Proudhon thought democracy in some ways worse than autocracy or dictatorship.) Later the Fabian socialist G.D.H. Cole declared that "[t]he crowning discovery of the nineteenth century was that democratic government made no difference to the life of the ordinary man."

Karl Marx used *democracy* before 1848 to mean the coming proletarian victory, but after that he tended not to find it a friendly word. In his *Critique of the Gotha Program* (1874), ridiculing those socialists who wanted to participate in democratic politics, Marx sneered at this "vulgar democracy" with its belief in "democratic miracles." The democratic republic is only "the last form of the state in Bourgeois society." Institutions such as parlia-ments and elections would presumably no more exist in the future socialist order than privately owned banks and factories. Several inferences from the Marxian or socialist point of view lent weight to this conclusion. If eco-nomic power is more important than political, then the elected legislature will simply be a tool of the dominant economic class, powerless to achieve reform or revolution on its own. "The man who employs governs." A capitalist order will have a capitalist polity. An elected legislature under capitalism can exist only at the sufferance of the employers. Why do they allow popular voting to exist at all? Perhaps because it helps legitimize the ex-ploitative order, providing a fig leaf to cover its shamefulness. If so, honest workers should be as suspicious of it as they are of other ruling-class ideologies or value systems. Real decisions in any case are not made by the lawyers and speechmakers, the "parliamentary cretins," as Engels called them.

To go all the way down this analytical road was to end in the camp of anarchists and syndicalists who spurned politics altogether, concentrating on factory or army where real power lay. If most Marxists did not go that far, they all in some degree saw a "superstructure" of law and rhetoric that masked a deeper and concealed foundation of economic reality. The proletariat could never be at home in the house of bourgeois parliamentarianism. It might perhaps exploit this product of capitalism's decay for its own purposes, to hasten the revolution, but it could never regard it as valuable in itself.

Socialist views of democracy hinged on the distinction between ends and means. "The end, socialism; the means, the Republic," said Louis Blanc. The "revisionist" Eduard Bernstein argued that the road to socialism might lead through and not around parliamentarianism; to revolutionary socialists such as Blanqui, clearly, around was better than through. In either case, the superior value was socialism. As an ideal system and the goal of history, socialism was the higher order mandated to replace an abhorrent capitalism. The latter coexisted with democracy; democracy might even be its political counterpart, "the political shell for capitalism," in Lenin's words. The future socialist society would doubtless in some sense be democratic, as a classless or universally beneficent society, good for everybody, perhaps no longer with domination (though Saint-Simonian socialists wanted an intellectual elite to rule). But would this socialist democracy have anything in common with bourgeois democracy? Was parliamentarianism—the system of elections, representation, "talking shops"—a specifically bourgeois institution, a trick played on the workers?

Pragmatic participation in the endless game of adjusting interests seemed to many socialists the basest kind of surrender to everything they hated. They expected a socialist civilization to supplant the bourgeois world, in which pragmatic (and often corrupt) democratic politics was being increasingly domesticated in the late nineteenth century. The antidemocratic strain in socialist doctrine may be found in its earliest proponents, such as the eighteenth-century writer Morelly, who advocated "the compulsory teaching of one orthodox moral philosophy," and the pioneer early nineteenth-century figures Robert Owen and Henri Saint-Simon. Owen was a patriarch who governed his own ideal factory before trying to establish branches of it in other places; Saint-Simon proposed a government of the scientific-technological experts.

Karl Marx has been seen as "a radical democrat" all his life.[4] That learned and astute commentator on Marx the late Sidney Hook said, "[T]here is not a line in Marx that justifies the dictatorship of a minority political party to introduce socialism, not even in the transition period." Marx spoke of "the dictatorship of the proletariat," but Lenin ominously misconstrued that famous phrase, it has been alleged. In fact, Marx and Engels did not bother to explain what they meant by it. One can as plausibly interpret it to mean the rule of a majority as the tyranny of a few. But in either case it assumes either the nonexistence of a minority or its ruthless suppression. Theory suggested that all nonproletarians would disappear naturally, like an obsolete species. But clearly theory left room for giving nature a helping hand in this process. Marxian democracy in any case seems to be one in which there is no significant dissent, because everybody has either accepted Marxism or conveniently vanished. Though he opposed Auguste Blanqui's insurrectionism, it is not clear that Marx disagreed with the famous French insurrectionist's reasoning in wanting a dictatorship of the "true revolutionaries." Blanqui demanded a dictatorship of the proletariat, a phrase Marx would adopt, which to Blanqui meant suppressing all political parties opposed to the revolution; the majority of the people may err and must be corrected by their natural leaders.

Marx was strongly authoritarian in debates about democratic procedures in the International; he opposed French proposals for universal suffrage in its meetings. You do not decide important matters on the basis of numbers. The majority might be wrong, that is, unacquainted with Marxian science. This may suggest recent reluctance by British trade union leaders to have their members vote on such questions as strikes.

Leninist revolutionary elitism thus had many predecessors within the social movement. Mazzini's Young Italy was a secret society of carefully selected professional revolutionaries prepared to lead a revolution "by and for the people." Lenin learned his elitism from Russian populist revolutionaries such as Tkachev and especially Chernyshevsky. Some of the populists, however, believed that if everybody could vote, the peasants would win and would support them. The shattering failure of the "to the people" movement of the early 1870s revealed the naïveté of this view, as 1848 had revealed it to Louis Blanc in France. Socialist faith in the people lasted only so long as they thought that the people would embrace socialist doctrines.

Among the many other socialists who contested Marx's supremacy within the movement, Ferdinand Lassalle called himself a democrat but fiercely opposed parliamentary government as bourgeois, and was even willing to bargain with Bismarck about a "social monarchy" that would join the working class and the aristocracy in a dictatorship aimed at the "egoism of the bourgeois class." (Lassalle, a flamboyant figure, cultivated aristocratic manners and was eventually killed in a duel.)

As an authoritarian creed, socialism could not be basically democratic. Talk as they might about democratic socialism (it is still invoked), socialists had an a priori rational idea of the proper, the indispensable, perhaps the world-destined form of social organization that it is essential to bring into existence. They might argue that an ideal people knows and wants this kind of social organization, that it is in the best interests of the majority, that tomorrow if not today everybody will recognize its superiority. A rather recent socialist tract, Douglas Jay's *Socialism in the New Society* (1962), seemed to assume that everybody would be a socialist and vote Labour if they were not kept from true virtue by a kind of Tory remnant of original sin; the proper education, and much reading of socialist tracts such as Jay's, should purge them of this frailty. But socialists cannot in the end escape the fact that their principle is not the principle of majority rule. If they do not fall into the trap of imposing it by the physical force of a minority, socialists must continue to live in what they regard as a fatally imperfect society while hoping for the conversion of everyone to their way of thinking. The only good situation is one in which everybody agrees about the obviously only correct way of life. As Charles Benoist put it in 1902 (*Revue des deux mondes*, October 15, 1902, p. 832), socialists think in terms of "absolute democracy."

Some socialist hostility toward democracy diminished toward the end of the nineteenth century. Karl Kautsky, August Bebel, and most of the immediate descendants of Karl Marx who led the powerful German Social Democratic party continued to believe as a formal creed in revolution followed by utopia, but in practice, arguing that people should not simply lie around dreaming of the Great Day, they approved taking part in democratic politics. It could be justified as an educational process, teaching workers the political skills they might later apply under a better system. But Marx had never ruled out the possibility of a peaceful transition from capitalism to socialism, and Engels toward the end of his life made the famous pronouncement that "[t]he time of revolutions carried through by small minorities at the head of unconscious masses is past."[5] "A party would be insane which decided on insurrection, as long as other, less costly and more certain methods were available," Kautsky added. Though reluctant to accept Eduard Bernstein's view that through democracy one might establish socialism, this leading German Marxist theoretician held what amounted to the same thing, that through the growth of socialist consciousness the workers might attain a real democracy. The French proletariat, Werner Sombart wrote in 1896, "is about to give up its Blanquist [i.e., insurrectionist] teaching, and is fighting the bourgeoisie by the same constitutional means as their comrades in Germany: in Parliament, in trade unions, in cooperative societies" (*Socialism and the Social Movement*).

Yet almost simultaneously Georges Sorel was calling democracy the mortal foe of socialism, and young Lenin had appeared in Russia, while

Gustave Le Bon maliciously noted that the real working class was quite conservative. The Social Democratic quasi acceptance of democratic processes was being questioned not only by French syndicalists and Russian Bolsheviks but also by British Fabians almost as soon as it was born. Fabian Tract No. 70 asserted that "[t]he Fabian society energetically repudiates all conceptions of Democracy as a system by which the technical work of government administration and the appointment of public officials shall be carried on by referendum or any other form of direct popular decision." Fabians claimed democracy as well as socialism as an objective. But democracy had been attained; "the difficulty in England is not to secure more political power for the people, but to persuade them to make any sensible use of the power they already have"—in other words, to be converted to socialism. What if they refuse?

Sorel, one of the three or four most influential political thinkers of the 1880–1914 era, was somewhat prodemocratic for a time during the Dreyfus affair but by 1907 was arguing that the socialist and democratic ideas are wholly opposed. He had grown disillusioned with the victorious Dreyfusards. Socialists had been tardy in rallying to the support of the falsely accused Jewish captain in this celebrated touchstone of political attitudes of the 1890s. Sorel considered socialist involvement in democratic politics a mistake, deflecting the workers from their all-important revolutionary purposes.

To which might be added the thought that socialism was always very much an affair of bourgeois intellectuals, not of plain people; "the workers" had a nasty habit of ignoring or even ridiculing the educated theorists who exhorted them to overturn the capitalist system. The latter felt its discomforts much more than the former. Upper-class intellectual socialists often frankly confessed an aversion toward actual workers. Bertrand Russell said of the famous Fabians, Sidney and Beatrice Webb, "Both of them were fundamentally undemocratic" (*Portraits from Memory*); a passage from Beatrice's *American Diary* (ed. David Shannon, p. 149) displays her frank contempt for ordinary, unintellectual people (much of which, indeed, Marx himself held). "Yes I fear my socialism is purely cerebral; I do not like the masses in the flesh," Harold Nicolson confided in a letter to his wife, in words many another Oxbridge-educated leftist could have repeated. Intellectuals who were prodemocratic in theory really got there via hatred of their society, projected onto its "ruling class"; the masses were assumed to be duped and drugged, but basically good if not thus corrupted or manipulated. The intellectuals projected fantasy images onto a people whom they did not really know. But this was "purely cerebral"; dealing with real people was quite another matter.

In Victorian England a vast gulf had existed between educated gentlemen and the "lower regions." Banker and literary critic Walter Bagehot, author of *The English Constitution* and editor of *The Economist*, asked his readers to try a serious political discussion with their footmen or housemaids, if they doubted this gulf. Socialist intellectuals of the next generation carried on this essential alienation from the masses, despite their theoretical approval of the masses. The alienation between a "civilized minority" and the masses in fact grew. In one notable passage in his *Autobiography*, Bertrand Russell declared that his generation, the late Victorian one, felt more kinship with the commonality than the next one.

> We believed in ordered progress by means of politics and free discussion. The more self-confident among us may have wished to be leaders of the multitude, but none of us wished to be divorced from it. The generation of [John Maynard] Keynes and [Lytton] Strachey did not wish to preserve any kinship with the Philistines. They aimed rather at a life of retirement among fine shades and nice feelings, and conceived of the good as consisting in the passionate mutual admiration of a clique of the elite.

In a broad context, socialism appears as the last of the dogmatic religions, a secular heir of Judaism and Christianity; as such, it was of the solidarist, organic, totalitarian type. The democracy it scorned was the pluralist, skeptical sort. Michael Rustin, in *For a Pluralist Socialism* (1985), appears to have been the first to endorse such a connection.

Notes

1. "If everybody's judgment is of equal value, only that is valuable which appeals equally to everybody. . . . There are only two good things which appeal to everybody, because they address the lowest instincts: money and physical strength. The result is that commercialism and athletics absorb the energies of men. . . . The final outcome must be that commercialism, if left alone, would devastate science and art, education and society, law and politics." Hugo Münsterberg, "American Democracy," in *American Traits* (Boston: Houghton Mifflin, 1901).

2. Hobhouse, *Democracy and Reaction* (London: Macmillan, 1904), and *Development and Purpose* (New York: Putnam's, 1913, p. 9). Among other examples of this are W.H. Mallock, *The Limits of Pure Democracy*, 4th ed. (London: Chapman and Hall, 1918), pp. 14–15; Oliver Wendell Holmes, Jr., in Max Lerner, ed., *The Mind and Faith of Justice Holmes* (New York: Modern Library, 1954), pp. 50–51.

3. Michels, *Political Parties*, English ed. (New York: Hearst's International Library, 1915). Michels saw organization as the inevitable enemy of pure, participatory democracy, not of the more pedestrian and pluralistic kind; parties might learn to elect their functionaries.

4. Alasdair MacIntyre, *Herbert Marcuse* (New York: Viking Press, 1970), p. 65.

5. Introduction to the 1895 edition of Marx's *Class Struggle in France*. Hans-Josef Steinberg, in *International Review of Social History*, vol. 12 (1967), pp. 177–89, argued that in context this celebrated dictum was less democratic than it sounds.

5

The Continuing Crisis of Democracy

End-of-Century Disenchantment

Retiring from politics in 1894, William Gladstone, the leading symbol and incarnation of a democratic polity in Britain, declared that the political world had changed in his lifetime largely for the worse. As leader of the Liberals this towering figure had presided over at least the beginning of their transformation from an aristocratic elite to a popular party. Championing the right of plain citizens to be heard and to participate in politics, and immensely popular among them, Gladstone had supported the suffrage extensions of 1867 and 1884 along with legislation for democratic local government, free public education, and other measures for equal opportunity. It was the decisive moment in Britain for democratization in the sense of Schumpeter's second variety of democracy, defended by Victorian oracle John Stuart Mill: equal-access democracy, of procedure not of condition.

But Gladstone's patrician nature never quite understood the mass democracy that the 1880s and 1890s brought in. His biographer S.G. Checkland observes that Gladstone's "system of thought was entirely undemocratic." "I am an out-and-out inegalitarian," he wrote to John Ruskin. To which we might add that the Tory leader who succeeded Disraeli as party head, Lord Salisbury, was much more suspicious of democracy than Dizzy had been.

It is hard not to see the great era of Gladstone and Disraeli (roughly 1865–90) as the golden age of parliamentary politics in Great Britain, marked by leaders of intellectual distinction, significant partisan issues, high public interest, and exciting elections. Significantly, it coincided not with a complete democracy but with a halfway one: the old patrician leadership interacted fruitfully with a still partly deferent populace, as universal suffrage and professionally organized political parties crept into the country only gradually.

It occurred to many that such success as popular government now had was really due to surviving elements from a predemocratic era. Charles Maurras alleged that French parliamentarianism was so bad because it was undiluted by king, church, or ancestral constitution. Emile Vacherot asserted that "the first condition of Parliamentary government is the existence of an aristocratic class." That British democracy worked only because of a unique preservation of monarchical and aristocratic elements was the conclusion of such notable commentators as Walter Bagehot, Henry Maine, and Erskine May. It also worked because a feeling of being a single family still prevailed despite social and economic inequality. The system of allowing opposition parties to assail the incumbent government peacefully, seeking to win an election not a civil war, could operate only where, as Lord Balfour memorably put it, a people are so fundamentally at one they can safely afford to bicker.

Even the United States had a constitution with roots deep in the past, interpreted by a sanhedrin of life-appointed judges who pretended to base their judgments on the literal and unchanging meaning of the venerable 1789 document—to the extreme irritation of pure democrats and social reformers but to the evident satisfaction of a majority of Americans. When democratization advanced beyond the limits set by this compromise with tradition, criticism of it mounted. Charles Maurras, incidentally, refused to classify the United States as a democracy at all; it was a feudalism of industrialists, tempered by relics of an older aristocratic tradition. Mill, who had earlier believed that democracy was at least a training of the mind and that "[u]nder a free system . . . truth never fails to prevail over error," came to think that democracy does not educate the masses or distill out truth.

Addressing the paradox of democracy's success accompanied by disenchantment, Graham Wallas in the introduction to his *Human Nature in Politics* (1908) observed: "At first sight the main controversy as to the best form of government appears to have been finally settled in favor of representative democracy." But Wallas wrote his book, probing beneath the official façade to explore the real ways of politics, because like his fellow British political philosopher L.T. Hobhouse he sensed that something was not quite right with the workings of democracy. "The golden radiance of its morning hopes has long since faded into the light of common day," he observed. "It is no longer possible to mistake the reaction against democracy," future U.S. president Woodrow Wilson wrote around the turn of the century (in *The Atlantic Monthly*, 1901). Its critics, John Morley noted in 1904, were as ten thousand. H.G. Wells said he "knew of no case for the elective democratic government of modern states that cannot be knocked to pieces in five minutes."

A leading French student, Georges Guy-Grand, in his book *The Democratic Process* (1911), was equally struck by the disenchantment that accompanied the success of democracy. No party of any consequence in France contested it; "democracy has become the legal custom of our country." Despite a few remaining monarchists and the beginnings of a fascist-like rumble, no one any longer seriously dreamed of replacing democracy, yet no one liked it either. "The democratic principle has gone forth conquering and to conquer, and its gainsayers are few and feeble," Sir Henry Maine (who didn't like it) conceded in his study *Popular Government* (1885). Its triumph was "universally recognized," Celestin Bouglé remarked in *Les Idées egalitaire* (1899). Yet this case-closed feeling coexisted oddly with an almost equally strong opinion, among the thoughtful and critical-minded, that democracy was either a failure or a fraud. It had few intellectual defenders, and the leaders of thought almost to a man spoke of a "crisis of democracy." The American Arthur G. Sedgwick almost summed it up in the title of his 1912 book *The Democratic Mistake.* Practical politicians would say, if they were as candid as Georges Clemenceau, "If I am a democrat, it is without enthusiasm."

In another book of 1912, Gustave Le Bon (*Psychologie politique*) went further: he saw a crisis of civilization at hand. Parliamentary democracy had become a mortal danger; "the basest interests of the multitude" ruled the elected representatives who, dreaming only of reelection, did not consult the national interest. A plebs eaten by envy and ruled by ignorance portended the breakdown of authority. Faced with this anarchy, the responsible middle class had no choice but to fight back in *le defense sociale.* Le Bon was one of the many pre-1914 anticipators of postwar fascism.

Even in Great Britain, about 1911 "the whole parliamentary process was beginning to be questioned to a degree unparalleled for two centuries," Robert Blake remarks in his history of the Conservative party. Elected politicians were a strangely dishonored breed, rated well toward the bottom of the social scale in the United States; Mark Twain held that "the only distinctly American criminal class is Congress." But hardly less so in France and Italy. And even a relatively low opinion of the British Parliament is suggested by a remark of Henry James in 1908 deploring "the immense waste of talk and energy and solemnity that Parliament is." Political parties, now regarded as essential to any parliamentary system, had "a tendency to wreak havoc in public life, to destroy right and justice, and to ruin individual character," Friedrich Paulsen remarked, in one of the milder things said about them.

If democracy was said to be a failure, even a disaster, others called it a fraud; the two criticisms perhaps contradicted each other, since it is hard to see how something that means nothing can be a menace. But the charge of fraudulence often really was saying that the system was not democratic at all. As will be recalled from chapter 4, one important body of thought saw democracy as only a disguised form of oligarchy or rule by an elite. Many doubted that the people really had all that much to do with government. For one thing, these critics perceived an alarmingly feeble public participation in elections or in the debate of public issues. Graham Wallas estimated the number actively engaged in politics in England at 10 percent, which suggested another variant of democratic elitism: the determined or obsessive "activists" who tend to dominate electoral processes were a small minority.

Jean Darcy, writing in *Revue des deux mondes* (August 15, 1902), calculated that the reigning cabinet, that of Combes, rested on the suffrages of under 25 percent of eligible French voters. Eduard Bernstein remarked in 1908 that in Prussia, where they were admittedly discouraged by the discriminatory three-class voting system, the percentage of eligible voters who bothered to cast ballots declined from 34.3 percent in 1862 to 23.6 percent in 1903. Hans Delbrück, writing in 1913, found [t]hat "the overwhelming majority of people [in Germany] do not take sufficient interest in politics to be able to form well-founded opinions . . . and to cast their votes accordingly." Speaking for the supposedly more democratic English, Herbert Spencer agreed that "[t]hose who adequately recognize the importance of honestly exercising their judgments in the selection of legislators, and who give conscientious votes, form but a minority." Armed with public opinion polls, later psephologists would be able to demonstrate conclusively how little the average citizen knows about leading political issues, but this was strongly suspected much earlier.

This apathy might partly be explained by that "fatalism of the multitude" which James Bryce noted in his famous study of American democracy (*The American Commonwealth*, 1888), a fatalism based on the knowledge of how little influence the individual citizen can exert on government. Thomas Carlyle had ridiculed a system pretending to be democratic under which "I have my twenty-thousandth of a Talker in our National Palaver," and Georges Sorel had observed that each of us is one ten-millionth a tyrant and every bit a slave. Size worked remorselessly against participatory democracy. Size was what was happening in the nineteenth century, as population multiplied (eight times in Great Britain over the century) and more and more of these masses become at least partly involved in the political process (*empowered* would be too strong a word).

Democracy meant the decidedly limited privilege of choosing every few years between two political oligarchies not all that different, usually, in their policies. As G.K. Chesterton put it cynically in commenting on the alternation of Conservatives and Liberals in Britain,

> The accursed power which stands on Privilege
> (And goes with Women, and Champagne, and Bridge)
> Broke—and Democracy resumed her reign
> (Which goes with Bridge, and Women, and Champagne).

Chesterton's coauthor Hilaire Belloc, who regarded the party system as oligarchic and corrupt ("the machinery of politics," he said in quitting politics, is controlled by "the dirtiest company it has ever been my misfortune to keep"), wished to replace Parliament by a representation of citizens through professions and occupations; but apart from any other consideration, there seems no reason to suppose that such a "corporative" system would prove any less prone to oligarchical control than the existing one of territorial election districts.

The plea that democracy needn't take a parliamentary form or, if it did, needn't have a partisan structure—the dream of "a republic that belongs to everybody and is no longer the plaything of a party" (Jules Lemaitre, 1899) —came from many directions: from guild socialists and syndicalists as well as from corporativists and seekers after a great leader. It appealed to socialists as well as conservative nationalists, united in their dislike of bourgeois democracy. Coming respectively from the extreme Right and the extreme Left, Charles Maurras and Georges Sorel joined forces in 1911 to form a Proudhon Circle, in memory of the great French anarchist who had been both socialist and conservative, but always an enemy of the state.

But this was in vain. One got back to the small community where face-to-face democracy might be feasible, but where was the nation? One faced the problem of size and representation on just another front.

Totalitarian Anticipations

Everyone knows that in the two decades after 1919, fascism, Nazism, and communism overran a Europe morally battered by the Great War of 1914–18 and almost destroyed democracy. What seems less well known is that the crisis started earlier; all the fascist and National Socialist ideas, for example, came from the decade or two before 1914 and were then picked up by pseudointellectual demagogues to be translated clumsily into hideous reality. As for Russian communism, Lenin, building on his interpretation of Marx, had worked out his ideas long before 1914.

Democracy was being assailed from every direction around 1900. Some of the reaction from scientists, artists, and socialists has been noted in chapter 4. The complaints continued with variations after 1900.

In Britain just after the turn of the century, a bureaucratic ideal of efficiency, associated with the scientific frame of mind, created an anti-democratic syndrome among Fabian socialists, social scientists, civil service reformers, and preachers of the cult of national efficiency. In his study of this movement (*The Quest for National Efficiency*, 1971), G.R. Searle noted that it spanned an ideological range from Fabian socialists to authoritarian imperialists such as Lord Milner. Government had become more necessary to the world, it was widely believed; not only socialists (and "we are all socialists now," a peer had said) but less ideological, essentially utilitarian reformers held that the modernized, industrialized urban society required that the state take over functions formerly handled privately or locally.

A great debate over social welfare legislation, involving a new conception of government's social responsibilities, took place between 1908 and 1911, with victory against stubborn opposition going to the New Liberalism against the old, of which it was almost the total opposite. In 1911 a plan of national insurance, administered by the state, began to replace the old Poor Laws as the remedy for poverty, indigence, and unemployment. During the immense excitement that accompanied this crisis, the House of Lords attempted to reassert its power by refusing to approve the new income tax but failed and had its powers legally pared down by a Parliament bill that not only explicitly barred the hereditary upper chamber from defeating legislation insisted upon by the House of Commons but established a salary for members of Parliament, thus helping to pry the legislative body loose from aristocratic control.

If the state was to take over all these (expensive) new duties of providing social welfare, was not greater efficiency in government necessary? Around 1906 William Beveridge, economist, administrator, and future architect of the welfare state, felt strongly antidemocratic, much more so than later. Ostrogorski and Graham Wallas had revealed, he thought, "the corruption and perversion of democratic institutions." It had become evident to him that "[i]n the last resort democracies must trust somebody or other with great and continual power if government is to be carried on at all."[1] Who is worth this trust? Hardly the wretches who, manipulated perhaps by sinister wire pullers, manage to get themselves elected by an ignorant populace. The only hope is in nonelected experts, professional "social doctors" committed to a disinterested standard of public service, scientifically selected and trained for their tasks.

The civil service system (pioneered in Europe by autocratic Prussia) had functioned in Great Britain since 1870 on the principle of selecting competently trained officials by competitive examination. As their problems multiplied, American cities discovered that a "city manager" was preferable to elected aldermen or a mayor, the latter probably devoid of professional administrative skills and corrupt (though to be sure it was discovered that the managers were not exactly immune from this disease). Training of a professional governing corps became the goal of one branch of American Progressives, in this era of Progressivism. (On the other hand, Progressives might agitate for the recall of public officials by popular vote.)

At the same time in the United States there was hope, which the example of President Theodore Roosevelt encouraged, that a new patrician class might arise to serve the nation selflessly. In her introduction to the translation of Faguet's *Dread of Responsibility* (New York, 1914), Emily James Putnam declared: "One of the most hopeful omens in our social future is the fact that there actually is growing among us a class of men who are willing to forego the financial rewards of great talents for the sake of serving the state."

Akin somewhat to the strain of thought that insisted on efficiency was one that accused democracy of fostering national weakness at a time of grave international dangers. This argument would be a special source of fascist appeal after 1919, but it was heard much earlier. From the 1880s on, patriotic nationalists in France vented their wrath against the parliamentary system, "the shameful politics which divides, oppresses, and ruins the country," a "pitiable anarchy," Etienne Vacherot called it (1887). In Italy, the biographer of Enrico Cenni says that "the production of such arguments was extremely large." In the form of government based on elected parliaments rent by faction, democracy meant weakness. At the same time such critics might support a monarchy based on universal suffrage, or a democratic Caesarism. After the ignominious collapse of General Boulanger's movement in France in 1889, when this "man on horseback" briefly threatened to overthrow the Republic, the Right tended to rally toward the Republic, but the Panama scandal and above all the great end-of-century Dreyfus affair caused second thoughts. After 1871, of course, the French brooded obsessively about their defeat and their fears of another encounter with an even stronger Germany. The hysteria produced by the great Affair cannot be understood without this background. Anything that weakened the nation was under suspicion. Many of the French blamed democracy for fatal national weakness.

On the Left, Georges Sorel and his friends identified the parliamentary republic with an execrable "tyranny of gold" to which they said they would prefer even a military dictatorship. Anatole France's Penguin Island, in the great satirist's work by that name, was democratic, which meant that "three or four financial companies exercised in it a greater power than that of the ministers of the republic." Sorel further identified democracy with modern decadence, from which some kind of neoprimitivism was necessary to restore community values. Chapter 4 has discussed the ambiguous attitude toward democracy of most socialists. Sorel was a renegade Marxist; like Lenin he had grown impatient with the "requiem socialism" of the majority Social Democrats, content to wait for a majority before installing the new order. A violent insurrection to Lenin was a means of gaining socialist power over the state; to Sorel it was an end in itself, restoring to degenerate democratic man the qualities of primeval heroism. This touched closely on the all-pervasive rhetoric of Friedrich Nietzsche, as well as on Vico's cyclical theory.

Around 1909 Martin Buber, prophet of a Jewish resurrection, was writing about "blood and soil" and the mystic racial soul in a way that can sound like Hitler with Jew in place of Aryan. Buber's dreamed-of new Jewish society would not only be integrally Jewish, soil-rooted, and attuned to nature, it would also be led by Nietzschean superior beings. He had been influenced by Nietzsche as well as by Max Nordau. Ritchie Robertson remarks that "Buber's vision of sturdy peasants tilling the soil of Palestine is simply a transposition to Asia of [Paul] Lagarde's vision of North German farmers"—Lagarde being generally recognized as a source of German National Socialist ideology. One might add that the Prague Bar Kochba Zionists fully accepted the identification of the *westernized* Jew with the worst features of a civilization sunk in empty and rootless materialism.

This kind of thinking was very common in the 1900s. The leading French example was Charles Maurras's integral nationalism, preached by his militant and popular (at least among students) *Action Française*. Maurras too was anti-Semitic. The most important French novelist was probably Maurice Barrès, who had traveled the road from an extreme Rousseauist subjectivism to a gospel of rootedness in French traditional culture, and an equally extreme French patriotism. Both Maurras and Barrès were direct founders of French fascism who greatly influenced Mussolini's Italian fascist revolution, something also true of the formidable Sorel, who migrated from working-class revolution to militant nationalism just before 1914.

Postwar totalitarianism picked up its storehouse of ideas from pre-1914 writers: from aspects of Nietzsche, Sorel, Barrès, Maurras, Le Bon; Darwinists, Futurists, Wagnerians, D'Annunzians; poets like Stefan George and William Butler Yeats, and many others, whose common denominator was disgust with democratic (mass) culture and democratic (parliamentary) politics. They projected the sense of a gigantic crisis of civilization or authority, a feeling of "all security gone," as Nietzsche's friend and teacher Jacob Burckhardt had put it in 1878: "Seitdem die Politik auf innere Garungen der Völker gegründet ist, hat alle Sicherheit ein Ende." Some of these writers sanctioned violence as a means of renewing a decadent society. Many of them talked about a renewal of national community, a *Gemeinschaft* (Friedrich Tönnies) or solidarity (Emile Durkheim) as an antidote to an anomic, fragmenting materialistic society. This *Völkisch* urge had already produced anti-Semitism in Austria, where Adolf Hitler as a youth learned it before the war from von Schönerer; and also in France, where mobs howled anti-Jewish slogans during the Dreyfus affair.

Also in the air was a decided penchant for superman heroes, charismatic leaders, an "audacious minority" who might rescue a world wasted by mediocrity and triviality, corruption and selfishness. Such a leadership might in some sense be democratic: it would stand for "a republic which belongs to everybody and is not the plaything of a party" (Jules Lemaitre); it would speak for all the people (at least all those who belonged to the racial community) and not special interests; it would recreate a primitive solidarity. In a sound democracy, D.H. Lawrence thought, the people obey their leaders, who have been selected by an organic, not a mechanical, process. This general will could even culminate in a single person, incarnating the collective people: shades of Robespierre and Napoleon. Granted, no such Caesar had made an appearance, except briefly and ludicrously in the person of General Boulanger. The thirst for one was nonetheless present.

Max Weber once declared that "[i]n a democracy the people elect a leader whom they trust. Then the elected one says 'Now shut up and obey.' People and parties must no longer interfere. . . . Afterward the people may judge him. If the leader has made mistakes—to the gallows with him!" His interlocutor, a prominent general, found that he could accept a democracy like that.

The issue of monistic versus pluralistic democracy was sharply raised in the United States in the early twentieth century by those numerous and strident voices who cried that the "new immigration" was a threat to Anglo-Saxon democracy. Professor John Commons (*Races and Immigrants in America*), Professor E.A. Ross, and others believed these non-Nordic hordes of unwashed Slavs and Latins, who poured in through the gates of Ellis Island from about 1880 to 1910, to be inherently unfitted for democracy. In the famous title of a book by Madison Grant, *The Passing of the Great Race* meant the passing of democracy, which, as J.W. Mecklin explained (*Democracy and Race Friction*), is possible only in a "small, intelligent, ethnically homogeneous" community, "united by common economic, religious, and political interests." Organic democracy once again reproached pluralism.

Professor Ross held that southern Europeans were both unintelligent and immoral (deficient in "ethical endowment") by nature. They were poor, Catholic, and accustomed to despotic government. They allegedly formed the clientele of city bosses. This sort of viewpoint was not entirely gutter journalism or lowbrow pamphleteering; it featured distinguished professors such as Ross and Commons, joined by such respected writers as the New England blue blood Morrison Swift. It included quite respectable historians who thought democracy was an Anglo-Saxon invention, born "under the oak trees of old Germany." Democracy, these people claimed, requires not only cultural unity but Anglo-Saxonness. Their prescription, like Hitler's, would have been to purge the body politic of all impurities and restore a community of like-minded, culturally homogeneous folk. And indeed the Viennese anti-Semites invoked as a model the Chinese Exclusion Act passed in the United States.

Other Americans such as Jane Addams, Waldo Frank, and Horace Kallen responded to this nativism by extolling the possible virtues of a democracy based on cultural pluralism. But the 1920s brought a movement in the United States to extend the restriction on immigration to other aliens, setting quotas to limit the numbers allowed in from some European countries as well as Asian ones.

World War I and Democracy

These mutterings of discontent gave way suddenly to the surge of primitive, communal emotions that marked the Great War of 1914–18. The relationship between the two things is seldom sufficiently noted. It is impossible to understand the war without understanding the incredible public support for it in all the warring countries. Greeted with wild enthusiasm at the start, as roaring crowds filled the streets to shout patriotic slogans (or, as in St. Petersburg, desecrate the enemy's memorials), the war held its backing amazingly well through the next four years of ghastly slaughter, inept military strategy, fumbling diplomacy, severe civilian as well as battlefield suffering. A million men volunteered in Britain in one of the greatest outpourings of patriotic zeal in all history. "Socialists who had vowed never to fight a capitalist war flocked to bear arms. Alienated intellectuals saw in the war a cleansing fire or flood that would wash away corruptions and lead to an apocalyptic revolution."[2] Old men tried to shoulder arms, while the young considered it a youth movement and feared the oldsters would spoil the fun by negotiating a peace. Women threw themselves into combat too, as never before. A strange sense of joy—"come and die, it will be such fun"—accompanied ancient archetypes of sacrifice, ritual redemption, rediscovered heroism. Some of this exalted, hysterical mood proved ephemeral, of course; the mystique of the 1914 "August days" could hardly last. In the end it gave way to a great disgust with war and its rhetoric. Still, this disenchantment scarcely eroded public morale until 1917 in Russia and 1918 in Germany.

Later this martial spirit seemed incomprehensible, even to those who had experienced it. Its existence has even been denied, because of a subsequent deep feeling of guilt among the intelligentsia about this treason, this desertion of civilized values in pursuit of martial glory (a classic case of Freudian repression on a mass scale).

The extraordinary way in which almost everybody rallied enthusiastically to the war, the intellectuals no less than the populace (if anything, more so), surely testified to some kind of psychic abnormality present in European society. Bertrand Russell stressed "unadventurous and dull lives" finding relief from ennui, "all the horrid duties of thrift and order and care." Then "the old primitive passions, which civilization has denied, surge up, all the stronger for repression."

But the most obvious disease for which war offered a cure was what Durkheim had called anomie, or Tönnies the lack of *Gemeinschaft.* Accompanying the war's sudden beginning was above all a sense of restored community, a reunion of all around a single common cause. It was, wrote German philosopher Max Scheler, a return to "the organic roots of human existence." "All differences of class, rank, and language were flooded over by the rushing feeling of fraternity," reported Stefan Zweig. From every belligerent country came similar testimony to an almost mystical experience of merging into the commonality, an experience to which alienated artists and intellectuals seemed especially susceptible. "Without parallel in history," Durkheim thought, was this revival of *le sens social.* An urge to wholeness amid the confusions of a fragmented urban society strongly affected the masses also (George Mosse, *The Nationalization of the Masses,* 1975).

So the war brought a temporary restoration of monistic, tribal democracy. This included preeminently an egalitarian thrust. "No more rich or poor, proletarians or bourgeois, right wingers or leftist militants; there were only Frenchmen," declared Roland Dorgelès. The war did more for a classless society than did Karl Marx. Max Weber initially saw 1914 as an uprising realizing the old dream of a *Volksstaat,* a people's state. In France it was compared to 1789 or 1792 (the armed people rising against monarchical invaders, which, according to François Furet, was a means of "integrating the masses into the State and forming a modern democratic nation"). In his *Mein Kampf*, Adolf Hitler talked about the army as a great equalizer: "In the Army a corporation director was no more important than a dog barber." Democracy as social equality clearly gained from the war. Some remembered fondly the camaraderie of the trenches and hoped that somehow it might be used as the basis of a new kind of society. One of these was Adolf Hitler. But the English essayist and artist Herbert Read also recalled that "[d]uring the war I used to feel that this comradeship which had developed among us would lead to some new social order when peace came. . . . It overcame (or ignored) all distinctions of class, rank, or education." Future president Friedrich Ebert in the German Reichstag, April 5, 1916, declared that "[t]he masses returned from the trenches" will demand equality and will have earned it. This feeling was found in all countries; those (if any) who came back from the trenches to England were promised "homes fit for heroes," in a catchphrase of the day.

The war experience did have a permanent leveling effect on manners and morals, evident in many areas. Thus, after the war "it was harder to tell what class someone belonged to by looking at their clothes," an Englishwoman observed.[3] Arnold J. Toynbee recalled how as a child in end-of-century London he watched the people in the streets and sorted them out by their dress, the working-class women with their shawls contrasting with the bonneted ladies. That was no longer so easy to do. Lord Curzon discovered to his dismay that an aristocratic manner was now a fatal handicap in politics.

A sweeping revolution in attitudes toward sexuality, a new frankness in speaking about such matters, now marked the sudden appearance of a generational estrangement. "It was very swift, this decay," the American writer Vincent Sheean recalled in his memoir *Personal History*. "When I left the University [of Chicago] in 1920 it had scarcely begun. Five years later it was, so far as I could determine, common among people of my age in the bourgeoisie. . . . The gulf between generations had suddenly become immense." Evelyn Waugh thought this was the first real generation gap in English history. This might or might not be "democratic"; it certainly was subversive of long-standing taboos and inhibitions characteristic of the ordered and class-structured society. Women gained the vote in Britain; their status in the post-1918 world, as they returned from front or factory to more traditional roles, was debatable, but they certainly profited from the greater freedom. The new freedom, or what Dora Black Russell called "the right to be happy," was taken up especially by the New Woman, who on the model of the central character in H.G. Wells's *Ann Veronica* (Dora's original inspiration) dared to have her romance and even her children outside the bonds of matrimony. The oldest of patriarchal institutions had begun to crack.

The war destroyed the venerable institution of domestic service: up-stairs/downstairs, the community of masters and servants living together as unequals in a microcosm of organic hierarchy, so beloved of the ancestral order in England, no longer existed. Women now found more career oppor-tunities outside of household drudgery.

Great Britain granted female suffrage just after the war. When John Stuart Mill asked for votes for women in 1867, he had received very little support. Just prior to 1914 Emily Davison and her "suffragette" sisters fought for the vote, which was foremost among their demands for sex equality, valiantly and violently, but in vain. It was now at last conceded in good part because women had served so bravely during the war—they were rewarded, like the lower class, for civic performance. But no such measure was enacted in France, which had experienced worse war trauma than Brit-ain (or Germany) and whose women had proved equally heroic. French conceptions of democracy were much more of the organic variety than England's; if shared danger and combat brought men and women closer together, this did not lead the women to demand separate rights. The argu-ment against woman suffrage in Britain had always been that the vote went with households and families; men exercised it in virtue of their role as head of the family, in a communal and hierarchical social order. Feminism was an aspect of the disintegration of this primeval solidarity, as society became a collection of individuals—an aspect of modernizing and plural-ization. So it is hard to say that the war caused the emancipation of women; it merely quickened an impulse already under way, as it tended to do with everything else. It was, in Marx's phrase, the midwife of history. (French women would get their ballot rights after World War II.)

There was no rush of women to public offices in the postwar decade. The Victorian era, when male democracy pushed its way forward, had seen less feminine political leadership than previous centuries. Queen Elizabeth, Queen Anne, Maria Theresa of Austria, Catherine the Great of Russia— these were only some of Europe's more notable rulers of the sixteenth to eighteenth centuries, at a time when crowned heads had real power. Victo-ria was a figurehead, and it is hard to think of any prominent woman who exercised political power directly in nineteenth-century Europe and the United States (undeniably they did so behind the scenes, as wives and mistresses of public figures). This was the time par excellence of "separate spheres," with men assigned to the public one. But despite their restricted access to higher education, women made significant contributions in literature and ideas, as well as in some of the professions. This last was not just as nurses; the Polish-born Marie Curie, working in Paris, made her way to the top of the world's scientific elite in 1903–11. But politics seemed a male profession. And this continued after the war despite female enfranchisement and fewer social constraints in general. Britain had to wait until 1980 for a woman prime minister; the United States has never yet elected a woman to the presidency. The revolutionary radicals who seized power in Russia at the end of the war were overwhelmingly a masculine society.

Between the two world wars people tended to assume that feminism had won its battles—the vote, legal equality, sexual emancipation, educational rights, professional opportunities—and there was no strong feminist movement until the rather unexpected "second wave" exploded in the 1960s. "Gone are the days of vigorous feminism and antifeminism," British anthropologist E.E. Evans-Pritchard wrote as late as 1955. "Surely these are 'issues that are dead and gone.' " The female vote was for a long time usually a conservative one (more religious, for example). Just as the working class defied all gloomy predictions by being conservative after 1867, so did the women after 1919. The right to vote in itself was less important than the electorate's consciousness and sense of grievance. The embattled radical feminists of a later generation used the democratic process, but also other devices of protest: "politics outside the system," pressure-group lobbying, the courts, publicity, and propaganda. Even earlier, feminists saw suffrage as desirable less for its own sake than as an emblem of equality; it was something men had and women didn't, and was therefore unfair.[4]

The history of twentieth-century feminism, which saw women first agitating violently for the vote, then relaxing after getting it, only to reemerge vigorously in a protest movement fifty years later with a whole new agenda of demands, indicates that it is the deeper social currents and cultural patterns that matter. Without a democratic consciousness, the formal procedures of democracy can mean little; these exist to permit the expression of public opinion, but if that opinion is not there, they are empty.

It was actually a small, activist elite of mainly upper-class women, joined by some men, who so vehemently demanded the vote before 1914. Their other proposals, such as sexual emancipation, relaxation of marriage vows, easier divorce, birth control, appealed as much to the masculine avant-garde as to sophisticated women. Much of this program actually came out of the writings of H.G. Wells, Bertrand Russell, and George Bernard Shaw. When that blue-blooded radical Bertrand Russell, who had campaigned for woman suffrage while embarking on an affair with the wife of the parliamentary candidate he supported, divorced his first wife in 1921, he married (much to her dislike) one of the first female graduates of Oxford

University's Girton College. Together Dora Black and Russell, before their separation ten years later, were to advocate and practice free love and open marriage. Dora had begun by reading H.G. Wells's *Ann Veronica*, the story of an emancipated woman. Wells had a romance and a child with the brilliant woman writer who called herself, after an Ibsen heroine, Rebecca West. All this was part of the interesting history of a notable literary and intellectual generation, but it had little to do with the great majority of people, women or men.

The sense of disappointment some women felt after achieving their long-sought right to vote was part of a general disenchantment with political democracy. That virtually everybody (except perhaps idiots and criminals) now could vote marked the completion of the long drive to democratize and left nothing more to work for on this front. George Bernard Shaw, in *The Intelligent Woman's Guide to Socialism* (1928), commented sardonically:

> If there were any disfranchised class left for our democrats to pin their repeatedly disappointed hopes on, no doubt they would still clamour for a fresh set of votes to jump the last ditch into their Utopia.

But there was none. The goal had been reached, and it was not utopia. Little, indeed, seemed to have changed. It was natural for reformers to look beyond democracy to a new goal, whatever it might be—socialism, fascism, Christianity, Zionism.

Max Weber headed a group of intellectually distinguished Germans who thought that their country lost the war because the German constitution proved inferior to the democracies, which adapted to the needs of the war. The parliamentary system nurtured the necessary war leadership. Lloyd George and Clemenceau proved able to mobilize the masses, whereas the Kaiser and the German war lords could not. The Russian autocracy fell while the French anarchy stood fast. The elective parliamentary system was an effective training ground for leaders, which was Weber's almost exclusive interest. He would have agreed with Lord Lloyd of Dolobran that "[t]here is no such thing as political evolution. There are only the consequences of wise leadership, the consequences of bad leadership, and the consequences of no leadership at all." How to get capable and honorable leadership seemed the central problem of democracy also to the philosopher Henri Bergson.

The democracies won the war on the political, moral front. They proved in the end to have the most stamina in a war of desperate attrition. Was it because they were democratic or because they commanded the most resources, or was there some other reason or combination of reasons? Parliamentary flexibility enabled the British as well as the French to change leadership during the war, Lord Asquith giving way to the more energetic and popular Lloyd George, while the Germans were stuck with a woefully flawed emperor and found no help from the Reichstag.

But the Russians overthrew their antiquated tsardom in 1917 to establish a short-lived democratic republic that could not reverse the course of a disastrous war. The October Revolution, a Bolshevik coup d'état, brought in a regime that quickly showed its contempt for democratic processes by forcibly dismissing the assembly that had been elected to draw up a constitution; it suppressed the other political parties and censored the press. ("We cannot allow the bourgeoisie to slander us," Lenin explained.) The Bolshevik dictatorship headed by Lenin then organized an apparatus of terror including the secret police; for them it was a question of class war to the utmost, in which only the law of survival counted. "The Terror and the Cheka [political police] are indispensable," Lenin declared, adding that they must be "merciless" to any foe of the revolution, that is, of the tiny Bolshevik party.

Nazism, fascism, and communism all "take their effective rise from the war of 1914" (Herbert Butterfield). The war broke apart Russian society and made possible the victory of bolshevism. It was defeat in war that prepared Germany for national socialism. But fascism appeared first in a country that was nominally one of the victors, Italy.

Regarding the war's success in rallying divided and purposeless communities to a moment of glorious solidarity, Hannah Arendt observed that "the strong fraternal sentiments collective violence engenders" are illusory, for "no human relationship is more transitory than this kind of brotherhood, which can be actualized only under conditions of immediate danger to life and limb" (*On Violence*). Such a democratic rally as that provided by the war rested on these fervent but transient emotions, and when they ceased, there was an almost equally intense reaction in the opposite direction. For many in the postwar years, war slogans turned sour in the mouth[5]—not least the one that said it was a war "to save the world for democracy." The postwar years were to produce an outpouring of antidemocratic utterances.

Notes

1. José Harris, *William Beveridge: A Biography* (Oxford: Clarendon Press, 1977), pp. 89, 314–15, 472.

2. See Roland N. Stromberg, *Redemption by War: The Intellectuals and 1914* (Lawrence: University of Kansas Press, 1982).

3. Valerie Steele, *Fashion and Eroticism: Ideals of Feminine Beauty from the Victorian Era to the Jazz Age* (New York: Oxford University Press, 1985), p. 237.

4. "Thus the issue behind the suffrage movement and behind the subsequent agitations over 'equal rights' is, and always has been . . . not so much a demand for the vote, which in itself might be described as a 'minor grievance' rather than as 'a grand old cause,' but a demand for a satisfactory answer to the fundamental question: 'Should a woman be treated as a human being, and if not, why not?' " (Vera Brittain and Winifred Holtby, 1927; in P. Berry and A. Bishop, eds., *Testament of a Generation* [London: Virago Press, 1985]).

5. "I was always embarrassed by the words sacred, glorious and sacrifice and the expression in vain. . . . There were many words that you could not stand to hear and finally only the names of places had dignity" (Ernest Hemingway, *A Farewell to Arms*).

6

Democracy at Bay between the World Wars

Aftermath of the Great Crusade

The effect of the war and the peace settlement of 1919 was a profound disenchantment among the victorious peoples almost as much as among the defeated. "No man who has lived through this [war] can believe again absolutely in democracy," D.H. Lawrence declared. In his study of Lawrence, one of the decade's leading oracles, Graham Hough remarked that "the belief that liberalism and democracy were in collapse was shared by much of the intelligentsia of Europe." The antipopular, elitist tone was virtually the keynote of this brilliant literary age, among its leading figures Oswald Spengler, T.S. Eliot, Ezra Pound, Lawrence, Yeats, H.L. Mencken, the later Freud. German high-culture writers, disenchanted with democracy, helped prepare the way for the demagogue Hitler, while Lenin's revolution in Russia, so appealing to a restive minority all over the world, totally eliminated the democratic element in Marxism.

Thus in the fashionable satirist Aldous Huxley, so different in other ways from his Victorian grandfather Thomas H. Huxley, we meet arguments that science has proved the inequality of man and that there ought to be an intelligence test for the vote (*Proper Studies*, 1927). Democratic inefficiency caused H.G. Wells to yearn for a governing guardian or Samurai class (*After Democracy*), while Bloomsbury aesthete Clive Bell (*Civilisation*, 1928) put the case for aristocracy more on cultural grounds. Bertrand Russell, though deploring the newer intellectuals for their snobbery, missed few opportunities to sneer at the philistines or at his friend and fellow philosopher Ludwig Wittgenstein for wasting his time on village peasants.

"I believe emotionally in democracy, though I see no reason to do so," the young Russell had stated. His lifetime of ambivalence on this point would make an interesting study. "He never did believe that men are born equal in ability," his daughter reported, "and he never felt at ease with stupid, ignorant or prejudiced people, though he was quite willing to devote his life to helping them."

Robert and Helen Lynd's cruel sociological dissection of mid-America's culture in their *Middletown*, a favorite of the 1920s and 1930s intellectuals, noted as one of its curious superstitions the belief that "if periodically given an opportunity to express itself, the choice of the majority of adult citizens . . . will fall upon the person best qualified to fill a particular post." Familiar too was the assertion that democracy is simply a fraud or an illusion. In *The Intelligent Woman's Guide to Socialism*, George Bernard Shaw declared that democracy "has never been a complete reality; and to the very limited extent it has been a reality it has not been a success."

What Oswald Spengler, German author of the internationally famous *Decline of the West* (*Untergang des Abendlandes*—"Downfall" would be a better translation than the usual "Decline"), called "the swindle of the democratic vote" was widely taken for granted in left-wing thought as well as Spengler's kind of right-wing thought: finance capitalists really call the tune using elections as a fig leaf for plutocracy. Or else it is the "managers" (James Burnham) or some other elite group who operate behind the façade to make the important decisions. Political "bosses" still ruled most major American cities; indeed, this was just about their heyday. Most of them, like Boston's James Curley and Kansas City's Tom Pendergast, were simply criminals, making little attempt to disguise their corruption. They would recede only after 1940, with the nationalization of social welfare. (The bosses, as Lincoln Steffens had pointed out in his insightful *Shame of the Cities*, represented a practical adaptation to the real problems of urban industrial society.)

Spengler's widely read historical synthesis (written by a German high school teacher just before the war and published right after it) saw the West as having peaked in the late Middle Ages; modern liberalism and democracy were products of its cultural and intellectual decay. The West's major flaw he saw as a "Faustian" or power-driven soul, rather like Max Weber's rationalization or Marx's capitalism. The cult of the common man is a reflection of the desertion of spiritual grandeur and art for crass materialism and creature comfort. Spengler's only rival in a positive hatred of democracy was perhaps Georges Sorel, the French anarchist turned nationalist who greatly affected Benito Mussolini and whose ideas were noted in chapter 5; much indeed of the fascist doctrine drew on pre-1914 ideas.

Among other scholarly works of an era stimulated by the war to a sweeping reevaluation of the past, Arnold J. Toynbee's massive *A Study of History* was begun in the immediate postwar years and published in six volumes, 1934 and 1939. Of these volumes easily the most impressive was vol. IV, a brooding prose poem laced with erudition on the theme of decline toward disintegration in all human societies or civilizations. Toynbee thought that "creative minorities" are always responsible for human achievements and that breakdown results from a lack of such creativity (rather a tautology, critics noted). An American critic of Toynbee complained that he said no good word for democracy. But in the growth stage of civilizations, according to the British savant, the people respond to the creative minority's leadership; it is only when a general disarray has set in that leadership becomes not creative but corrupt. Still, democracy was acceptable to this great historian only when it was "Christian," and for modern "pagan" democracy with its idolatrous worship of mankind itself (Collective Humanity) and its nationalism, he usually had scorn. To him, as to Spengler, the past couple of centuries, the "democratic" ones, had witnessed nothing but breakdown.

Another major work of scholarship characteristic of the 1920s, on the perennial subject of the ancient world's decline and fall, Michael Rostovtzeff's *Social and Economic History of the Roman Empire* (1926) attributed Rome's collapse to erosion of high aristocratic values by the plebs: it was a cultural failure, with culture being defined as aristocratic. (Yeats: "Base drove out the better blood/And mind and body shrank.")

A swarm of theorists suggested aristocratic or Caesaristic alternatives to democracy in post-1919 Germany (for a discussion, see Walter Struve's *Elites against Democracy*, 1973). These included socialists as well as conservatives. Some of the latter, for example, Othmar Spann, wanted a return to a medieval social and political structure, though how this was to be accomplished remained a mystery.

The distinguished French political veteran Tardieu wrote after his retirement of his disenchantment with the parliamentary system of which he had had such long experience (see *La Reforme de l'état* and *L'Heure de la décision*, 1934). Another prominent figure who rejected liberal democracy after 1919 was the Jewish liberal industrialist and intellectual Walther Rathenau, assassinated by a military gang in 1921.

Of all the antidemocratic arguments, by far the favorite of this postwar generation was that which condemned democracy as cultural degradation. If the prevailing intellectual mood of the 1920s was tied to perceptions of a general regress that had culminated in the 1914 apocalypse,[1] the new and crasser popular culture much strengthened this tendency. Radio broadcast entertainment, movies, Tin Pan Alley music, commercial advertising, and mass-circulation journalism were the startling projections of new technology combined with urban mass society. Young Americans who rebelled against the "emotional and esthetic starvation" of American civilization (see their 1922 manifesto *Civilization in the United States*) blamed it on democracy, which summoned to their eyes visions of Babbitts and Gantrys (Sinclair Lewis's memorable characters), provincial dolts gabbling about the superiority of the United States because it was democratic. Later much honored, the "common man" summoned up to this "civilized minority" images of the shopgirl mentality, the common man as "boob" (H.L. Mencken); of people who voted for Prohibition (the Noble Experiment struck many intellectuals as a crushing example of popular stupidity as well as persecution mania), who harassed nonconformists, sympathized with the Ku Klux Klan, banned the teaching of Darwin, elected Warren G. Harding president. Even when more innocently employed, this common man, generally conceived in the image of a small-town businessman, was a buffoon who joined ludicrous lodges and got drunk at American Legion conventions.

Europeans saw their own high culture threatened by something similar; "modern England is Blackpooling itself," J.B. Priestley lamented (meaning roughly Coney Islanding itself). Others said, Americanizing. A procession of European writers visited the American scene and pronounced it a menace. (*America the Menace* was the actual title of one such book.) Bertrand Russell, whom the American civilized minority paid well to hear insult their national culture ("America persecutes Americans for the opinions it hires foreigners at great expense to express," he noted), painted that culture as a bastard offspring of Puritanism and advanced technology, receiving the worst features of both: an intolerant materialism. With his usual bent for paradox, Russell defended democracy in a 1927 debate with Will Durant on the topic "Is Democracy a Failure?" To him the worst thing about the Americans was that "they lack liberty, leisure, education, culture" (1930). "What is best worth having can only be enjoyed by a cultural aristocracy." André Siegfried, in *America Comes of Age* (1928), pronounced the United States a land without real art and culture.

It was certainly extraordinary that the land of freedom should be accused of lacking it; but a decade that included the great Red Scare of 1919, the Scopes trial, the rise of the Ku Klux Klan, Prohibition, and the Sacco-Vanzetti case as its leading landmarks impressed the intelligentsia, at least, as remarkably illiberal, bent on the persecution of religious and political and social nonconformists. Amid it all the new urban popular culture seemed to threaten civilization itself.

The influence of Nietzsche, Sorel, and Spengler combined with the Bolshevik Revolution to produce a Vichian cyclical image: total degeneration followed by total and barbarous renewal. The apparent cultural collapse of the West into the inanities of popular culture reinforced this sense of profound decadence, the senescence of a civilization that had now outlived its creativity, "an old bitch gone in the teeth," as Ezra Pound called it. The feeling of decline and fall worked its way into almost all of the era's leading literature and history; we need only recall the great landmarks *The Waste Land*, *The Man without Qualities*, *The Rainbow*, *Under the Volcano*, or any of a score of others. In most cases this profound sense of catastrophe included an association of democracy with social decay—a view as old as Plato, but now revivified. Democracy is the normless confusion that is left when an integral culture has fallen apart. ("Things fall apart; the centre cannot hold," which became possibly the most quoted line in modern poetry, came from Yeats's 1920 "The Second Coming".) Proust as a symbol of this ghastly leveling of values has the old Baron de Charlus, now witless, bow to everybody without distinction, meaninglessly. The destruction of a vital culture leads to a kind of mechanization of the soul expressed in the mechanical adding up of votes, "mathematical equality."

Left-wing satire of parliaments and politicians weakened the Weimar Republic thus preparing it for Hitler, as Harold Poor notes in his biography of Kurt Tucholvsky. The 1920s politically was the age of Stanley Baldwin and Calvin Coolidge, simpletons who made a joke of politics. A parade of obscurities passed in and out of office in the struggling German republic too, as was also largely true in post-Clemenceau France. At least they seemed so in the atmosphere of the Lost Generation's great letdown. The bumbling prose and corrupt politics of Warren G. Harding, who seemed like something out of a Sinclair Lewis novel, led on to the bewildered Puritan in Babylon, Calvin Coolidge. Infiltrated by the Ku Klux Klan, the Democratic party offered nothing better.

A quasi Marxist like Walter Benjamin, railing against the cheap and standardized culture products manufactured in Hollywood or New York, while seeking to blame this on "monopoly capitalism" found himself conceding that the masses love it, they "insist on the very ideology which enslaves them," and thus he slipped into using the term "democracy" rather than "capitalism" as his *Schlagwort* ("The Work of Art in the Age of Mechanical Reproduction"). Soviet Russia in the 1920s still was culturally as well as economically unformed; the brilliant crew of pre-1914 Russian artists and poets of the "silver age" still mostly clung to a faith in its future, though one by one they dropped off, and a Stalinized Russia developed an ugly, standardized architecture and literature dictated by the new political bosses.

Fascism and Nazism

What regime did the intellectuals really want or expect to succeed a degenerate democracy? Many of them hailed Mussolini as well as Lenin, without knowing much about either one; later they would regret this. This political irresponsibility of the intellectuals was to become, in fact, almost the scandal of the century. In the 1920s they were implicated in fascism, a decade later in communism. "It is a myth that the Nazi movement represented only the mob," George Lichtheim remarked. "It had conquered the universities before it triumphed over society." French fascist intellectuals of the 1930s included truly first-rate writers like Maurice Barrès and Georges Bernanos. Better known is the thirties intellectuals' infatuation with Soviet communism, but Nazism and fascism did not lack distinguished backing among the intellectual and spiritual leaders of the time, including prominent scientists. (If Einstein fled Germany and denounced Nazism, another Nobel Prize winner, Johannes Stark, stayed and praised it.) Italian fascism and German national socialism appeared to embody the archetypes celebrated in the words of many a prominent poet, novelist, theorist. Carl Jung was alleged to have felt a momentary attraction to Hitler; Martin Heidegger certainly did.

"I don't believe in democratic control," D.H. Lawrence declared. "The thing must culminate in one real head, as every organic thing must . . . an elected king, something like Julius Caesar" (letter of 1915). Lawrence wanted a hierarchy of elections, so that each person would vote for someone he/she actually knew; it was the dreadful inhumanism of the mass election, each person with one vote, that appalled him: the poison of mathematical equality. But at the top of the pyramid there should be both a dictator and a dictatrix (Lawrence believed in the radical difference of the sexes but also in their equal value). Lawrence's "anti-democratic sentiment consorts with an almost religious veneration for the individual human person," Graham Hough remarks in *The Dark Sun*. The great novelist did not admire Mussolini and would surely have loathed Hitler. But there was a certain spiritual kinship, recognized by Bertrand Russell when he crudely accused Lawrence of being a fascist.

Shaw, Sorel, the American Lincoln Steffens, and others were as enthusiastic for Mussolini as for Lenin (oddly, it seemed later); they saw both as strong men slaying a degenerate parliamentarianism and affirming fresh values. If these heroes were violent and murderous, did not a decaying civilization need the strong medicine of barbarism to purge and renew it?

Fascist thought rejected atomistic individualism and affirmed a renewal of community; it demanded a total revolution against what Hitler called "this entire world of opinion," meaning that of selfishness, decadence, corrupt parliamentary politicians. To its followers fascism, like the war that preceded it, initially offered a chance to revivify a world grown old and cold and weary, cleanse it of its corruptions, renew a sense of purpose. That to this end it enlisted a kind of democratic element (democracy of the first sort, totalitarian and not pluralistic) might even enhance the fascist appeal. Contemptuous of upper-class elites, the fascist parties were led by outsiders and little people and appealed unabashedly to popular prejudices, of the sort liberal democrats usually deplored or ignored but that were all too democratic—xenophobia, anti-Semitism, antimodernism in the arts, anti-intellectualism. The "average man" almost everywhere in the West "was patriotic, didn't much like Jews, hated modern art and snobbish intellectuals, was cynical about politicians, the Church, and other Establishment institutions, had little patience with legality if it stood in the way of getting things done, believed criminals should be punished more severely, etc."

In burning the novels of Kafka and the paintings of Klimt, in outlawing Einstein and Freud and denouncing all "modernisms" in art, literature, and thought, Hitler was much more on the side of the "average man" than were the educated elites. The 1920s brought a sharp escalation in the cultural war between the "civilized minority" and the great philistine majority. Hostile audiences had booed Stravinsky and thrown vegetables at post-Impressionist paintings just before 1914, pronouncing them incomprehensible; the 1920s brought even more provocative modernist creations, launching Joyce's *Ulysses* and Surrealist poetry and art at a public just becoming enamored of tabloid newspapers and Hollywood movies. In his youth Adolf Hitler had watched the glittering Vienna scene of modernist art and architecture as an outsider. Refused admittance to the Vienna Academy of Fine Arts and forced to live virtually as a vagabond, he gained from this a hatred of all sophisticated decadence, which he blamed on the Jews. In this profoundly significant cultural conflict, Hitler was more nearly on the side of the man in the street.

Fascism was a response to the collapse of order and authority and integral community that the masses felt as deeply as anyone (more so than the classes); it was a rebellion against permissiveness, pornography, cynicism, "decadent" sophistication associated with the artistic and intellectual rebels. Nazism, Hitler's biographer Joachim Fest writes, appealed to people "with a strong but directionless craving for morality"; people not very sophisticated, not very bright perhaps, certainly not learned, but concerned, indignant about corruption and official arrogance, convinced that sturdy traditional values were being undermined. Perhaps, as psychoanalysts argued, they were types naturally subservient to authority. Simone Weil, no fascist but a left-wing anarchist-socialist, observed that "[h]ierarchism is a vital need of the human soul."

A profile of the Nazi voter describes many in the lower middle classes, no doubt, but also many workers and farmers—"little people." Even the Soviet Marxists sometimes called fascism a revolt of the masses, though they also called it the dictatorship of big capital—quite wide of the mark so far as concerns its origins and rise to power, at least. The Nazis screamed insults at bankers and financiers and excoriated "Jewish capitalism," in a muddled but deeply populist way. Robert O. Paxton has defined fascism as "a mass anti-liberal, anti-communist movement, radical in its willingness to employ force and in its contempt for the upper-class values of the times, sharply distinct not only from its enemies on the left but also from its rivals on the right, traditional conservatives" (*Vichy France*, 1972, pp. 228–29).

Fascism/Nazism's mortal foe was pluralistic democracy, with its divided national will and its weakening liberties, but the fascist ideal much resembled Jacobin democracy in seeking a brotherhood of all the racial comrades. In practice, while producing monstrous tyrannies and injustice, it often overthrew established elites to make a place for new men. "Hitler's notions were violently democratic" in some ways, Keith Robbins remarks. Hitler himself said that "National Socialism is the true realization of democracy." ("We wild Germans are better democrats than other nations," he exclaimed on another occasion.) Hitler always put himself forward as a plain man of the people, risen from poverty, a private in the army, a foe of the rich and privileged.

The elections between 1928 and 1933 that featured the rise of the Nazis brought remarkably high numbers of people to the polls in Germany, ranging from 75 percent to 89 percent of eligible voters. Hitler was undeniably the popular German choice in the 1930s. What if a majority chooses to reject parliamentary and libertarian democracy? If democracy means simply a regime, of whatever sort, that meets with the approval of a very considerable majority of the people, then Hitler's could claim to have been democratic. Hitler came to power in 1933 in a legal, "democratic" way, via elections and the approval of the Reichstag, not by a coup or revolution. The National Socialists won 37 percent of the vote in 1930, far more than any other political party; under the normal rules of parliamentary politics it was hard to justify keeping them out of the government. The Reichstag passed the Enabling Act, which granted Hitler's chancellorship unusual powers—not entirely different from the United States Congress's voting unprecedented emergency powers to newly elected President Franklin Roosevelt in 1933 to deal with the economic crisis. The Reichstag renewed the 1933 act in 1937 and 1941, and in 1937 Hitler had his authority confirmed by a plebiscite, in which, to his disappointment, he won a mere 84 percent of the vote. He wanted 100 percent. Meanwhile he had also been elected president. In a whirlwind of propaganda and ideology he used his powers to mesmerize the German people into believing in his vision of a single, united racial community: "one people, one state, one leader." This extraordinary process cannot be understood except in terms of the organic, totalitarian version of democracy. There was an echo here of the participatory village democracy, the premodern community that of course had never been tolerant or legally egalitarian.

Nietzsche had remarked in 1886 that "[t]he democratizing of Europe is an involuntary arrangement for the rearing of tyrants." He meant that the appeal to unrestricted popular opinion would bring to power the most irresponsible demagogue. Worst would drive out best in a political Gresham's law. In this sense the soil of democracy nurtured Hitler. Hitler found an echo in the common man's all too unappetizing opinions—his anti-intellectualism, xenophobia, crudeness.

> Our evil *Daimon* to express
> In all its ugly nakedness
> What none before dared say aloud,
> The metaphysics of the Crowd.
>
> —Auden

More frequently people said that the failure of democracy had paved the way for Hitler; what they meant by democracy was the Anglo-Saxon rules of elections and parliaments, but there could be other varieties of democracy.

Hitler's brand of "German democracy" aroused such intense hatreds during its frenetic and disastrous period of power (1933–45) that it was seldom associated with democracy elsewhere; its foes used that word to stand for their horrified opposition to Nazism. Some however always saw the Nazi state as a "hyper-democracy" (see, for example, W. Martini, *Das Ende Aller Sicherheit*). It was a government based directly on the masses, without institutional and social checks; Hitler did away with independent centers of power, destroying the trade unions and intimidating the judiciary, persecuting deviant intellectuals and trying to force education, art, architecture, everything into one National Socialist mold.

Germany had perhaps in the past failed to develop sufficiently the judicial and legislative institutions that filter, if they do not block, the immediate popular will. What J.L. Talmon named "totalitarian democracy" thus again became a fearsome danger. If the Nazi state was a menace to civilization, its flaw was a deficiency less of democracy than of constitutional liberalism. Parliaments traditionally had a lower prestige in German culture than they did in English. The liberal theologian Ernst Troeltsch had pointed out in an essay titled "The German Idea of Freedom" that Germans undervalued voting and politicking, while showing a greater concern for inner spiritual and intellectual freedom, which was influenced heavily in the formidable German tradition by Lutheranism as well as by Kant and Hegel. Was this necessarily "undemocratic"? Only, perhaps, from an Anglo-Saxon bias.

But people who fought against the Axis powers in World War II almost unanimously accused them of being undemocratic. This association did much to shape the view of democracy as liberalism. If it was pointed out that the great majority of the German people did seem to support Hitler, the reply in the Allied countries was to condemn the German people en masse, often on grounds suspiciously akin to racism, for having deserted the principles of democracy and the common heritage of western civilization. A considerable body of literature examined the German past in order to locate where the land of Kant and Goethe had gone astray. The Prussian style had always been autocratic and militaristic. (No matter that Hitler, a low-born southern German, hated the Prussian aristocrats and generals, who in turn provided much of what little resistance to the Nazis there was in Germany.) Bismarck had crippled German democracy at a crucial point in its development, preparing the way for Hitler, it was said. (No matter that in temperament and style Bismarck and Hitler were far different.) Japan, loosely allied with Germany and Italy, was said also to be a fascist state, considerably straining the definition of that elastic term. Wartime propaganda depicted the western democracies, Great Britain and the United States, as defending democracy against fascism, its polar opposite.

The Soviet Union as an ally fitted uneasily into this picture; but, as in World War I,[2] ways were found to convert Stalin's regime into a democracy. It is true that from September 1939 to June 1941, when Hitler and Stalin fashioned a marriage of convenience, intellectuals who followed the Moscow party line (by no means an insignificant number) claimed that democracy was really the same thing as fascism. But this phase ended and was forgotten in a surge of wartime solidarity with the Soviet ally, which was now portrayed as having close kinship with American democracy.

Communism and Democracy

The western intellectuals who switched to communism in the 1930s usually joined Sidney and Beatrice Webb in declaring Soviet Russia to be really more democratic than the decaying capitalist West; no parliaments, to be sure, but good riddance, replaced by "economic democracy" or "proletarian democracy." "To accommodate the Soviet Union," historian J.D.B. Miller remarked, "Mr Wallace [the fellow-traveling American vice president and 1948 presidential candidate] invented five kinds of democracy." The Soviet Union was "a great democracy," American writer Theodore Dreiser asserted. In his book *Europe, Russia, and the Future*, the veteran British socialist G.D.H. Cole expected the USSR to "reinvigorate" democratic institutions in the countries it occupied during World War II. Scholar and Labour party adviser Harold Laski, conceding that "there could not be democracy in the Soviet Union in the sense in which the democratic concept has meaning in Western civilization," thought this was a small price to pay for the total reshaping of human nature under communism (*Faith, Reason, and Civilization*, 1944). Just before the war, American left-wing pundit Max Lerner had argued (in *It Is Later Than You Think*) that what was needed was "a militant democracy," which seemed to mean one ruthless enough to wipe out the capitalists and impose "collectivism" by force. The American Socialist party split in 1934–36, a sizable number deserting the traditional position to support seizing power with a minority rather than wait for a majority.

If the regime in the USSR could be called a democracy, the term did indeed seem to be losing what fragile connection it once had to reality. Once they had seized power amid the crumbling society of war-ravaged Russia in 1917, the Bolsheviks (a small number, at most 15,000 strong) quickly institutionalized a completely authoritarian regime and defended the idea that power must come from the top, from an elite, Lenin's "salt of the salt," not elected from below but co-opted from above. "The will of the proletariat is sometimes given effect by a dictator," Lenin explained. Nothing could be more dangerous to the revolution than actual popular rule, which meant ultimately the benighted peasantry. Kamanev observed that if you allow democracy in the Party, tomorrow you will find it demanded for the workers, and finally "even the peasants will have to have it!" "The masses are the masses and they will always be led by someone." Soon after the Bolshevik coup d'état of November 1917, Lenin ordered his troops to dismiss the constituent assembly elected to draw up a democratic constitution. Thereafter his party never attempted to base its legitimacy on the popular will in any but some ultimate metaphysical sense, namely, that the Bolsheviks incarnate the will of history, which in the end, after fierce battles, will bring about a state of happiness for all.

Lenin's more moderate rivals within Russian Marxism, the Mensheviks, were not in principle any more democratic than the Bolsheviks: "Martov had, no more than Lenin, the remotest intention of allowing party organization to develop on democratic lines," Leonard Schapiro wrote in reference to the pre-1914 Russian Social Democratic party. Their governance would certainly have been milder than that of the Bolsheviks, whose leader, Lenin, with the aid of the Polish aristocrat Dzerzhinski, organized an apparatus of secret political police to smell out and terrorize any opposition that might appear. This dictatorship, justified as necessary in a pitiless class war, was supposed to be temporary, of course, but as utopia retreated further and further into the future, the reality of Soviet life degenerated into Stalin's bloody tyranny, from which it has scarcely yet recovered.

Replacing Alexander Dubcek after Czechoslovakia's brutally suppressed experiment in democratic communism in 1968, Gustav Husak said that "cheap gestures and slogans about democracy, freedom and humanism and the so-called will of the people" are "naivete and political romanticism." This was the settled view of the new ruling class that resulted from the Russian Bolshevik revolution of 1917. The originally democratic soviets, or workers' committees, became oligarchies in a process that illustrates Michels's "iron law": an elected legislature of the soviets delegated power to a central executive committee, which was dominated by a small number of insiders. In this way the Bolshevik party, also of course highly centralized, gained control of the soviets. Only one party was allowed, since after all there was only one proletariat. Outlawing of opposition parties was extended in 1922 to include other socialists, who had been denied equal rights from the beginning, then to "factions" within the ruling Bolshevik party; any members who dared to criticize the party policy, once it had been determined, became also subject to arrest and execution.

This concentration of power in an omnipotent executive reminded many of the old Russian tsardom, but the Lenin-Stalin model was even more powerful, doing away with any semblance of an independent judiciary, for example. The goal was to forge an instrument of action and undivided will without parallel in previous history, in order to force backward Russia to industrialize quickly—an ideology of extreme dynamism and titanism. The party rationalized its brutality by the creed of titanic energy. "We communists are people of a special mould," Stalin boasted. "We are made of special stuff." Here were echoes of Nietzsche's superman, an idea found indeed among some of the early Bolsheviks. But "progress through coercion," which is the subtitle of a recent study of Peter the Great, had been a Russian custom ever since that titanic figure lashed backward Russia into the mainstream of western history early in the seventeenth century.

In his study of the attempted Hungarian revolt in 1956 against communist rule backed by Russian tanks, Noel Barber quoted the reply of the prime minister to a student delegation: "You have no right to declare your sympathies with Poland, because the Central Committee has not yet come to a decision on the subject." The Party's top leadership made decisions that were expected to be accepted by everybody. Local Party committees became bodies appointed by the Central Committee. The Central Committee then took its orders from the small Politburo. In the course of time one man would decide the membership of the Politburo. Trotsky, in a reversal of Kamenev's sequence cited above, said that first the Bolshevik party claimed to speak for the masses, then the Central Committee spoke for the Party, and finally one man spoke for the Central Committee. Behind all this lay the perfected apparatus of spying and terror. As Robert Conquest writes, "'Who will rule Russia?' became simply 'Who will win a faction fight confined to a narrow circle of the leadership?' " In his picture of the Soviet inner circle, *Conversations with Stalin*, Djilas noted how remarkably cut off they were from the outer world of Russian society, getting drunk and playing crude party games to pass their time.

It is nevertheless significant that the Communist leaders had a democratic conscience; they wished in some sense to be thought of as democratic. Lenin obviously thought his police state a temporary thing, to be changed when the emergency was over (of course, it never was), and before his untimely death in 1924 he worried a great deal about the course things were taking. Some Communist party members protested (to their ultimate ruin) about the increasing lack of freedom within the Party; there was supposed to be, on Leninist principles, "intraparty democracy" in the form of free debate prior to a major policy decision, though afterward everybody (Party members or not) had to support the decision. It was these critics that Stalin dealt with in the famous "purge trials" of the mid-1930s, when he forced them to confess to other crimes such as treason and sabotage, as if admitting that criticism of the leadership alone was not quite a mortal sin. And even Stalin had an elaborate constitution drawn up and adopted in 1936, which bore no relation whatsoever to what actually happened in the USSR. The cynical thought this was simply to deceive gullible outsiders, but in part it reflected the hope that in the end, after long and bloody preparation, there would indeed be a (perfect) democracy in the Soviet Union.

In his book *Democratic Theory* (1962), Giovanni Sartori claimed that all these ideologists, fascist or communist, really wanted democracy; they were led into sanctioning dictatorship, terror, and mass murder by their impatience and their simple-minded belief that one might obtain a perfect society by exterminating the wicked. There is some truth in this, though in the USSR a deep corruption set in with the institutionalization of terror. In the course of bloody struggles against the peasants, who were the mass of the people, beginning during the savage civil war of 1918–21 and continuing with the enforced collectivization campaign of 1929–31, the Party had become brutalized; the only survivors were hardened fanatics who unquestioningly obeyed the Party's commands from on high.

One might, of course, blame all this on the lack of sufficient civic consciousness and democratic institutions rooted in Russian society. Why did the Russian people allow the dictatorship to develop, and why did the Bolsheviks give up on a revolution from below? It was because there was so little established foundation for self-government among the masses. The long legacy of Russian history under the tsars had contributed to this absence of local self-government. Ivan the Terrible and Peter the Great had by the most violent and arbitrary means set the example of change from above. The answer to this was that the peasants had their communal institutions, which the war and revolution had strengthened, while the soviets of workers and soldiers had begun the revolution democratically in 1917 (as they had in 1905), only to be destroyed by the revolutionary centralizers. In 1921 the soldiers and sailors of Kronstadt base, who had virtually begun the revolution, rebelled against Lenin's government in the name of soviet democracy. The revolt was ferociously suppressed. The revolution of the people had been destroyed by an organized power elite. (The desire of the peasants to own their own land ran counter to the Bolshevik hierarchy's insistence on collectivization.)

Those who reconciled Soviet communism and democracy could only do so in some ultimate sense, supposing that democracy will exist after the dictatorship has hammered a new humanity into shape (by liquidating a goodly percentage of its present members). "The utopian liberals," American Communist luminary Corliss Lamont wrote in 1937, "believe that vast social changes can be brought about with the same politeness and restraint that characterize an afternoon tea-party." Endowing these "vast social changes" with an absolute value, the Communist true believer thought virtually any price worth paying to bring them about. Since such a utopia became increasingly remote, one must suppose that those western intellectuals who continued to approve and defend the Stalinist regime really did not value democracy. "The truth of the matter is that totalitarianism is a doctrine very flattering to intellectuals," Jonathan Sumption claimed. They were seldom happy with the drift and muddle of pluralistic democracy, together with its implicit denial of any single truth or standard of value. In their notorious seduction by Stalinism in the 1930s, what they sought, as those who went through the experience testified, was a new dogmatism, "the intellectual comfort and relief found in emerging from a tragic predicament into a 'closed system' of beliefs that left no room for hesitation or doubt" (Arthur Koestler) and "progress toward a new community of belief" (David Daiches).

"The once zealous spokesman for democracy and free speech became an inflexible apologist for Stalinist totalitarianism," his biographer says of the American Communist and fellow traveler Scott Nearing. (An early convert, Nearing left the Party when it tried to give him orders, yet remained a staunch defender of all Soviet policies.) That so many western intellectuals, who were fierce nonconformists and freethinkers, became uncritical supporters of such a tyranny—the scandal of the century, one might argue—has suggested to some that their need for a healing faith was so urgent that it blinded them to reality. There is evidence that they knew much of the truth about Russian horrors but were prepared to overlook it. They condoned the sacrifice of human lives and liberties to the faith they had found after long agony of soul and were not about to abandon at any cost. Democracy to them was a pallid cause compared to this dramatic if bloody vision of the apocalypse.

One might add that both the fascists and the communists eventually became more or less good democrats. After the collapse of the bureaucratic and authoritarian communist system in the Soviet Union, and throughout Eastern Europe, in 1989–90, Communist parties renamed themselves Socialist or Social Democrat or Workers' parties and competed at the polls, often with success. The Italian Communist party had earlier accepted the principles of pluralism to play a role as one of several political parties contending for office; after 1989 it dropped the name of Communist altogether. Not only that, but in Italy there was a resurrection of the Fascist party, led by a man who once called Benito Mussolini "the greatest statesman of the century" and who became probably the most popular political leader in Italy in 1995, not as a would-be hero-leader but as a democratic politician. Perhaps, belatedly, these extremists of Right and Left had learned to resist what a French critic called "the totalitarian temptation."

However that may be, in the interwar years they stood as rival champions of militant ideologies equally contemptuous of a degenerate parliamentarianism and what Mussolini called "the lie of universal suffrage."

Other Democratic Failures

Other places also failed to sustain democracy in the post-1919 years. The nine new states planted in Eastern and Southeastern Europe in the "Balkanization" that emerged from the war, for which the disintegration of both the Austro-Hungarian Dual Monarchy and of the Russian Empire was chiefly responsible, lacked secure foundations in history and ethnicity. Their attempts to introduce parliamentary government usually failed. Poland, restored to independence for the first time since 1772, found that such a government "was ill-suited to coping with the fractious ethnic, social, and economic problems of the country," as Keith John Lepak remarks (*Prelude to Solidarity*). "The weak governments, the constantly feuding multiple parties, and the corruption of the parliamentary era" evoked widespread revulsion and led to a quasi dictatorship under Marshal Pilsudski, military hero of the war against Russia that ended in 1921 with a Polish victory over the newly created Red Army.

Assassination of a representative on the floor of the parliament brought an abrupt end to Yugoslav democracy, and a king governed by decree after the first few years until his own assassination in 1934; civil war was to break out with the coming of World War II. There was also a personal monarchical regime in Rumania. The old-fashioned monarchy seemed to have much to recommend it; countless people in all parts of the dismembered Dual Monarchy were said to wish that "Papa Josef," the last of the Hapsburg emperors, would return, and if allowed to vote on it, a majority of Bavarians would surely have favored bringing back the Wittelsbachs. Among the successor states of Eastern Europe only Czechoslovakia managed to make democracy work. Austria, left abandoned as the rump of the old empire, and denied the right to join Germany as most of her citizens would have preferred, underwent severe civil strife. A façade of democracy in Hungary concealed actual dictatorship; elections were fraudulently manipulated. A country with as many problems as Austria's, now shorn of all its possessions, could hardly afford democracy.

At the other end of Europe, Spain passed from autocratic rule through a brief and unstable republic to a bloody civil war that was the most famous event of the 1930s. Between 1923 and 1930, General Miguel Primo de Rivera governed in the name of the king. His was a somewhat enlightened dictatorship, but he encountered liberal opposition and was forced to resign, after which the king soon "withdrew" also and a republic was proclaimed. Its five years of life were marked by bitter political strife between Left and Right, with both of these blocs themselves divided. The first republican government embarked upon the confiscation of property, cut back funds for the army, and assailed the church. New elections in 1933 brought a swing back toward the conservatives. The Asturian miners then rose up in rebellion, while Catalonia tried to secede. Further elections in 1936 produced a lurch back to the Left, causing a military-led rebellion against the republic. Bitter class animosity, the religious question, and regional ethnic minorities combined, many said, with the headstrong Castilian temperament to create the worst possible conditions for parliamentary government. From 1936 to 1939 Spain became a battleground in which outside forces intervened to turn it into what looked like a climactic struggle between fascism and communism. Mussolini and Hitler sent aid to the nationalist rebels, Stalin helped the republican Loyalists, while the western democracies, including the United States, declared a plague on both houses. There actually were not many fascists or communists in Spain, until these outside forces intervened to take control of the war. Volunteers from Britain, France, and the United States joined some anti-Nazi Germans and others to create a 40,000-strong International Brigade to fight in defense of the republic, but some of them came away disillusioned at the way the communists persecuted other left-wing groups.

This passionate and dramatic crusade, enlisting the intellectuals of the world and producing some great works of literature, was thus less a defense of democracy than of socialism or communism. The victory of the nationalists and consequent establishment of a right-wing military regime seemed (though in fact General Franco was much less a "fascist" than a traditional clerical-military authoritarian) to underscore the lesson of the decade as a battle for the minds of men between the two opposing ideologies of fascism and communism, both hostile to democracy. This notion of an apocalyptic struggle between two faiths, in which democracy was a bemused bystander, dominated the decade's thought and poetry. As Cecil Day Lewis wrote:

> private stars fade in the blood-red dawn
> Where two worlds strive.

One had to choose between Hitler and Stalin; there was no third way.

Ironically enough, the long-expected outbreak of another great war came when the two dictators buried the hatchet, sinking it into hapless Poland as they signed the Nazi-Soviet pact in 1939. This was the climax of a diplomacy in which further weakness of democracy seemed exposed.

Foreign Policy and the Coming of War

Quite a few analysts blamed democracy for the erratic policies that led to World War II. Challenged by National Socialist Germany's bid to overturn the Versailles Treaty and restore Germany's hegemony in Europe, vacillating politicians representing an irresponsible public in France, Britain, and the United States between 1934 and 1939 refused to face the Nazi menace, opposed rearmament, preferred to "appease" Hitler; then they abruptly changed and, after selling out Czechoslovakia in 1938, decided to fight for indefensible Poland in 1939. The democracies, France's Paul Reynaud declared, neither armed themselves nor allied themselves, until too late. But they could not even follow through to the end the only other option, which was surrender (disguised as "appeasement").

The weakness of the 1919 peace settlement, it was frequently said, was that it got the worst of both worlds, insulting the Germans without mortally wounding them. The inequities of the treaty preyed on the democratic conscience of the Allies, and they gave in to Hitler's demands for equality and self-determination after they had refused such favors to the weak Weimar Republic. British prime minister Neville Chamberlain found Hitler's demands meritorious ("on account of racial affinity or of just claims"), and indeed it was hard to argue that Germany was only claiming the same rights as other states (to arms equality, freedom from military occupation, admission of German minorities in Czechoslovakia and Poland, merger with Austria). But then having conceded the point in the cases of Austria and the Sudetenland, Great Britain and France reversed themselves and decided to fight for Poland. The United States had withdrawn to sullen isolation in the 1930s, a considerable majority of her citizens convinced that U.S. entry into World War I had been a ghastly mistake and that the British and French were as bad as the Germans.

This uncertain diplomacy, the consequence of public mood swings, continued on the whole during the war, the outcome of which left much of Europe in Stalin's hands. Tocqueville long ago had noted, in *Democracy in America*, that "it is especially in the conduct of their foreign relations that democracies are decidedly inferior to other governments," being inherently incapable of "designing a plan and sticking to it," while also keeping it a secret. "Foreign policy requires the use of almost none of the qualities which are congenial to democracy, on the contrary it demands the development of almost all those which democracy lacks." In the realm of foreign relations, the democratic propensity to compromise often produced fatal results. In facing a determined adversary, one can resist firmly or else decide the battle is useless and give in with good grace. What is dangerous is to waver, to half-resist, to shout defiance and then appease, to do the opposite of what Theodore Roosevelt advised; to speak loudly but carry a small stick.

Tocqueville's allegation, often repeated by others, compelled American secretary of state Dean Acheson to publish a book in 1962 on the "real and imagined handicaps" of democracy in foreign relations; others too have attempted a rebuttal. Whether or not it is true that democracy necessarily handicaps foreign policy, in the game of power politics between 1935 and 1940 the harassed politicians of the West were no match for the dictators. Germany's Adolf Hitler, pursuing his path toward war in 1939, felt a sovereign contempt for the leaders of the democracies, France and Britain. "I have seen these little worms at Munich," he said, referring to their appeasement of him by deserting Czechoslovakia in 1938 to save the peace. He could issue his threats and make his diplomatic moves free from their handicap of having to keep a wary eye on public opinion, fearful of doing anything that might disturb their fragile hold on office.

Democracy seemed to select its leaders primarily on the merits or otherwise of their role in domestic issues. Thrust into the American presidency in 1945, and forced immediately to make urgent decisions about the peace settlement and the future of the world, Harry Truman said, "I didn't know anything about foreign policy." In this respect, he was typical of American politicians. If in this case the matter turned out better than might have been expected, the answer would be Lord Bryce's, who, commenting on the way the world's greatest democracy selected its top leader, observed that "success in a lottery is no argument for a lottery." In the 1930s, when Hitler was on the prowl, President Franklin Roosevelt was wholly preoccupied with urgent questions of Depression-fueled economic issues, as was true also of the beleaguered leaders of France and England. Roosevelt's tendency to choose his diplomatic appointees from among "wealthy campaign supporters, academics, military men, and old friends" (Arieh J. Kochavi) stood well within an old American political custom too. Since foreign affairs were not very important, one could use them as a dumping ground for patrons and incompetents.

Soviet Russia was also in the throes of vast internal changes that incapacitated her for a strong foreign policy. The weakness of Hitler's foes could thus not be blamed entirely on "democracy." It was the result of weakness, and an absolute as well as a democratic regime might suffer from weakness. If the specific defect of western foreign policy seemed to have been a kind of muddled indecisiveness, there was also sentimentalism. Pacifism was abroad, of course, the result of a deep reaction against the slaughter of 1914–18; everybody was vowing never to fight again, *nie wieder Krieg*. Bertrand Russell could hardly be accused of muddleheadedness when in 1936 he published a pamphlet advocating surrender to Germany. The only alternative was war, he saw, and that was even worse. In the event Russell could not act on his logic and supported the war against Hitlerite Germany. But the strength of antiwar feeling, nourished on vivid writings about World War I, slowed the pace of determination to rearm and resist.

Such feelings had been prevalent in Germany too; probably the most moving and widely read novel about the war, transferred memorably to the cinema in 1932, was the German Erich Maria Remarque's *All Quiet on the Western Front (Im Westen Nicht Neues)*. Hitler changed all that, by the sheer force of his will and his command over the German people— the triumph of a sort of democracy. At any rate one might agree that parliamentary democracies can usually act less quickly and decisively than dictatorial governments, that they tend to produce compromise strategies, which are weak ones in a domain that requires clarity and decisiveness, and that dependence on public opinion may lead to abrupt swings as well as to simplistic positions.

Decisions about foreign policy are uncomfortable for democracy because they are probably more shaped by conditions beyond control. Democracy must depend for its effectiveness and plausibility on an assumption that there are alternative policies, some of which are better than others in dealing with a not wholly recalcitrant reality. If what governments must do is wholly determined by a set of implacable objective forces, what basis is there for preferring one form of government over another? An elected parliament would be forced to do the same things as an absolute monarch, no doubt more clumsily and slowly. The pure democratic model has the people making decisions about what is best to be done, among a number of possible choices, and transferring this decision to their representatives. Though admittedly no decision is entirely free from constraining circumstances, there must at least be some room for choice and free will.

This is less true in foreign policy, because decisions are forced by the actions of other countries that a government cannot control. The German people willed Hitler, and the Americans and British had to react to this. Their peoples might vote for the ostrich policy, and in fact did so for a time. (The British public overwhelmingly approved a peace referendum in 1936 that proposed that the League of Nations do something about Germany while Britain disarmed.) But in the end they could not avoid the unpleasant facts of an international situation they could not change. The war forced itself on publics regardless of their wishes.

It is true that decisions about domestic policy often have constraints and that in fact it is hard to draw a clear line between foreign and domestic questions. (Where does a tariff act fall?) But in general a particular people and government are more in control of their own destiny when the issue is a purely internal one. To decide whether to build more roads, or to change the educational system, or to prohibit the consumption of alcohol, does not much depend on what other governments do or want. The democratic process is supposed to consider various possibilities and decide on the most desirable one. Not so when the enemy is at the gate and allies are in danger.

It had been a part of the democratic ideology that wars would vanish when the people gained control of governments. The main cause of war was said to be an aristocratic feudal-warrior ethos, or the irresponsibility of a ruling caste cut off from public opinion and corrupted by its power. Even Tocqueville conceded that democratic nations are naturally peace-loving. Erasmus had long ago contended that the common people sacrifice their lives in quarrels that concern only princes. "Their governors had fallen out," Carlyle explained, "and, instead of shooting one another, had the cunning to make these poor blockheads shoot." Count Tolstoy was even more demagogic: "Those who devise and prepare for these plunders and murders, and who compel the working people to carry them out, are but an insignificant minority who live in luxury and idleness upon the labor of the workers." This strain of thought, with roots in Christian millenarianism that it shared with the socialists, considered the greed of rulers or the irresponsibility of elites as virtually the only significant causes of war. The powerful liberal-bourgeois school of economics, led by Cobden and Bright in England, varied this only slightly in holding that war would disappear when people learned to devote themselves to production and trade, as individuals, causing both aristocracy and the state to dwindle away.

Events were to cast serious doubt on this picture. Much of nineteenth-century left-wing rhetoric dwelt on the need for the people to rise up in holy wars against their oppressors, whether foreign or domestic. Mazzini, the archdemocrat, said that "[t]he people armed in a holy cause" is the most inspiring spectacle known to man; it "awakens to a kind of inspired life and exalts to enthusiasm capacities for struggle and sacrifice." "I hail the glorious emancipating battles of humanity, from Marathon down to our own Legnano." War, Mazzini added, is a great crime "when not sanctified by a *principle*." But when it is so sanctified, it is sacred. Marx and Engels, as well as their socialist rival Proudhon, thought that war was the great locomotive of human progress. The latter, a famous anarchist-socialist, was a particularly enthusiastic extoller of war, which he called "the basis of our history, our life and our whole being." In 1848 Marx and Engels called for "implacable struggle, war to the death against the Slavs . . . extermination, terrorism without stint." The great democrat Charles Péguy in 1914, and Julien Benda in 1940, launched powerful arguments against those who would deny the Republic the right to defend itself in war against the foes of liberty (see Benda's eloquent "Pacifism and Democracy," in *Foreign Affairs*, 1941).

So the assumption prodemocratic ideologists often made, that undemocratic government was the chief cause of war and that popular control of foreign policy would bring an end to war, can hardly be seriously maintained. Why had Chateaubriand, reversing the liberal bromide, declared that "[d]emocracy means war"? World War I showed how popular war can be. In 1914 a few opponents of the war argued, as did the British Union of Democratic Control group, for example, that a few professional diplomatists had made the crucial decisions for war, having already tied their hands by secret treaties the public did not even know about (such as the Anglo-

French understanding about naval operations in the event of war with Germany). They could hardly deny, however, not only that the war was immensely popular—in the last analysis the chief cause of the long war was surely an incredible popular support for it—but that the decision to fight rested on a manifest national interest that any government would have had to recognize.

Halford MacKinder, in *Democratic Ideals and Realities* (1919), was among those who claimed that the democratic spirit largely ignored foreign policy, as did the socialists. The Fabian essays of 1889 contained not a single examination of foreign policy or international relations, and the Fabians, as Beatrice Webb confessed, never had a philosophy covering this area. ("Such political philosophy as I possess," she cried in 1914 at the onset of the war, had not equipped her to understand "racial wars." Socialists generally alleged only that the triumph of socialism would bring an end to all war.) The heated American presidential election of 1912, immediately prior to World War I and featuring three parties with able leaders—probably the best of all American campaigns—scarcely discussed foreign affairs at all. The traditional American ideology regarded this topic as almost immoral; only decadent Europeans, wedded to force and fraud, had foreign policies. Alliances between states, balances of power, indeed anything about "power" at all, were wicked and essentially antidemocratic or nondemocratic. Count Leo Tolstoy, the powerful Russian preacher of social reform, declared that "the great majority of people" take no part in wars or preparations for wars except against their will; those who devise and prepare for "these plunders and murders" are a small minority living in "idleness and luxury." This was not far from the Cobden-Bright English liberalism, which saw war as resulting from aristocracy and bound to disappear in an epoch of commerce.

The Liberal party that held office in Great Britain in the eight years before 1914 reveals an almost total separation between its ideals and its practices. Dedicated overwhelmingly to domestic issues, it talked of foreign affairs, when it did discuss them, in terms of disarmament, arbitration, no alliances, and Anglo-German reconciliation. They cried out against any friendship for despotic Russia. Yet the actual Liberal government went on secretly developing a virtual alliance with France, rearming, playing the game of balance of power and diplomacy against Germany, and making various imperialist "deals" such as the 1907 one with Russia over Persia. This actual governance of foreign relations occupied another world than that of the democratic ideologues. When the war came, the latter in the main adjusted uncomfortably, deciding that Russia was a democracy, Germany a despotism, and that war must be waged to "make the world safe for democracy."

This argument against democracy in foreign relations, that it suffered from a total lack of realism, obviously depends on associating democracy with a kind of utopian mentality that in fact contained elements of Christian pacifism, socialist indictment of capitalism, and general moral righteousness discharged against a wicked world. As the "peace movement," it occupied a special niche in the political and moral constellation, flourishing before 1914 but even more in the 1920s and 1930s, when great tides of fervent opinion, led by churchgoing women, such as produced the Kellogg-Briand Peace Pact "outlawing war," swept through the world. The peace movement was not the same as democracy. There was an affinity, obviously, at one time. But in 1940–41 as in 1914, the democracies turned warlike with a vengeance.

Public opinion in regard to war is generally both confused and inconsistent. People may initially support a war, and then, turning against it, deny that they ever had done so, rather as Bertrand Russell was caught in a flat lie about an opinion he had once held regarding war with the Soviet Union, which he had changed and then expunged from his memory. Popular opinion will flay as antidemocratic the leaders it originally encouraged to undertake the conflict. Such was the case with the notorious Vietnam War in the United States; it is often forgotten that American military intervention in Southeast Asia, which eventually became so unpopular, was approved by a substantial majority of Americans in its early stages.

"If the United States had been governed by an autocrat not subject to public opinion, the war in Vietnam would almost certainly have been brought to an end several years earlier," a writer remarked in 1973 (*Times Literary Supplement*, May 11, 1973, p. 520). Vietnam also supplied a glaring example of the ill effect of democratic tendencies to compromise; President Lyndon Johnson, listening to both hawks and doves among his advisers, pursued neither peace nor war with any determination and ended by getting the worst of both worlds.

On the other hand, public opinion may indignantly oppose military intervention only to reproach leaders later for not having taken such action: Reginald Bassett, in his *Democracy and Foreign Policy*, found this to have been true for the Manchurian crisis of 1931–32, and much the same analysis could be applied generally to the response to Hitler's aggressive actions in the 1930s: condemned in hindsight, "appeasement" was overwhelmingly popular at the time, when it counted.

In the United States in the early 1930s, liberals pushed a constitutional amendment to require a national referendum before the government could declare war; within a few years this became an embarrassment as most of them wanted to bring the United States into war against the Axis powers.

"Democratic enthusiasts clamored for popular control of foreign policy and then complained when the popular veto ruled out war except in self-defense," as Keith Robbins observed. They in fact supported the highly personal diplomacy of President Franklin Roosevelt, which tended to by-pass both Congress and the State Department.

In the great American debate of 1939–41 about whether to enter the European and Asian wars or remain neutral, interventionists and isolationists both copiously invoked democracy. The former saw the chief issue as defense of liberal and democratic societies against the "totalitarianism" of Nazi Germany and (until June 22, 1941) Soviet Russia. The isolationists or neutralists replied by insisting that a class-ridden, monarchical Britain was no more democratic than Germany. This apart from the Marxists, who believed that Germany and Britain were both "capitalist" and nothing else mattered. "The intellectuals who are at present pointing out that democracy and fascism are the same thing depress me horribly," George Orwell wrote in January 1940, forgetting that he himself had occupied this position not long before. Pro-Soviet *compagnons de route* were at that time presenting this argument. Both sides framed the question (of war or peace on Hitler's terms) with reference to democratic ideology. But in the end it was power, not ideology, that counted. In order to defeat Germany and her ally Japan, the Anglo-American Allies warmly welcomed the Soviet Union as an ally after Germany attacked it in 1941; as in 1914, reasons were quickly found to deem Russia a great democracy rather than a monstrous tyranny. But the Allies moralized the war as a struggle against monstrous evil, and thus insisted on total victory without compromise—"unconditional surrender." So, lurching from pacifism to total war, the democratic polity sowed the seeds of future conflict. "Wars in chain reaction," as Raymond Aron argued in a notable contribution to the literature on war, result from wars waged *à outrance*, which end in total victory leaving vacuums of power as well as bitter hatreds that engender new wars. Such, allegedly, has been the tendency of democratic wars. Democracy cannot fight limited wars for limited objectives but, once it has blundered into a war, must moralize it and fight it to the utmost. "The war of peoples will be more terrible than the wars of kings," Winston Churchill had predicted before 1914, without realizing he would live to prove the point. Others, including Karl von Moltke, had said the same: "It will become a war between peoples which will not be concluded with a single battle but will be a long weary struggle with a country that will not acknowledge defeat until the whole strength of its people is broken."

The tendency of democratic publics seemed revealed in the slow, sometimes stupid, but often powerful tides of mass opinion regarding international problems. Subtleties are beyond it, and compromises with the enemy strike it as immoral. The flexibility that enabled eighteenth-century rulers to switch sides and go in and out of a war for tactical reasons is unthinkable in a democracy. That kind of action seems cynical, but it enabled states to avoid anger and thus escape treating the defeated in a way that bred revenge. The vindictive peace settlement of 1919 led to World War II, in which the policy of unconditional surrender led to total destruction of the enemy with subsequent vacuum-of-power conflicts. With this in mind, Walter Lippmann was among those who questioned whether democracies are inherently capable of waging war "for rational ends and to make a peace which would be observed and could be enforced." The post-1945 clash of the USSR and the western bloc chiefly over control of Central Europe was once more constructed as an ideological struggle, between democracy and communism. Hans Morgenthau, in his *In Defense of the National Interest* (1951), complained that when the Americans decided to make a response to the grievous weakness in Europe, they put the matter "not primarily in terms of . . . the maintenance of the European balance of power, but in terms of a moral principle." The conflict could not be between the United States and the Soviet Union; it had to be between "totalitarianism and democracy." In the view of Morgenthau's school of realists, this made the problem worse, by inflaming it and befogging the real issues.

The answer to all these indictments of democracy in foreign policy might be, for one thing, that inconsistency and unpredictability, or shrinking from hard choices, or moralizing the issues, or refusing to confront the realities of power, are not monopolies of democratic governments. The undemocratic ones often exhibited them too and handled their foreign affairs just as badly. We have noted Napoleon III's horrible mistakes. Neither the fascist nor the communist dictatorships carried out foreign policies that were models either of success or lucidity. Consider Stalin's lurches in the 1930s, which included inadvertently helping Hitler to power in 1933 and then, after trying clumsily for a popular front against Hitler, forming an alliance with him in 1939, after which the Soviet dictator refused to believe the Germans would attack Russia in 1941 when all the rest of the world knew of it.

The conduct of foreign relations is a frustrating and difficult art that is seldom done well by anybody. American mistakes could as well be attributed to a lack of experience in foreign relations, a result of the long period of relative isolation from the outer world and the turning of national energies inward. No doubt an enlightened despot, a Bismarck or Metternich, is preferable to a weak elected leader burdened by a fickle populace; but then a bad dictator is worse. This restates a judgment as old as Aristotle, that rule by one can be either better or worse than rule by many.

Bismarck, like Britain's Lord Salisbury, thought that you could not count on any alliance made with a democracy because the regime and the policy might change at any time. Soviet foreign minister Andrei Gromyko complained, when facing a new American president in 1977, that "[o]ne cannot talk about stability when a new leadership arrives and crosses out all that has been achieved before!" Advantage, perhaps, to the despot, except that maybe long-term alliances between states are not the best way to peace, as 1914 may have demonstrated. Or perhaps a democracy may indeed stick to an ally for a long time, as in the case of Great Britain and the United States.

Nevertheless a considerable literature echoed Morgenthau, especially after 1945, in probing democratic weakness in policy making during a more testing period in world affairs. We turn to that era in the next chapter.

Notes

1. "The Victorians had begun to be dwarfish and misshapen. Their Twentieth Century successors were abortions. Through the mists of the future one could see a diminishing company of little gargoyles and fetuses with heads too large for their squelchy bodies, the tails of apes, and the faces of our most eminent contemporaries, all biting and scratching and disemboweling each other" (Aldous Huxley, *Point Counter Point*).

2. See J. Dover Wilson, in R.W. Seton-Watson et al., *The War and Democracy* (London: Macmillan, 1914), who argued that Russia has "a fundamentally democratic spirit."

7

World War II and After: Democracy in Low Key

Democracy in World War II

A spate of books published during the war testified to a swing toward democracy. Among wartime books on democracy in the United States and the United Kingdom were Edwin Mims, Jr., *The Majority of the People*; Carleton K. Allen, *Democracy and the Individual*; Henry Steele Commager, *Majority Rule and Minority Rights*, all denying any insoluble contradiction between individual liberty and majority rule; Julian Huxley, *Democracy Marches*; C.J. Friedrich, *The New Belief in the Common Man*; Henry A. Wallace, *The Century of the Common Man*. A collection edited by a Marxist literary critic, Bernard Smith, titled *The Democratic Spirit*, reprinted selections from canonical Americans from Roger Williams to Carl Sandburg. Composer Aaron Copland wrote a "Fanfare for the Common Man," who seemed at last to come into his own. He had triumphed over the *Führerprinzip*.

This applies especially to the Anglo-Saxon democracies. The situation was somewhat different in France. Defeated, humiliated, and partly occupied by the Germans, France engaged in an orgy of self-reproach in which, as before 1914, democracy was sometimes blamed for the failure. This was the case not only with those who attempted to rally around the regime of General Pétain in unoccupied France, but also with so relatively independent a thinker as Emmanuel Mounier. He blamed "liberal democracy" for the fall of France: "We believed that it was parasitic, like dust or lichen, but we failed to recognize that it was venomous, eating into France as surely as spiritual evil or social disorder" (November 1940). But in the end almost all reputable defenders moved away from Pétain, resistance to the Nazis drew Frenchmen of all sorts together in an antifascist unity, and the Free French returned in triumph with the victorious Allies in 1944. Free French leader Charles de Gaulle preserved some of the animus against parliamentary democracy, however, in his vision of a kind of neo-Jacobin nation united in an organic democracy that shunned political factions and parties and that was incarnated in a great leader.

Strictly speaking, "the leadership principle" is not undemocratic, in the context of organic democracy. In this kind of folk democracy, the leader is chosen spontaneously, raised on the shield—"we recognize the man," the British Tories still said—and granted full power to act as director of the community. It was this kind of archaic folk community that the low-born Adolf Hitler thought he could restore to Germany. The great conflict of World War II was really between the two kinds of democracy, not between democracy and "dictatorship," a more pejorative term than "leadership." To complement it, the term *totalitarian* came into usage at this time and took on sinister qualities.

Totalitarianism, originally Mussolini's term, was used to embrace both Hitler's and Stalin's attempt to destroy all nonconformity and to force everyone to subscribe to the same values, those of the one people or party. The opposite of this was more nearly individual liberty or minority rights or pluralism. But almost always this liberalism was called democracy. Similarly, the National Socialist ideology asserting the racial superiority of "Nordics" or (loosely) Germans was taken as a sign of antidemocracy, though in fact it underscored the democracy of the German people; they were all supposed to be superior beings and, as such, equal.

The "common man" of Allied discourse tended to vanish in clouds of rhetoric, like "the people" in earlier discourse (perpetuated in Carl Sandburg's "The People, Yes"). The concept owed something to this war's mystical vision, not as powerful as that of World War I but a strong vision of everybody coming together to defeat Hitler and the Japanese warlords. The egalitarianism of army life was saluted on Broadway in an Irving Berlin musical. London, of course, underwent the moving experience of a people standing together almost alone during the German bombing raids of 1940–41. There was Shakespeare in the underground shelters during air attacks and in Laurence Olivier's film production of *Henry V*.

Once again, the western democracies had, after all, won the war and in doing so demonstrated considerable efficiency. James Burnham had predicted the Nazis would win the war because of superior efficiency; he cannot have known much about the real situation. It would be closer to the mark to say the Nazis lost the war for want of efficiency; consider their resounding defeats in the intelligence war and their failure to produce the atomic bomb. While suffering little damage from their own defectors, the Allies gained enormous advantages from the services and information of those inside Nazi Europe, including some in Germany, who hated Hitler's new order. The only effective traitors within England and the United States were those who gave their primary loyalty to the Soviet Union, and in this war that country was an ally of the western democracies. (Kim Philby and other British moles probably did something not only to ensure that no deal was cut with any non-Hitlerite German group, thus forcing the invasion and occupation of Germany, but also to see that the Communist resistance movement triumphed over its rivals in Yugoslavia.) In the struggle for men's minds during the great global war, one could plausibly argue that liberal democracy had triumphed over fascist totalitarianism.

When attempts were made to define it, this 1940s version of democracy strove to give it a social welfare component. The war followed closely on the Great Depression with its rebellion against laissez-faire economics, its American New Deal of government-administered welfare, its Keynesian school of new economic theory stressing the role of the state as economic stimulator. The welfare state had earlier beginnings, of course, reaching back at least to the New Liberalism of the years just before 1914, which had seen Great Britain imitate Bismarck's Germany in enacting the national insurance principle of government-administered old age and unemployment payments, with an income tax to help pay for it. At the same time in the United States the Progressive movement featured an intellectual campaign against "chaotic individualism" that would, it was hoped, strengthen democracy by bringing about a more equal distribution of wealth and a more responsible attitude toward the destitute. The Progressive drive to subject industry to regulation and punish or break up the trusts accompanied their interest in democratic reforms, such as direct popular election of senators, direct primaries, and initiatives and referenda. Emphasis on this kind of statist economic reform as democratic (see, for example, Weyl, *The New Democracy*, 1918) was more pronounced in the United States than in Great Britain.

Now the new economics and the experiences of the 1930s, followed by wartime planning for war production, demonstrated the ability of human intelligence to plan for full production. A book by the famous Czech statesman Edvard Beneš in 1939 (fateful year for the republic he headed) called *Democracy Today and Tomorrow* urged augmentation of state services in a vaguely socialist direction, as did Wallace and Friedrich, cited above, the latter titling a chapter "Planning for the Public Good." The ideological climate of the war, in which the Soviet Union between 1941 and 1945 was an ally, nourished an impulse to draw on Stalin's model, not indeed to its extremes of political elitism and repression, but in its principle of state socialism—perhaps a nice blending of American capitalism and Russian socialism might work best. A 1940 manifesto by western intellectuals in a fine flight of rhetoric asserted that "[d]emocracy ... must be redefined: no longer the conflicting concourse of uncontrolled individual impulses, but a harmony subordinated to a plan; no longer a dispersive atomism, but a purposive organism" (Herbert Agar et al., *The City of Man: A Declaration on World Democracy*, 1940). This was the thrust of much World War II rhetoric in the Allied countries; compare John Dewey, *Freedom and Culture* (1939), and above all the famous British Beveridge Report of 1942, "Full Employment in a Free Society."

William Beveridge was a belated convert to the welfare state, which he had once thought inconsistent with democracy and individual liberty. Such doubts now vanished. That "planned production for use not profit" was superior to capitalism's chaos and greed, all right-thinking, that is, left-thinking, intellectuals accepted in principle, if not always in the Russian practice. Such views came not just from Marxian dogmatists but from such anti-Communists as Albert Einstein and Bertrand Russell, the paladins of thought. Sometimes the term was *collectivism*, a bit less frightening than *socialism*. Historian Paul Addison remarks that "[t]he intelligentsia worked with great success to establish collectivism as the conventional wisdom for all thinking people." "Collectivism," in British usage, meant nationalization of some basic industries combined with centralized state administration of welfare and social security, along with trade unionism, the unions being given special powers and protection by government.

When T.S. Eliot asked Karl Mannheim whether his "planning" was not an undemocratic concept, "Mannheim replied that democracy as he saw it involved the availability of leading positions to the broad mass of the people, who were selected according to certain principles not identifiable with wealth."[1] In other words, whatever served to improve the economic condition of the masses, and hence their opportunities for career advancement, was democratic. To which one might object that a socialist system, or some other paternalistic order, ruled by experts and without any place for popularly elected bodies, could claim to be democratic on this definition. But Mannheim's usage was very common.

Democracy in Low Key

After the rhetoric of the war of ideologies had died away, sometimes leaving, as after World War I, discordant echoes, the term *democracy* tended to fall back into a much lower-keyed discourse in the West. There was no sharp and bitter rejection, as after World War I; democracy, if not pushed too far, seemed decidedly a good thing, as an antidote to the strident totalitarianism that had just come close to destroying the world. The discourse of 1939–45 had upheld democracy as the opposite of Nazism. Democracy was a Cinderella whose humble virtues shone forth after the gaudy sisters, fascism and communism, turned out so badly. "Their fanaticism," Bertrand Russell wrote, in the end "roused the hostility of the world" against the Nazis and led to their downfall. One-time elitist Gaetano Mosca after living under Mussolini came to feel that "the defects of parliamentary assemblies are merest trifles compared to the harm that inevitably results from abolishing them."

This latest apotheosis of democracy presented her in the guise of moderation and common decency against the overwrought idealism of those "smelly little orthodoxies," as George Orwell called them, that plagued the world. The mood carried into the fifties, when disillusionment with the communist "god that failed" seeped through the intellectual community. The idea of democracy shaped by clashes with totalitarian dictatorships of both Left and Right was a subdued variety. It stressed the inevitable imperfections of any political society. It conceded democracy's defects. Democracy was seen not as an "ideology" but as the opposite: "There can be no ideology of democracy," Christopher Martin wrote in praising "political apathy." Peter Calvocoressi discussed "Democracy in Low Gear" (*The Listener*, March 5, 1964). Two cheers for it, not three, E.M. Forster recommended in a famous essay.

In *The Revival of Democratic Theory* (1962), Neal Riemer suggested that democracy is suitable to a "heterogeneous, ambiguous, paradoxical" world. In *The Democratic Prospect* (1962), Charles Frankel expressed content with the kind of government and society that, rather than seeking to inflict on us some strident dogmatism, leaves us alone to search each in our own way for the good. Julien Freund suggested we reject *la politique* and enthrone *le politique*: down with the total ideology, up with the practical adjustment of differing viewpoints (*Le Nouvel Age*, 1970). Such an outlook was not far from the conservative theorizing of Michael Oakeshott, prestigious in England in the postwar years. No political "system" or theory is valid in politics. "Every claim in the sphere of human affairs to an absolute truth," Hannah Arendt argued, "strikes at the very roots of all politics and all governments."

The trouble with such low-key defenses of democracy, stressing its negative virtues, was that they could easily slide into a resigned rejection of the whole idea. "Democracy is out," T.E. Utley wrote in 1955 (*Spectator*, January 21). "It is the theme of almost all intelligent writing about politics today that ... majority rule as an institution has a permanent and increasing tendency to produce either dictatorship or bankruptcy or both." "It can hardly be denied that democracy no longer inspires the same enthusiasm as it inspired in Rousseau or the men of the French Revolution," Bertrand Russell observed in 1952. Among the best known novels of the 1950s, William Golding's *Lord of the Flies* was a parable on the theme of failed democracy. Marooned on an island, a group of boys find themselves in a Hobbesian state of nature; their efforts to establish democratic government lead only to a brutal dictatorship.

It has been noted earlier that the idea of progress favored democracy; the reverse was also true. Political and cultural pessimism meant a rejection of democracy's claims to be the last and best of human governances. There can be no guarantee of the victory of democracy over tyranny, Reinhold Niebuhr pointed out, since there is no guarantee of any victories in this world. No political order can overcome the taint of imperfection inherent in human affairs. It is a bent world, never to be entirely straightened out; its troubles are from eternity and will not fail. Such a diagnosis threatened any system's claim to success. But other forms of government had not usually claimed to have the final answer that would overcome this imperfection; despotisms or oligarchies more often invoked this view of ineradicable evil in their defense. Granted, C.S. Lewis, the tremendously influential source of a sophisticated return to "mere Christianity,"[2] said that he was a democrat because of original sin: men are "too wicked to be trusted with more than the minimum power over other men." The pessimism that had caused Maistre and Schopenhauer to reject democracy now served as a defense of it. If all men are base, how can rulers be exempt from this frailty? Niebuhr, another prominent representative of the return to Christianity, who wrote much in criticism of democracy, accepted it so long as it is not elevated to the primary object of worship and thus made idolatrous (see also Arnold Toynbee); democracy is the least bad of possible governments in an imperfect world. This was, however, hardly an argument most democrats would find congenial.

Probably the most widely read serious book of the decade, George Orwell's *1984* (1948) voiced a warning against the imminent danger of "a centralized slave state, ruled over by a small clique." If its most obvious target was the Soviet Union, which Orwell had assailed at a time when most of his fellow British intellectuals thought this a shocking heresy, and which he had satirized in *Animal Farm*, *1984* also targeted aspects of western democratic society as well as the totalitarian ones. Its popularity lay largely in its appeal to those who believed their own British or American governments were encroaching more and more on personal liberty. The chief source of this threat, as Orwell saw it, lay in the triumph of technology and its accompanying bureaucratic mentality, and the treason of the intellectuals who manufacture lies and distortions for the ruling class. Orwell's enemy was not democracy but modern industrial society, and his remedy seemed to lie in a return somehow to simpler times and less corrupted people—to a kind of Rousseauist bucolic utopia. Democracy could stand for the good old days before urban anomie had created a society of strangers. "My chief hope for the future is that the common people have never parted company with their moral code," wrote this singularly honest and appealing writer. In this respect Orwell joined those disillusioned pessimists who despised the masses slightly less than they loathed their betters. Still, his picture of what, he feared, contemporary society was or was about to become depicted the total defeat of democracy by forces of social and moral decay.

Voter apathy plumbed new depths in the 1950s. British Labour party membership fell precipitously, from more than a million in 1951 to less than 200,000 in 1980, according to Peter Jenkins—a reaction from the exaltation of its 1945 triumph, which suffered severe disenchantment in the 1950s. Academic students of politics dwelt on the electorate's unattractive qualities; the people were ill-informed, uninterested in political issues, irrational in their judgments. "An extraordinary world," Auberon Waugh called the voters' one, "half make-believe, half ill-digested fact, swayed by deep unbudgeable prejudices or by an occasional reckless spirit of the moment" (compare Le Bon in 1912: "fantasy, illusions, chimeras"). Peter Pulzer claimed to have established that the 25 percent of unaligned or floating voters, who commonly decide the outcome of elections, is not the most intelligent and responsible part of the electorate but the least (see his *Political Representation and Elections in England,* 1968).

That the man in the street lacks the understanding and the knowledge to form an intelligent judgment on most public issues was hardly a new insight, but it seemed especially noteworthy now. He showed for the most part little concern about the issues. This *incivisme* killed the Fourth Republic in France and, a generation later, seemed to imperil the Fifth, which Charles de Gaulle had created in order to circumvent the frustrations of party politics. Local elections brought out fewer than 50 percent of the voters in France. In 1965 a student of American politics found apathy "on a scale unknown anywhere else in the Western world."[3] The percentage of Americans who bothered to vote was lower than in any other major democratic nation; this was in the most thoroughly democratized of all countries, in some ways, with the deepest national tradition of democratic faith.

It had once been a commonplace that the mass of people were not up to the demands of judging wisely on political issues. "I do not think the public ever think," a character in Disraeli's novel *Tancred* remarked. "How can they? They have no time." But the late twentieth-century citizen steadily gained not only more leisure from long, toilsome labor, but also more education. The average workweek had declined since Victorian times, roughly from 60 hours to 40 hours, and educational levels had risen even more dramatically, with a special leap forward for higher education after 1945. Less than 1 percent in 1900 entered university in Britain, distinctly a privilege of the upper class; only a tiny minority even went to secondary school. By 1960 the latter level was almost universal, and 25 percent were going on to some kind of advanced education. With more leisure, more wealth, and more education, surely the people could now become informed and intelligent voters. The process itself, Mill had thought, in one of his few arguments in support of democracy, would make them so; democracy is an educational process. As they practiced it, citizens would grow ever more intelligent and knowledgeable.

But this did not seem to happen. Late twentieth-century people spent the leisure awarded to them on a hundred other things: participating in or watching sports, watching television, exercising; looking after their personal appearance, their health, their love life; figuring out their income tax, playing with their personal computers, vacationing. Programs on television, viewed by tens of millions, were seldom about public affairs; telecasts of that sort, a few of which were presented from a sense of duty, were usually confined to Sunday mornings or subsidized "public" stations, which had few viewers. The great majority regarded these programs as unutterably boring. The popular shows were about murder, terror, invasions from outer space, sex, preferably all of these together; or sports events, games, cartoons, comedy, and other trivia. Those serious people who defied the general trend were more likely to devote leisure hours to eastern religious meditation than to political meetings.

If there was more leisure time, there were far more distractions for modern urban man and woman. And their personal problems were far more time-consuming than in simpler times when finding a mate and keeping one, as well as selecting a career and training for it, had not required a great deal of planning and anguishing. (You followed your father's trade and married the girl next door.) The rates of mental illness, alcoholism, drug addiction, divorce, child abuse, crime, suicide, and other indices of social dysfunction suggested that more people today are desperately confused and unhappy in their personal lives; no time to worry about public policies.

Plain people, perhaps, could not be blamed for a failure to grasp the full dimensions of public questions when the experts themselves had become confused. There was no longer any accepted or dominant school of economics, for example; on the major issues, such as whether there should be government intervention in the economy and, if so, what kind, there was basic disagreement among distinguished economists. The economy, they would murmur, is too complex to yield to any simple formula; there are no "invariant laws," no "certainties." Even the hard scientists proved poor guides, changing their minds as often as the economists, or psychologists; they first issued dire warnings about "global warming," stimulating a rash of drastic measures to reduce carbon dioxide emission, and then decided the whole thing was a mistake. The public, even if disposed to have a serious opinion, could hardly find one that was not debatable. Thus the complexities of postmodernist life defeated the old model of a single truth that all the people would gradually learn to recognize and accept.

"Apathy" is perhaps in need of definition; the evidence for it was that people did not bother to go to the polls, even on serious issues, or to take part in political debates. But this attitude itself may have been a serious or informed one. People may have refrained from voting in the spirit of that Shavian character who said that "like most intelligent people I never vote." They had seen through the fraud of democracy. Or a withholding of judgment can be the expression of a point of view: I do not like any of the parties/candidates/positions; I do not think there is a positive solution to the problem; I have not seen enough solid evidence on the basis of which I can intelligently judge. The very imperfection of the democratic process may force noncommitment. Thus, when in 1979 a third of the Scots did not vote on an urgently important referendum about Scottish autonomy, this was not because they didn't know or didn't care about the question, but because they were honestly ambivalent: there were good arguments both for and against Scottish independence or autonomy.

When all excuses have been offered for the failure of the citizens of democracies to understand the issues and to vote (bear in mind that many elections brought out no more than 15 to 20 percent of the eligible voters, a turnout no better in Europe than in the United States), there remains no alternative but to admit that the large majority of people do not want to be bothered with the complicated questions of public policy they are supposed to grasp, and that this has not improved nor is it likely to. "Few people," Pulzer wrote, "are sufficiently interested in politics to follow or discuss current affairs regularly, or re-think their position in the light of this information from one election to the next." Not many thoughtful political observers would have disagreed with this estimate. The direction of everyday life in the ensuing years offered little promise of change. If anything, the rise of distractions, such as popular television programs and movies viewed at home, and computer games for young and old, made for even less time and inclination for a serious interest in public affairs and issues. Perhaps it was significant that the once lavishly subsidized Center for Study of Democratic Institutions (California) was reportedly reduced in 1975 to living off the proceeds from a book written by one of its senior fellows, *The Joy of Sex*.

It is true that political interest was subject to extreme volatility. In France, between 1951 and 1962, only a small proportion of the French people indicated much interest in politics. (The largest party of all was those who did not vote.) Gaullism revived interest, with the presidential election of 1965 setting an all-time high of 85 percent voter participation. Later, apathy and disgust set in again. The evident lesson, reenforced by the Kennedy years in the United States, was that charisma is only a fleeting antidote to voter apathy. The Gaullist Fifth Republic, installed in 1958 after the post-1945 Fourth had lost all credibility, sought to escape the deadlock of parliamentary politics in a much-divided country by giving more power to a president elected on the American plan, separately from the legislators and able to appeal directly to the people via plebiscite against the parliament, and installed for seven years, a good deal longer than the American presidential term.

The Left no more than the Right—if anything, even less so—found democracy in the sense of popular rule appealing. The people in fact continued their habit of opposing nearly everything the enlightened vanguard regarded as progressive. Nearly 90 percent of the Harvard University faculty supported presidential candidate George McGovern in 1972, so he lost by the largest margin in modern presidential history. The term *silent majority* became an epithet of contempt. A liberal writer found it "sad" that conservatives should "point to the popular voice" in support of their positions. But, replying on behalf of the conservatives, William F. Buckley denied this aspersion (*New Republic*, April 8, 1978; *National Review*, May 26, 1978). (Everybody speaks respectfully of the people's wisdom when his viewpoint has a majority but speaks scornfully of the rabble's ignorance when it doesn't.) It came to be conventional wisdom that an excess of popular opinion is an evil to be guarded against; governments tried to time their hard decisions to come as far away as possible from an election. A liberal commentator in the *Manchester Guardian* in 1978 found "the thought of the unfiltered popular voice playing around with" complicated modern technological questions a "terrifying" one. This had changed little since John Stuart Mill argued in the nineteenth century that the intelligent minority should prevail over the stupid majority, or, otherwise put, that the majority must respect limitations on its power in the name of reason.

Political activists enjoyed sailing against the wind, struggling for unpopular causes and perhaps enjoying the experience of mild martyrdom. They contended with the sodden passivity of the masses. If their cause won in the end, it was not perhaps because they won an electoral majority. Most of the striking changes in the United States, generally applauded by liberals, such as racial desegregation, legalized abortion, toleration of pornography, abolition of capital punishment, emerged not from the legislatures or public opinion but from the Supreme Court, the one undemocratic source of power in the United States. When British jurist Lord Devlin argued in 1964 that law should reflect the sense of the community, he outraged not only liberals but most other lawyers; Devlin's legal populism was assailed from all directions as about the most ridiculous opinion any learned man ever held. Schoolteachers denounced the practice of requiring approval of any new spending on public schools by a popular referendum, because this almost always defeats the proposal.

Theoretical writings probed democracy's weaknesses or inconsistencies. R.G. Collingwood's *New Leviathan* repeated the point that "[e]very democracy is in part an aristocracy, and every aristocracy is in part a democracy." The majority does not and cannot rule; if it did, the result in a modern state would be disastrous. The influential Oakeshott school of conservatism associated democracy with eighteenth-century utopian rationalism. Politics is an irrational or "practical" realm for which no general principles can be prescribed. The same view may be found in Hannah Arendt's striking political writings. This seemed to be a return to Edmund Burke, who had declared that there are no general truths in politics.

Needless to say, the path of cultural democratization continued to arouse alarm, as with the coming of television the mass media continued their assault on aesthetic values. Walter Lippmann's *The Public Philosophy* (1955) can serve as an example; the distinguished American critic and columnist issued something like a call to defend the high aristocratic traditions of Europe against an upstart massism threatening the extinction of all civilization as well as public order. This sense of cultural doom was of course a century old by this time and had been repeated in each generation from Flaubert on. Its futility as well as its repetitiousness tended to cause it to wane. Democracy is "inherently hostile to the first rate," wrote Thomas Griffith in a book called *The Waist-High Culture*; many others echoed his lament. "What we are witnessing in all the arts . . . is the liquidation of 500 years of civilization," Jacques Barzun lamented. In an era when literacy, if not sanity, seemed menaced by the global village's television culture, the civilized minority might have been expected to intensify its scream of horror. But the very hopelessness of that cry caused it to lapse into a mutter.

Mass higher education having arrived everywhere, few of the voices that used to deplore it (a long tradition extending from John Henry Newman's Victorian *Idea of a University* down to Robert M. Hutchins, Abraham Flexner, and José Ortega y Gasset in the interwar period) were any longer heard. "More is worse," Kingsley Amis muttered, but for better or worse more had come to stay, everyone realized.

Power Elites and the New Left

The best means of selecting rulers and managers is "by cooption among the members of each branch of the service, as promotion normally ensues in armies, banking houses, universities and ecclesiastical hierarchies." So thought the veteran philosopher George Santayana, in *Dominations and Powers* (1951). Pareto's "fluid elite" reappeared as the "meritocracy" in sociological literature.

The favorite study of academic political scientists in fact now became "power elites." Professional scholars armed with computers endlessly labored the point raised at the end of the nineteenth century by Pareto and Mosca, that democracy merely produces another sort of elite governance. But now it was added that a multiplicity of elites prevents dictatorship, making the people at least semisovereign.[4] There are many elites, and they cancel each other out by being in competition. The condition of a free and modernized society is "polyarchy" (Robert Dahl's term). And this pluralism of oligarchies is better for liberty than an undiluted popular-will democracy. In Geoffrey Gorer's words:

> I should say that the characteristics of democracies as we have known them and their chief claim to being a more desirable political system than any alternative lies precisely in the fact that the locus of power cannot be precisely determined, that the specialists in power, the people who have come to the top of the power hierarchy . . . do not have a monopoly of social power; their influence and their predominance are modified by those of individuals at the top of other socially recognized hierarchies.[5]

Alfred Weber (1946) went so far as to argue that the best weapon against the rule of the masses is "freedom and democracy." Pluralist democracy is a safeguard against the rule of the "people" in a totalitarian manner. This, of course, is what used to be claimed for constitutional liberalism.

Power, on the analysis of Bertrand de Jouvenel (*Du Pouvoir*, 1948), has increased steadily and incrementally regardless of forms of government. Present democratic governments are far more powerful than any medieval or early modern kings, who had to act as tyrants precisely because they exercised such a limited range of power. Their theoretical power was greater but their practical power, limited by technical constraints, was less. (If they caught some rebel or outlaw, they could deal with him with far fewer limits on their power, but they couldn't catch very many.) The size of governments had immensely grown over the centuries. These early rulers lacked money, cadres, administrative structure. Roland Mousnier estimated that in 1500 there was about 1 official of the state to every 1,000 people in western Europe; in 1565, after a crucial era of state making, the ratio was 1 to 76. Today the ratio is more like 1 to 15 or 20. Robert H. Ferrell in his biography of President Harry Truman says the executive branch of the United States government grew from 600,000 employees in 1933 to 2 million in 1953. Today it is 3 million. (The State Department in the nineteenth century had consisted of three or four people.) The president's own White House staff grew to be so vast that he lost control of it.

The number of junior ministers in the British Cabinet increased from none before 1832 to 15 by 1914 and 64 in 1995. By a heroic sacrifice Prime Minister John Major had managed to cut back to this number from 65. The same principle that decrees that no equality is ever lost ensures that the size of government is never diminished.

And so modern man is actually less free than he was in the days of absolute monarchies: more subject to a variety of compulsions, from going to school to paying taxes and needing a license for almost everything, and more spied upon and informed upon, with reams of information about his life on record. If in desperation he sought to numb his mind against these pressures, he could be arrested and fined for using illegal substances. If he joined a religious commune and refused to pay his income tax, the feds might gun him down.

Appraisals of democracy like everything else vary widely from decade to decade, if not from year to year. In 1956 Robert Dahl (*Preface to Democratic Theory*) argued that "moderation" and "social peace" resulted from American democracy. It hardly seemed so a dozen years later. Some of the rebellious youth who flourished in the 1960s dreamed of a purer and better democracy, direct and immediate. A rage against establishments and authorities swept the intellectual community. Voting, elections, ministers, cabinets—how bourgeois! New Left ideologues sought to "put an end to politics" or to practice only a politics of confrontation and direct action. Or to "unstate" politics, bringing it down from the remote chambers of national power to the streets. Only the revolutionary mob is socially authentic, thought Jean-Paul Sartre. In this anarchist utopia each individual would be self-regulating and the group would be naturally harmonious.

Despite slogans about "power to the people" and "participatory democracy," these prophets of revolutionary violence were in fact consumed by a

Nietzschean contempt for the masses. "Real men—most of them—sicken him," it was said of Herbert Marcuse (Maurice Cranston, *The New Left*, 1971, p. 116), a judgment amply born out by Marcuse's own words (for example, *Essay on Liberation*, 1969, p. 68 ff.). Neil McInnes observed that "Marcuse's aristocratism is the leading feature of his criticism of democracy, of industrialism and of the mass distribution of cultural works." The young radicals' democracy seemed to consist of being somehow allowed to "do their own thing," away from an urban, industrial, bureaucratic mainstream they abhorred. There was a curious inconsistency in these unkempt outsiders' claim that they represented "the people"; the paradox said something about the ambivalent status of the concept democracy. Their leading organization in the United States was Students for a Democratic Society. They declared that the absence of real democracy justified the "civil disobedience" so much in fashion. They could, in brief, choose to disobey those laws they didn't like. "I dream of some day living in a democracy," one of these anti-establishment figures declared. "Some day we will participate actively in running our own lives in all spheres of work and leisure." Apparently, to judge from the exhortations of Jerry Rubin, this would be after murdering their parents and many other figures of authority.

West German Socialist chancellor Willi Brandt said that "the democratizing of our society" is the task of this age. French politician Pierre Mendes-France wrote a book calling for the rejuvenation of democracy via participation. President Charles de Gaulle called for it too, meaning a healing somehow of the rift that separated the average citizen, who "has no grip on his destiny," from government. Whatever their naïvetés, advocates of "participatory democracy" focused attention on one striking fact: that the standard sort of political democracy actually is based on nondemocratic social institutions. Democracy does not run through all our social institutions but is a kind of façade on the surface of society. Business enterprises no more than educational institutions, nor for that matter governmental bureaucracies, make use of democratic methods of operation. Professors are not chosen by vote of the student body any more than corporation managers or military officers or diplomatic agents are hired, fired, and promoted by popular acclaim. This is hardly a matter of the economic versus the political; if practically all businesses are autocracies or oligarchies, so are universities, hospitals, and other public institutions where technical qualifications come into play, as is true of virtually all of them. Those involved in these institutions which govern everyday life would say that democracy destroys them, by substituting ignorance for expertise and undermining directional authority.

Perhaps it is because everything else is so firmly authoritarian that political society as a whole could be democratic. Democracy at the national level in a sense is possible only because there is no democracy at the local level: if the government of the whole state or nation is meaningfully democratic, then it must possess the authority to overrule the actions of any small unit within its boundaries. In the United States, a law passed by one of the states of the union that is in opposition to federal law cannot be enforced. If a state, or each small unit such as a factory, a village, or a university, were to have full powers to govern itself, there would be no central government to exercise the popular will via elected representatives.

Those who wished to extend the principle of democracy to everything, to bring about the *Entstaatlichung* of politics, thus took on a formidable task, assuming they were serious about it. Perhaps the radical students simply wished to embarrass the hated establishment by exposing its cherished values as frauds or hypocrisies. But they could rightfully assert that the existing kind of democracy was inadequate. A Yugoslav writer, in that year of revolt both East and West, 1968, observed that "the impotence of the citizen before the powers that control his life" was virtually as great in the western democracies as in the eastern communisms. "That's the meaning of all your demonstration marches, your letters and petitions left at Downing Street or the House of Commons" (*The Listener*, June 27, 1968). "Politics outside the system," meaning in effect the mob or the act of terrorism, came into being out of a deep frustration at the hopelessness of politics inside the system to accomplish any meaningful change.

Insofar as experiments in workers' comanagement of business enterprises, or other forms of participatory democracy, were made, they were subject to the same problems that afflicted democracy in the first place. Why does democracy turn out to be so imperfect that we have to have a participatory revolution to establish the real thing? Will not the same thing happen to *this* democracy, that is, domination by an elite? The distinguished sociologist Ralf Dahrendorf noted that participation tends to self-destruct as it is extended. For it means the creation of new organs of politics that fall under elite control and become just additional pressure groups in the pluralist order.

Studies of experiments in industrial democracy usually showed that a large majority of employees do not want to "participate" in running the company, because they lack the requisite aptitude or interest. Even if they do, they must resort to electing their representatives, for in an enterprise of any significant size not everybody can sit on the company board; this is not much more feasible than having every citizen sit in Congress. So one came back to the problems of representation and alienation, at just a slightly lower level. Interest in industrial democracy or self-management faded after some initial interest. In 1973 Jürgen Habermas (*Kultur und Kritik*) claimed as one of the New Left's enduring achievements this democratizing at the level of institutions and not merely the state. But, like his other examples (the depatholigizing of mental illness, the decriminalization of crime, the de-aestheticizing of art), the *Entstaatlichung* of politics scarcely made much of an impact on the real world, except perhaps in the universities, where its influence was debatable. Industrial "self-management" proved a disastrous failure that contributed to the collapse of Yugoslavia: workers short-sightedly voted for immediate wage increases at the cost of both investment and expanded employment.

The New Left's political activities were seldom on anything like a practical level. The hippie culture did participate somewhat in the American election of 1972, which saw the crushing defeat of Democratic presidential candidate George McGovern.

The reader of a representative literary document left behind by that unusual campaign, Hunter S. Thompson's *Fear and Loathing on the Campaign Trail '72*, gets the impression that amid much profanity, consumption of alcohol, and pot smoking these would-be kingmakers didn't like the other Democrats any more than the Republican opposition, which they thought truly loathsome. McGovern's leading campaign manager turned out to be "an evil bastard," and the campaign was run by "technicians." Most other Democratic politicians were corrupt or time-serving "old politicians" (there was now supposed to be a "New Politics"), whom Thompson characterized as "old hacks and ward-heelers." Nor did the young leftists really like each other very much. McGovern himself failed to get his case across to the public because, according to Thompson, he was "goddam maddeningly inept." But the voters were to blame for their "apathy, stupidity, and laziness." Why bother with politics anyway?—a wretched game. And so they all got stoned and wrecked the airplane on the way back to Washington. It had all been a nice "happening," which undeniably shook up the old pols. That their candidate lost by the largest margin in presidential history the new politicians seldom blamed on their own views or personalities. Thompson's own desire was for a "genuinely radical" leader who would confiscate all inherited wealth and decree a 100 percent excess-profits tax. But such candidates were in short supply, and so after puzzling over the shattering McGovern defeat at the hands of Richard Nixon, Thompson could only head back to the fashionable ski resorts of Colorado to organize local Freak Power. Nothing showed more clearly the distance between this "democratic" element of intellectual sophisticates and any possible politics.

The far left of the New Left engaged in terrorism and assassination, or milder "civil disobedience" lawlessness, which led to a strong public reaction against the whole movement. Their leaders urged children to murder their parents (Jerry Rubin) and everybody to kill policemen (Timothy

Leary). If these sentiments represented the movement, what was intended was less a democracy than a general pandemonium.

Much of the rather confused image of democracy in this eventful decade emerged in Jacques Ellul's *Illusion politique* (1966). He protested the "politicalization" of life, and the "technological society" he had berated in another popular work; also the old ideological mythologies, which screen us from existential reality (a bow to the fashionable existentialist philosophy). Public opinion, he agreed, is a menace to sound public policy when aroused. Yet beyond politics and beyond ideology, Ellul visualized some sort of future for democracy—exactly what is difficult to say, a utopia evidently of free, mature individuals in a totally sincere society. Student rebels of the 1960s shared some such fuzzily hopeful vision, though it was difficult to characterize them as mature. They were certainly unlikely democrats, violently hostile as they were to the whole mainstream society and culture. The puzzle remains why, especially in the United States, they so persistently described their goals as "a democratic society." The answer might lie in their perception that, as it stands, the western "society" as distinct from politics is not at all democratic. Given the chance, however, to take part in university governance, the students generally found it too boring; they were the least likely of bureaucrats too.

Postmodernist Democracy

But the "postmodernist" intellectual era, alienated from its own alienation, brought the common man somewhat back into vogue. Modernism with its violent rejection of mass culture lost status, and with its decline the time-honored complaints about cultural and intellectual degradation diminished in force and frequency. In the late democratic era intellectuals moderated their tendency to sneer at the masses and bash the bourgeoisie. Perhaps it was because they had been bought off with university appointments. If they complained it was against the government for not giving them more. They might cultivate their own esoteric gardens of hyperspecialized research and vow never to pander to popular taste. "Not for us is the limelight and the applause of the public at large. . . . The economic scholar works for the only coin worth having—our own applause." Thus asserted Paul Samuelson in the 1961 presidential address to the American Economics Society, a disavowal rendered somewhat ironic by the fact that his university textbook earned hundreds of thousands of dollars. But they did not shout *odi profanum* quite so loudly as in former times. Poets previously confined to bohemia now found comfortable niches in universities. Art, lavishly subsidized by the government, was successful big business.

Postmodernist critics even asserted, more or less seriously, that Las Vegas architecture was as good as Le Corbusier's, Raymond Chandler could be stacked against Cervantes, and Mickey Mouse might hold his own against Puck. The structuralist vogue of the 1950s and 1960s had undercut content to reveal the formal similarities of high and low art. On one hand, public television, recorded classical music, mass reproduction of works of art (whatever the concern of intellectual mandarins about their lack of "aura") brought the old high culture much nearer the masses than ever before. Opera stars became international celebrities rivaling sports heroes in their popularity. And, on the other hand, the mass media imposed a uniform culture; postgraduate students and blue-collar workers watched and read more nearly the same thing than at any time in the past. The gap closed from both directions: if more clerks and laborers, now perhaps college educated, listened to and read the "classics," highly specialized Ph.D.'s might be illiterate outside their own narrow area of expertise or might perhaps self-consciously take up the study and collection of comic books.

Their ghastly mistakes regarding communism and socialism severely shook the confidence of the intellectuals in their political judgment. The average man had proved politically shrewder than the intellectuals. ("The man in the street, I'm sorry to say, is a keen observer of life," W.H. Auden belatedly conceded.) Postmodernism saw Adam Smith, once considered the nadir of bestiality, win a belated victory over Karl Marx, just as Disney triumphed over Dali. The collapse of the socialist ideal has been called the greatest failure of the century; it was recorded not only in the surrender of the communist world to the marketplace but in the abasement of the British Labour Party, routed by a grocer's daughter preaching hard work and competition, and by a wave of divestments and privatizations all over Western Europe. To survive, the Labourites had to become converts to all this. The whole era of the intellectual, beginning with fin de siècle aesthetes and leading on to Leninist fellow travelers, had ended in the postmodern triumph of capitalism and mass culture. Many intellectuals lamented their political impotence, or turned high conservative, or just quietly rejoined the kindly race of men, perhaps by way of a career in academia or the mass media, with the rewards from which they could insulate themselves from the vulgar crowd via travel, home entertainment, PCs and VCRs, the Internet, and all sorts of dazzling products of the electronic age.

They could, of course, find in democracy a subject for new fashions in interpretation. Democracy, it seemed, had deconstructed itself, in the terminology of this intellectual fashion. Max Weber and others had already done that. In realizing itself, democracy destroys itself: masses of voters can only be handled by concealed elites. Masses of people considered as equals necessitate rules, which means bureaucracy, which in turn means elites and arbitrary decisions. As every citizen knows, more and more of the real power to determine vital issues falls into the hands of administrative officers controlled with the greatest difficulty by popular or legislative will—or into the hands of courts of law, whose arbitrary verdicts may bear only a remote relationship to the laws they are supposed to be applying. Parliament, as Andrew Mar observes in *Ruling Britannia* (1995), no longer counts for much. It is becoming ever less powerful.

In another analysis, the spread of knowledge and power (access to influence) through society—surely in one sense a victory for democracy—brings about numerous parties and innumerable pressure groups, which undermine the stability necessary to a workable democracy, such as a two-party system provides. As the public becomes better informed and less inhibited, it becomes at the same time and by the same token more demanding and critical. Democracy deconstructs itself by producing greater popular discontent with any government, even a democratic one. These numerous political clienteles, diluting the consensus on which democracy rests, also make legislation much more difficult and legislative assemblies less manageable.

Harry Eckstein, in his *Theory of Stable Democracy* (1961), had developed the paradox that too much voter participation is a danger to democracy. James W. Ceaser, in a study of presidential selection, found most informed people looking for anything to temper the raw populace, which begets "demagoguery" or worse. Left to their own devices, the people would probably give the presidency to some sports hero or television personality. Too much democracy, one might say, is the mortal enemy of democratic government.

Notes

1. Roger Kojecky, *T.S. Eliot's Social Criticism* (New York: Farrar, Straus, and Giroux, 1972), p. 170.

2. *The Screwtape Letters* was reprinted eight times within a year after it came out in 1941 and has since been read by millions; it may have converted more people to Christianity than Billy Graham. Those it converted were more likely to be, like the New York City Jewess Joy Davidman, whom Lewis married, former atheists and communists.

3. Walter Dean Burnham, "The Changing Shape of the American Political Universe," *American Political Science Review* 59 (1965), p. 27.

4. E.E. Schattschneider, *The Semi-Sovereign People* (New York: Holt, Rinehart, and Winston, 1960); Harry Eckstein, *Theory of Stable Democracy* (Princeton, NJ: Princeton University Press, 1961). Cf. Donald J. Devine, *The Attentive Public* (Chicago: Rand McNally, 1970).

5. *The Danger of Equality and Other Essays* (London: Cresset Press, 1966).

8

Democracy in the Contemporary World

Democracy in a World Setting

The democratic doctrine, with its central shrine in the United States of America, had of course always taken for granted the ultimate worldwide triumph of democracy. This was a version of the historicizing that the nineteenth century bestowed on all its favorite causes, transferring to them the Judeo-Christian sense of a grand design and final purpose in history. This faith in democracy's inevitable spread throughout the world appealed especially to Americans, who conceived their national destiny as spreading the gospel after being the first to bring it to fruition. They were the chosen people, fated for long to be scorned and isolated because they were the only pure ones in a corrupt world, but certain at last to convert the heathen. All the great American struggles and crises were expressed in terms of this democratic drama. The Civil War had saved democracy, then World War I was called a war to "make the world safe for democracy." Similarly, World War II brought forth mountains of rhetoric on the same theme: the criminal aggressor nations whose goal was democracy's destruction had to be totally destroyed.

But for a long time even the Americans worried little about democratizing most of those vast portions of the world that lay outside Europe and its offshoots. Their own ventures in imperialism fell far short of the British and French models, because something in the democratic credo rebelled at its forcible transfer to others. There was an enormous debate about this in 1898, when fate threw temptation in front of the United States in the form of a crumbling Spanish empire in Cuba, Puerto Rico, and the Philippines.

Was it undemocratic to spread democracy by force of arms? In joining the imperialist push, did the United States desert its role as the one pure people and become as sinful as the rest? If it refused, was it not shrinking from a sacred duty to move out of isolation at last and save the world? Or were these yellow and brown and black peoples really capable of receiving the message? Even those who claimed that more sordid motives actually underlay the hesitant decision to imperialize could not deny the vehemence and earnestness of this American national debate.

This tentative 1898 toe-thrust into the chilly waters of imperialism did not lead on to a full plunge. Between 1922 and 1934 the United States governed Haiti after marching the marines in to restore order and, hopefully, plant the seeds of democracy, but the latter did not happen. Progressive doctrine denounced such interventions as "dollar diplomacy" and viewed them as shady conspiracies of the Right. A Democratic hero-president, Woodrow Wilson, had admittedly sent the troops into Haiti, but another, Franklin Roosevelt, brought them home; being a good neighbor meant minding your own business.

World War II, however, which the Americans entered with a vengeance, produced the idea of an "American Century," such as the influential publicist Henry Luce preached. The time had come at last when a world that had become "One World" (as presidential candidate Wendell Willkie affirmed) must repeat the lesson of the Civil War on a global scale; it could not endure divided against itself, half slave and half free. This was the dominant theme of American political rhetoric from 1941 to 1945 and for some time afterward. The only way that the United States could honorably enter the sordid arena of international politics was to reform it completely. Faced with the evident necessity of becoming an active world power at last, rather than a sullen loner, the American republic covered its retreat from purity with a cloud of ideology about recreating the world in a new image, one that repudiated power politics and selfish national interests. The League of Nations and then the United Nations, both destined to some cruel disappointments, owed their creation mainly to American enthusiasm, at least in their image as bearer of a wholly new moral order of world politics (though it was Tsar Alexander I of Russia, or his mistress Julie de Krüdener, who first conceived this idea in their Christian Holy Alliance of 1815).

Not the least important change in the post–World War II era was the emergence of a host of new nations, many of them formerly ruled over as colonies, or dominated as protectorates, by Europeans. Decolonization began right after the war, with the enormous and wrenching experience of British withdrawal from India. But wars in Southeast Asia and Algeria marked a French effort to hold on to colonies until new president Charles de

Gaulle decided in 1962 to concede Algerian independence. The United States relinquished the Philippines; the Dutch more reluctantly surrendered Indonesia. In the 1960s two conservative leaders, de Gaulle and British prime minister Harold Macmillan, presided over a massive withdrawal from the African regions their countries had seized in the great imperialist scramble of the 1880s—responding, as Macmillan put it, to the "winds of change" that were blowing in a new Asian and African consciousness, and perhaps a European crisis of confidence. Peoples who were apparently simply becoming slaves of the forceful Europeans won their independence and gained some measure of autonomy to choose which way they wanted to go. This mighty process had its supreme moment in the 1960s but sent disturbing waves through the entire world for all the rest of the century.

This Third World sought to identify itself as a third force during the cold war hostilities of western and Soviet Russian blocs. Its peoples struggled with an independence for which they were often ill prepared as they searched for political and economic systems that worked for them and were recognizably their own. They might decide to imitate one or another of the European models or to adapt these in some way to their own cultural traditions.

The great world historian Arnold Toynbee tried to define the ways in which a civilization can deal with the impact of a stronger, aggressive, "radioactive" force from outside, as much of the rest of the world has had to deal with the West in modern times. It can refuse all compromise and try desperate resistance, as the Jewish Zealots did when faced with the Roman Empire in ancient times, and as the Islamic fundamentalists do today. Or it can, as the Herodians did, adopt the ways of the potent strangers, seeing no answer except to imitate them—a path deliberately chosen by, for example, Kemal Ataturk in modern Turkey. Or, as is more usual and, Toynbee thought, more creative (the way of Paul, on the Jewish analogy), the victim of social aggression can respond by selectively borrowing from the aggressor while retaining its own distinctive features. The impact of the West on Asian and African cultures and their responses to this challenge in the last two centuries is perhaps the greatest theme of modern history.

This was usually supposed to be in some sense democratic, but initially some of the developing peoples saw Soviet communism as a hopeful model. Dominant in virtually all of black Africa was a western-trained elite who, whether communists or liberal interventionists, wanted to plan their new society from above; the 1960s produced one-party states, great leaders or "redeemers," dictatorships of one sort or another. In worshipping charismatic leadership figures, the African masses were behaving in accordance with an ancient human order of things, such as had characterized medieval

Europe and other archaic societies. But as modern nation-states, most of them were deeply flawed by being made up of older local, tribal societies that had been flung together by the accidents of European colonial rule. They were not yet a social unity, on which any system of government by agreement must rest. This precondition of the democratic era had taken Europe many centuries of patrimonial monarchy to create. And so the steady sound of falling parliamentary regimes, on paper, in the Third World of *jeunes états*, replaced by various sorts of dictatorship, sometimes effective and sometimes not, provided the background for a wide-ranging discussion of the preconditions of democratic government as understood in the West. This was against the background of sloganizing about world democracy as the expected goal of history after the terrible world war.

The complete failures of their grandiose and ill-conceived plans for economic development discredited many of these African leaders, often plunged their peoples into civil strife, and led them to abandon state planning for some degree of free-market economics. This might include attempts at political democratization. Their European and American creditors insisted that they must be "democratic" and were naively dismayed, and angered, when this did not happen. In actuality, attempts to enact sweeping reforms, in effect to telescope stages of development, required some kind of elite guidance; the infrastructure of a capitalist market economy needed as much central planning and tending as a socialist state-owned one.

The experience of modernization in the past half century or so in numerous parts of the non-European world sharply reveals how resistant traditional cultures are to political democracy of the western variety, insofar as it rests on secular, skeptical foundations. Pluralism is distasteful to unmodernized societies and may appear to them as a form of unwelcome western-based corruption. Toynbee told how his Arab friend listed parliaments along with alcohol as examples of deplorable western imports. Much of the problem of democracy in new African sovereignties, in which one-party governments tended to emerge, grew out of the persistence of premodern communitarian mentalities quite unable to conceive, much less accept, the apparent cynicism and decadence of a pluralist society. Such attitudes may be found even in some European-derived civilizations, in South America, or in sophisticated Asian ones.

Democratic Preconditions

When political scientists began to examine the special conditions under which democracy can succeed—as, faced with a disconcerting number of failures in new political countries, they increasingly did after about 1960—

they usually concluded that excessive division on basic matters, whether of race, culture, class, or religion, is a severe handicap. As Niebuhr and Sigmund put it, democracy "cannot afford too many rifts in the organic forms of community established by a common language or race, or too localized and serious divisions within the community as a result of divergent religious loyalties." Eric Stokes, reviewing L.H. Gann (with Peter Duignan), *Colonialism in Africa* in 1970, noted that "[f]or him liberal democracies with their panoply of civil liberties are the exotic product of relatively homogeneous national communities in the West, whilst most African states are plural societies in the ethnic, if not in the economic sense." Compare Bernot Marrah (1942):

> The enemies of democracy in the modern world are primarily the forces·that tend to destroy the homogeneity of nations, and introduce principles of division which go beyond differences of opinion, and rend the society asunder by conflicts of doctrine, or of real or alleged interest, in which there is no common ground to form the starting-point, and the finishing point, of argument.

And yet, others found the opposite to be true: democracy does not flourish in a society that is too organic. A high valuation of consensus and community may impede acceptance of (western-style, pluralistic, parliamentary-partisan) democracy, with its competitive individualistic features.

Myron Weiner thought this to be the case in India, others in Japan and in Latin America. Monistic democracy does not willingly accept pluralism and retains its democratic (consensual) features only so long as incompatible cultural elements do not intrude; when they do, it may react in a fascistlike, intolerant direction.

A degree of social and economic independence for individuals qua individuals is a necessary condition of political democracy. In England, the nineteenth-century client of a great patron, who automatically voted as his landlord or employer directed, had to be able to stand on his own feet before his vote could mean anything. Even after he gained a secret ballot (perhaps democracy's greatest single victory) he had to learn not to continue to vote for members of the upper class out of an almost instinctive "deference."

So either too much pluralism or not enough impairs democracy's prospects of success. As Bertrand Russell wrote (in *Power: A New Social Analysis*, 1938):

> Democracy, if it is to succeed, needs a wide diffusion of two qualities which seem, at first sight, to tend in opposite directions. On the one hand, men must

have a certain degree of self-reliance. . . . But on the other hand men must be willing to submit to the decision of the majority when it goes against them. Either of these conditions may fail.

For much of Western Europe a happy if precarious medium existed by the end of the nineteenth century, a halfway house on the evolutionary road from traditional to modernized society. The serious problems of our own democracy today result from the steady erosion of a common cultural foundation, an ever-increasing pluralism to the point of cultural anarchy. (This will be discussed further in chapter 9.)

The preconditions of democracy can be numerous and conflicting. It was long the Englishman's view, still conveyed in Erskine May's Victorian tract *Democracy in Europe* (1878), that the "lesser breeds without the law" included Continental types, tempestuous Frenchmen and authoritarian Germans as well as wild Russians, who were, May thought, destined to be "the everlasting abodes of despotism." Only your true-born Briton has just the right combination of freedom and discipline. Even more recently, Geoffrey Gorer argued that only Protestant cultures, marked by a keen sense of guilt, can evolve the political style suitable to democracy. (This would seem, oddly, to qualify the Prussians but not the French.) Reinhold Niebuhr had thought that "the ultimate presuppositions of the Judaeo-Christian culture" along with technical skills were democratic essentials.

A reasonable conclusion is that what we call "democracy," and assume must be good for everybody else even if it must be forced on them, turns out to be a complex mixture of many things peculiar to our history and culture, some of it coming from very undemocratic sources, all of it built up through centuries of special experiences in the European as well as the American past. It doesn't work particularly well even for us. Individual countries work out their special customs, some of which are very peculiar, to make it manageable. (A study found that Italy is one place where the way things really work departs most widely from the way they are supposed to work on paper.) Other societies, which have not undergone the peculiar centuries-long experience of Western Europe, Great Britain, and the United States, are expected to absorb this overnight, taking, as it were, a prescription filled out in Washington and bought at the World Bank pharmacy and that was supposed to act immediately.

Daniel Lerner, in *Passing of Traditional Society* (1958), was rather typical of learned opinion at one time in viewing democracy as the end product of "modernization." It may be nearer the mark to say that democracy flourishes best at a certain moment halfway between traditional and fully modernized. If so, some of the still undeveloped societies might look forward to a period of relatively successful democracy, only eventually to follow the others into decadence.

Democracy in the Late Twentieth-Century World

Let us postpone further discussion of the question about democracy's status in the world until we have conducted a brief factual survey of the situation. A preliminary hypothesis is that in the world at large there seems no long-term historical trend either toward democracy or away from it, but rather a kind of steady-state condition in which some peoples, wearying of authoritarian tyranny, rebel in the name of democracy, while others get fed up with it after a season of anarchy and opt for some promising strong man or the army. They will probably reverse the roles in a few years. The model that best fits the state of democracy in the contemporary world is that of ebb and flow, overall steady state.

In 1970 Robert Dahl foresaw no great change over the next generation in the evolution toward "polyarchy": some switches back and forth but overall a steady-state equilibrium (*Polyarchy, Participation, and Opposition*). It is not clear on the basis of what evidence he believed this, but his intuition was generally correct. Democracy flourishes after a season of negation, as in Italy after fascism, when for a time interest in electoral politics was high, only to fall off as the inevitable disenchantment settled in. Examples of countries that fluctuate between dictatorships and more or less democratic, parliamentary regimes may be found all over Latin America, where some countries appear to have virtually institutionalized this alternation.

Democratic ideology once assumed it to be the foreordained culmination of human history; its critics saw it as a stage on the way to total collapse. Neither apocalypse appears to be likely, though both have been freely predicted. Books such as Robert Moss's *The Collapse of Democracy* (1975) were at least as numerous as confident assertions of democracy's certain ultimate triumph. In 1980 William G. Bowdler, assistant secretary of state for Inter-American Affairs, testified before the Senate Foreign Relations Committee that "the observance of democratic practices is widening" in Latin America. But about the same time David Collier edited a book titled *The New Authoritarianism in Latin America* alleging a "recent resurgence" of antidemocracy. It would be hard to say who was right. Since then there have been about as many reverses for democracy as successes. In 1994 the United States sent troops into Haiti to "restore democracy," as it had done in 1914, when the process of restoration lasted twenty years.

Democratic regimes fail to satisfy the expectations of their citizens and lose their popularity; they have too little established "legitimacy" to survive a time of troubles. The expectations are so high, and in most countries the prospects of satisfying them so low, that the fate of any regime is almost sealed. A military or charismatic dictatorship rising on the ruins of some swamped experiment in parliamentary government will also fail; it has avenues of suppression and coercion denied to democracy, but these may well backfire as mass consciousness rises, and if the nondemocratic regime does fall it may leave behind a correspondingly greater deposit of dislike, guaranteeing a fairly long run for the opposition.

So, it may seem, one gets a steady back and forth between democracy and despotism, trying perhaps all kinds of in-betweens, such as military dictatorships that permit a façade of democracy, or the familiar "tutelage" ideologists who say our one-party dominance is only temporary, tomorrow we will establish democracy. (Such a position was reached notably by the founder of modern Chinese politics, Sun Yat-sen, who had begun as a democrat but by 1923 believed that a period of "tutelage" under the Chinese National Party, the KMT, was a necessary preparation.) Colombia arrived at an agreement to let the rival political parties alternate in power, which not surprisingly led to extreme voter apathy. Regimes regarded as stably democratic—Uruguay, Chile, India—lost their democracy, only to regain it eventually (perhaps only for a season).

One may even see democracy as being in retreat. Disturbing to the advocates of democracy, one would think, is the tendency among the world's developing countries for necessary modernizing "reforms" to require authoritarian governments. Democratic ideology traditionally put the two things together: as a society emerges from the tribal or patrimonial stage, it urbanizes and industrializes and also democratizes, all part of the same evolution. But in fact all over the world, elites who want their peoples to escape from agrarian poverty to raise their standard of living by manufacturing, producing, and exporting find that this program is not popular. Developing a complex market economy requires expert guidance over a long period of time; a technocratic dictatorship seems necessary, elections are an obstacle, the masses have to be "tutored" for a while.

The new Russian (ex-Soviet) leadership was almost engaged in forcible liberation, imposing the free society by fiat. Its goal was not to satisfy the popular will but to devise a workable economic order; what had triumphed was not democracy but capitalism (or some new kind of capitalistic socialism). So likewise many Third World countries have tried to modernize their economies. If the new order included some democracy, it was largely a byproduct of the other reforms.

Market reform needs strong government. It is seldom popular in the short run. The market economy requires laws and institutions that western states take for granted, forgetting that they had to struggle for centuries to establish them. The features most needed by a free-enterprise economy are those that uphold the validity of contracts and enforce the rules that surround buying and selling of property. This is not a matter of democracy, but of laws and courts; a nondemocratic political order could do this as well, perhaps better.

The most important basis of a capitalist economy is the individualism that is marked not only by personal responsibility and the widespread distribution of property, but also by habits of economic efficiency, what Max Weber meant by "rationalization." Such individualism is exemplified in Adam Smith's "economic man," who carefully calculates and acts to his personal advantage. If these features are present in the members of society, there will also be a tendency toward democracy in that such self-reliant citizens will not easily surrender to an arbitrary government or allow their rights to be infringed; they will quickly and effectively defend their personal liberties. But this may not mean that they uphold government by elected parliaments.

The dilemma of needing to use despotism to install democracy or the economic foundations of democracy confronted American policy makers early in the cold war period. An American diplomatic adviser looking at Iran in 1946 "believed that democracy could be handed down from the top, provided there was economic reform from the bottom up. He felt that a strong central government could offset the weaknesses of an immature democracy (that is, a democracy in which the voting franchise had been extended to an illiterate peasantry), which, he believed, inevitably led to nationalization crises and Communist gains. This stronger central government, carefully monitored, could use statist methods early on to implement economic reform. Then, as democratic capitalism rose up to meet the state, statist intervention would decline."[1] The scenario closely resembles the much more recent trend all over the developing world. If American policy supported the shah's authoritarian government in the hope that the eventual upshot would be Iranian democratic capitalism, there were obviously some miscalculations.

Progressive portions of the non-European world seem less and less impressed with the democratic model. They want free markets and less government intervention, but democracy may look to them, as it looks to Singapore's Kishore Mahbubani, as involving handicaps rather than aids to the economic growth they seek. The veritable explosion of productivity in East Asia, from the little "tigers" Singapore, Hong Kong, South Korea, to China and India and Indonesia, joining the fabulously successful Japan, has produced an explosion of confidence as they threaten to wrest world economic leadership from the haughty Europeans and Americans. (Mahbubani points out that "East Asia's GDP is already larger than that of either the United States or the European Community.") They are less disposed to imitate the West uncritically. The United States, they point out, is dragged down economically by an array of social problems that include high rates of crime, drug addiction, alcoholism, family disintegration, welfare dependency. Are these the results of an undue emphasis on individual rights, an ineffective political system, a loss of respect for authority? (No need to worry about that in Singapore!) It may be illogical to think so, but obviously what has gained many of these areas prosperity is not democracy in the sense of elected parliamentary governments or extensive individual liberty, but strong leadership, education, and the work ethic. "There are often places," *The Economist* lamented (February 1995), naming Singapore and Malaysia, "where democracy [by which it meant civil liberties] is seen as less important than order. . . . The temptation to emulate them must be strong."

Senator Daniel Moynihan, then U.S. ambassador to the United Nations, was quoted in 1975 as saying that "democracy is where the world was, not where it is going." Twenty years later, the dominant pattern seemed to be not so much antidemocracy as quasi democracy: a strong leader, legitimizing his power by a façade of democracy via referenda, actually ruling in cooperation with the military, and prepared to bully or dismiss an elected parliament if it tries to oppose him. Often this leadership was enlightened in the sense of trying to restructure and modernize the economy. But since such reforms were at least temporarily painful, they were not popular. Democracy in the sense of the popular will was out of step with the society of individual freedoms and economic competition.

A survey of the world's democratic status is almost an impossibility, because so much of the world is in flux. The number of new sovereignties on the earth tripled, increasing by a hundred or so during the decolonializing flood of the 1960s and 1970s, then swelled still more with the breakup of the Soviet Union in the 1990s. A majority of these more or less *jeunes états* are still struggling to find their political identity. They are highly unstable, but so are most places in Europe and its offshoots.

The following is only a sampling to give some idea of democracy's status in the world at the end of the twentieth century.

Africa

In Algeria, a national election was canceled in January 1992, when it appeared the result would be an undesirable victory for Islamic fundamentalists, who were extremely opposed to all form of modernization. To them any democracy is wrong because it allows the word of God to be judged by men. The unconstitutional (undemocratic) act of canceling elections was taken by those who wanted to save pluralistic democracy from its enemies, who could claim, as we know, to be democrats in one profoundly illiberal sense of the word. Since 1992 the fundamentalists have resorted to assassination and terrorism while the government, under a military dictatorship, has responded in kind, outlawing the murderous Islamic liberation army. A notable defeat for democracy under any definition.

"Tribal" massacres took a toll of several hundred thousand lives in Burundi and Rwanda. ("Tribal" or "ethnic" is what bewildered westerners called these bloody quarrels, but it is difficult to ascribe them to anything tribal or ethnic. Most anthropologists and historians find little evidence of any real differences between the Hutu and the Tutsi peoples, except that almost everyone, except the Twa, whom they both persecute, thinks he belongs to one or the other group, like Republicans and Democrats.) Peoples riven by such ancient and deep-seated feuds are not, of course, ready for democratic procedures. Other African countries ravaged by civil war were Angola, Mozambique, Sierra Leone, Ethiopia. The latter country struggled in the 1990s to restore constitutional order after the flight of the "Marxist" tyrant Mengistu, under whom a Red terror took an estimated 100,000 lives in 1976–78. In Zaire, two governments competed for governing power amid growing anarchy.

After the capture and killing of Liberian president Samuel Doe by rebels in 1990, a divided army and contending warlords led to almost total anarchy; other African states intervened, attempting to restore constitutional order. In Chad the old colonial ruler France, acting still in loco parentis, demanded (as a condition of economic aid) that this land of nomads and poor farmers establish democracy; when elections were held they bred violence, kindling rivalries between the different religions and regional loyalties. As in strife-torn Sudan, Muslims in the north opposed animists and some Christians in the south.

The latter country had a frightful civil rights record, from the western point of view; any dissent from Islamic orthodoxy was banned and ferociously punished. The Sudanese government was a grim theocracy with military backing. Yet Khartoum called itself a "party-free" democracy. Elections, which the opposition labeled shams, attracted few voters and only one viewpoint was permitted. Such a situation is found widely, as we know, and may indeed almost be called the present global norm. Sudan, one of the most extreme antiwestern regimes, very like neighboring Libya, was a prototype, or travesty, of organic-style democracy. Kenya was in many ways quite different, but its longtime and much respected leader, Daniel arap Moi, made no secret of his dislike for multiparty democracy, which he accepted only under pressure from the West and did not permit to express much opposition to his government.

Egypt too, one of the most modernized of African countries, had a muzzled press. Elections in Egypt illustrated the extremely low rates of participation typical of non-European elections throughout the world. Thus in the national election of late 1995, observers found between 5 percent and 10 percent of the registered voters showing up at the polls in Cairo (*Le Monde*, December 6, 1995). While the well-established government of Hosni Moubarak and his National Democratic Party, in power since 1981, aroused little enthusiasm, the feeble opposition was even less credible. It of course complained of unfair election practices (including the symbol of a revolver used on the ballots to represent it), but it could just as well have blamed its own intellectual poverty. In any event the Egyptian masses obviously thought the elections of little significance. Nigeria, largest of all African lands and rich in natural resources, had lived for some years under a military regime that occasionally mentioned possible future elections but never got around to arranging them. Civic spirit there was reported in 1995 as abysmally low. Little criticism of the government was allowed.

Guinea, long under the dictatorship of Sekou Touré, permitted *no* criticism of the regime and exiled distinguished writers such as Tierno Monenembo, as did Zaire. The military dictatorship in Nigeria, which has postponed elections time and again, shocked the world in November 1995 by executing, along with others, a world-famous writer, Ken Saro-Wiwa. The Ivory Coast, a relative democratic success, was less secure after the death in 1994 of its patriarchal figure, Felix Houphouet-Boigny. In the last analysis the people relied on that oldest and most basic of human sentiments, the attachment to a leader, a father.

It is not difficult to see why L.H. Gann wrote (in 1970) that "[t]he rules of habeas corpus or of Western parliamentary institutions have little or no future in Africa." A quarter of a century later he might have wished to qualify this judgment slightly, but not very much.

Latin America

The twentieth-century history of Argentina consists of alterations of power repeatedly between military dictatorship and turbulent democracy. Juan Peron's ten-year Argentine dictatorship fell to an army coup in 1955. Then after another experience of partisan politics, "democracy had lost its last remnants of respect among much of the population," as the Swiss newspaper *Neue Zürcher Zeitung* reported; another general encountered virtually no resistance when in 1966 he dissolved the legislature and all political parties and forbade all political activity. But there was another stormy upsurge of Peronism preceding still another coup. The military junta that held power in Argentina between 1972 and 1983 was responsible for extreme violations of human rights, including the assassination of leftists, but this was less a cause of the junta's fall than was the humiliating defeat in the Falklands War of 1982. Democracy returned in 1983 as a chastened army deferred to civilian leadership. The new order seemed to do well, but the future obviously has to be reckoned uncertain. The leading political party is still Peronist. The president, Carlos Menem, conformed to a pattern many saw as setting the fashion for Latin America, and indeed for much of the rest of the world (for example, Indonesia, Russia, the former Soviet Union states in Central Asia): a strong president, relying on military support, controls the elected parliament, reducing it to more or less of a sham and ruling by decree; he gets himself reelected to long terms by ballot-box manipulation if necessary in order to install supposedly enlightened structural changes in the economy. (Menem was reelected by a large majority in 1995.)

This resembled Peru's president, Fujimori, who disbanded parliament in 1992 in a "civil coup" supported by the army in order to change the constitution. In April 1995, Fujimori won an impressive electoral victory, gaining some 64 percent of the votes cast, amid the usual questions about ballot-box fraud. Fujimori, unhappy with "parties," wanted to be a popular dictator; his foes accused him of "authoritarian" tendencies. He had dealt effectively with the long-standing terrorism of the leftist Shining Path guerrillas and was seemingly committed to progressive (free-market) economic policies. But would he have received a majority in a free election in which most Peruvians cast ballots without fear? History might repeat itself: in 1919 Augusto Leguia, after his election, allied with the military, bullied the legislature, exiled his opponents, but lasted only until 1930.

Brazil's Fernando Henrique Cardoso also hoped for reelection and a long-term, quasi-dictatorial presidency. So did Ecuador's Sixto Duran Ballen. Brazil's political history much resembled that of its southern neighbor. The military chiefs who seized power in 1964 muzzled the press and imprisoned critics of the regime. Under this dictatorship Brazil flourished for a time, bringing inflation under control and attracting foreign investment; later, after a return to civilian rule, inflation became a virulent fever. Much of the history of South America suggests an unfortunate linkage between benighted politics and enlightened economics, and the reverse.

The Venezuelans overthrew a dictatorship in 1958. But forty years later they seemed thoroughly disillusioned with democracy. Two ex-presidents, one of whom had fled the country, were charged with corruption. Dismal economic conditions, including 70 percent inflation, reflected the performance of an anti-libertarian government. In 1995 this regime was desperately trying a fascist-like patriotic-nationalist campaign in order to bolster its sagging popularity.

Chile was approaching chaos in 1973 as a result of a ruinous attempt at a socialist revolution by the democratically elected Allende government. Amid hyperinflation, food shortages, and a breakdown of order, an army coup overthrew Allende, who committed suicide. The military dictatorship proceeded to terrorize the Left. Under General Pinochet, it ruled until 1989, when an election preceded by a referendum defeated his regime. Regarded as a loathsome tyrant by the Left, Pinochet used his power to establish a free-market economy; East European countries after 1989 adopted his privatization program as a model. The Chilean economy grew rapidly in the 1980s. A democratic success had turned into an economic horror, while the ensuing dictatorship was a political monstrosity with enlightened economic policies. Could Chile find and keep a stable regime that permitted economic growth while respecting civil liberties and democratic procedures? Perhaps, but the past record hardly encouraged much optimism.

The instance of a nation being governed by a single party, claiming a monopoly of power and regarding any opposition as unacceptable, was not confined to the Soviet Union and other communist states. Indeed, it was almost the standard in evolving countries of the "undeveloped" or developing world. If this was true in decolonialized Africa after 1960, it was hardly less so in Latin America. Mexico was a prize example. The PRI (party of the Revolution) has held a monopoly of power in Mexico since 1929. For a long time it was indeed by most accounts overwhelmingly popular. But times changed, and an aging PRI grew corrupt. When opposition groups began to emerge in the 1980s, they were at first suppressed. When international public opinion forced free elections, and it began to seem that the PRI might actually lose or prove embarrassingly short of a huge majority, the party resorted to tactics reminiscent of earlier North American city "bosses": intimidation of voters, disqualification of opposition voters, fraudulent counting of votes, ballot-box stuffing. The government used its powers to deny opposition groups access to news media. In 1994 the assassination of a presidential candidate evidently grew out of this attempt of the old guard to hang on to power at any cost.

Electoral frauds went on in front of outside observers in the 1994 election. In the eyes of its veterans, the PRI was by definition *the* party of the people—the party of those who had made the revolution in the name of the people—and any opposition to it was ipso facto reactionary and undemocratic. They found it hard to accept that democracy means a free vote in which they might lose. To think that Mexico was in fact divided, and that each side had as much right to be heard as the other; to think that the PRI, in brief, was not uniquely right and specially privileged, struck at deeply entrenched feelings that in fact may once have been almost universal. Did democracy mean the rule of the Party of the People (the People's Revolution), or did it mean leaving matters to a majority of the voters? Encapsulated in this dilemma were questions of the two basic kinds of democracy.

Outside observers frequently spoke of "fledgling" democracies in Latin America as if these countries were just starting out on their political careers and might be expected to improve with time. But the practices and patterns mentioned above have been going on for at least a century. One is reminded of Oscar Wilde's quip that the youth of America was its oldest tradition. It would be more logical to assume that ingrained customs will continue to assert themselves in Latin America; this old and in many ways rich civilization is not very well suited to democracy.

Asia

Burma received many nominations for the worst government in the world, a title held steadily since 1962. This military dictatorship of socialist tendencies led a country endowed with many human and natural resources on a steady downward path, governing "with the malignity of an unending natural disaster," as one journalist put it. Though surpassed in sheer horror by neighboring Cambodia, this Burmese regime achieved the miracle of a rice shortage in one of the world's richest rice-growing regions. Whatever explained the ineradicability of this sad military-based dictatorship, there were no signs of any significant change as of 1995.

Singapore seemed to combine most successfully a capitalist system and ethic with a highly authoritarian government; indeed, this was the formula by and large for all the East Asia "tigers" that have so successfully vied for world economic leadership in the past few decades. They aspired to import the West's dynamic society without its accompanying vices of crime, drug addiction, corruption, family disintegration, and so on. Singapore, sharing some of the radical Islamicists' violent horror at the West's permissiveness, refused to allow any concern for the rights of those it saw as criminals or degenerates to inhibit severe repression of misbehavior. But many a westerner, as well as perhaps many a resident of an "undeveloped" country, secretly envied this achievement. Those who, like Singapore and South Korea, aspired to join the select club of "tigers" were surely more numerous in the world, alas, than those who sighed for a liberal and democratic order.

India's democracy was turbulent to the point of anarchy. In June 1975, Prime Minister Indira Gandhi had declared a state of emergency, censored the press, and arrested hundreds of opposition leaders, in order, she said, to "defend democracy against its enemies." This did not prove the end of Indian democracy. No one, not even a Gandhi, could kill the free spirit in the land that invented it. But India was prone to fall into crises, to be racked by discontents of many kinds, and to see distracted governments resort to illegal repressions. It displayed in extreme form a model familiar throughout the world: a nation impatient with any regime, including a democratic (parliamentary) one, that does not meet demands for better living conditions. A strong popular presence, perhaps too much democracy, made for the precarious existence of a workable parliamentary order; there was no stable structure of political parties, leading, as so often happens in such a situation (for example, Germany in 1930–33), to popular disgust with the "party system."

In 1979, James Jupp (*Sri Lanka: Third World Democracy*) presented Sri Lanka (the former Ceylon) as a successful Third World democracy. This was just before it collapsed into a ruinous civil war, still going on in 1995 without much hope of settlement. This was an "ethnic" division. Such conditions of severe "cultural pluralism" had seemed to doom democracy in Malaysia too.[2] Thailand scarcely had this excuse but nonetheless passed through a series of unconstitutional seizures of power, the latest one in 1992. This alertly modernizing country seemed to have virtually institutionalized the coup.

Indonesia was fortunate, perhaps, in having one party and one leader under an arrangement that might on the most generous view be called qualified democracy with the leader's permission. A tame parliament was packed—for example, by having 100 of its 500 seats reserved for army officers appointed by the president—and its role was carefully orchestrated; a small token opposition party, within strict limits, was duly licensed. Some members of the legislature who dared to be outspokenly critical of president and party in 1995 were summarily sacked, as if they had been disloyal soldiers or corporate employees. People made jokes about how members of the parliament sat, listened, and collected their salaries. The government closed down an overly outspoken magazine in 1994. The benevolent and popular President Suharto, who came to office via a military coup in 1967, ran little risk from this token legislature; most Indonesians seemed happy with the arrangement. Nor did the outer world much criticize so stable a regime except to remark occasionally upon its disgraceful actions in the interior of Irian Jaya (western New Guinea), where Indonesian military forces had, according to informed estimates, killed as many as 150,000 Papuans in the past twenty-five years or so. Indonesia, a vast and sprawling country, had done well economically under Suharto's enlightened dictatorship. Why run the risk of upsetting it? Someday, Suharto hinted from time to time, there might be a stronger parliament and more criticism permitted. For the time being Indonesia would have to be listed as one of the false or pretend democracies: enough window dressing to gain respectability. What might happen when Suharto passed on, of course, pointed to a problem endemic in monarchy throughout history.

Indonesia, in a curious and interesting way, has proclaimed a national ideology of toleration—everybody swears a solemn oath that they will believe anything they like, so long as they believe something. This is a way of adjusting the organic to the pluralist order.

In the aftermath of gaining their independence after the breakup of the Soviet Union—which really was more nearly Russian imperialism—five Central Asian states reverted to dictatorial rule. Early in 1995 President Nursultan Nazarbaev of Kazakhstan disbanded parliament and declared his intention of ruling by decree, pending a future election. Members of Parliament threatened to defy the order and meet as an alternate assembly— shades of the English, 1640—but this did not happen. Parliament had voted against privatization and other free-market measures. Here again, in order to set up what many in the West saw as democratic reforms, that is, free enterprise and competitive capitalism, it was necessary to resort to dictatorial government, for such measures were not popular. But Nazarbaev won an overwhelming victory in a referendum (April 29, 1995) that extended his term five years without an election. Though outside observers questioned the fairness of this vote, there seems little doubt that a large majority of the people, wishing to avoid turmoil, wanted the strong ruler and gave lower priority to democratic elections. "Democracy," said President Nazarbaev, "is only just knocking on our door. You don't have to mourn for something you never had."

In neighboring Uzbekistan events took a very similar course. President Islam Karimov, who had been the Communist boss in pre-1989 days, decided to extend his presidency from 1996 to 2000, and though he had this idea approved by Parliament and submitted to a popular referendum, there was suspicion that this was not really a free vote. Observers suspected intimidation, but more likely the communitarian instincts of a largely unmodernized people impelled them to fall in line with their leader. Only one party's nominees were permitted; no genuine opposition was allowed. The successor party to the Communists, now styling itself the People's Democratic party, held almost all the seats in the High Assembly. Whether this was antidemocracy or just a different kind of democracy, it was not western style. These leaders were former Communists, and it seemed that only the names had changed in the government of these peoples. The Leninist-Stalinist dictatorship had appealed to them not because it was enlightened, as its westernized intellectual creators supposed, but because it was antique. But observers noted a general disgust among the Uzbeks with the hypocrisy of a democratic façade that concealed rigging; the tensions here, in addition to strong regional rivalries, stemmed from the opposing pulls of old tribalism and new democracy.

There was the same pattern in the other Central Asian republics. Turkmenistan's president had already had his term extended. The president of Kirgizstan too had dismissed parliament and found ways of electing one that he found more to his liking. In Tajikistan, the boss of the old Communist regime headed a government challenged by the Islamic Renaissance party, while several thousand Russian troops tried to keep the peace.

Virtually alone in the world (except for Cuba and Vietnam), China was a Communist-ruled society that refused to recant or to crumble, overtly at least. The Red mandarins who continued to govern the most populous nation in the world with an iron hand scandalized the world by shooting down students who assembled in the spring of 1989 in Tiananmen Square, making that incident a symbol of infamy. After more than fifty years in power, during which they were supposedly transforming China into a modernized society, China's rulers did not dare permit a popular election or permit the people to assemble peacefully. The Chinese Communist party, like all the traditional Communist parties, believed in principle in rule from above. It was self-elected and accountable to nobody; its top leadership controlled appointments to the bureaucracy to which it delegated the power to carry out the policies decreed, as in the former Soviet Union, by a few people in the policy-making Party committee (Politburo). A National People's Congress, carefully screened, assembled two weeks every year to endorse everything the leadership wanted. (In 1995 for the first time in history the NPC showed some signs of independence, voting only 63 or 68 percent approval on a few issues rather than the customary near unanimity.) What legitimized this dictatorship in its own eyes, of course, was its monopoly of truth, in the form of a Marxist science of society to which kingdom the Party leaders somehow held the keys.

On the other hand, unlike the USSR prior to 1990, the Chinese Communist rulers had permitted a great deal of economic liberalization. This led to a spectacular economic boom in the 1980s. The Chinese took to capitalism as they had never taken to communism. But the Communist party dictatorship remained, apparently determined to preside as a ruling mandarin elite over a process of economic liberalization. (But huge inefficient state-owned industries remained too and were a drag on the economy.) Amid the perils and problems, not so say horrors, of economic development and modernization, with bureaucratic corruption, gangsterism, terrible environmental pollution, the rulers sometimes seemed to have lost control of the situation in the 1990s. Local autonomy was increasing; the decrees emitted from Beijing, like those from Moscow, often had little effect, and the Party leadership seemed mystified about everything except one point, that it intended to hang on to absolute power.

In western eyes it was an anomaly that a country that had seen vast social and economic changes in recent decades could undergo no political changes whatsoever. Surely economic pluralism must sooner or later lead to political pluralism? But China had no experience of democracy; the huge country had been governed for 2,000 years, with interludes of civil strife, by a despotic monarchy and a carefully selected elite civil service, based on a Confucian ideology upholding the people's subservience to supposedly wise teacher-governors. The 1911 revolution, led by western-influenced democrats, quickly deteriorated into local warlordism. Sun Yat-sen, the revolution's moral leader, who (influenced by American ideas) had initially believed that China was destined for democracy, had to admit the necessity of an authoritarian regime to "prepare for democracy"—the first of many such strategies from newly independent countries of the Third World. Both wings of the party Sun Yat-sen founded deserted democracy. (Sun's successor, Chiang Kai-shek, who had driven out the Communists in 1927, became sharply disenchanted with western democratic ideas. See his 1942 *China's Destiny*.) Broadly speaking, the Asian leaders during the first national revolts against western colonialism, c. 1905–45 (the turning of the tide is often dated from the impact of Japan's defeat of Russia in their 1904–5 war), had held to the goal of establishing a western-style type of parliamentary democratic, liberal government. The vision faded, if it did not die, when the attempt was made to put it in practice.

After the Communists gained control of the central government in China soon after World War II, there was no more talk of tutelage. It is true that the mercurial, perhaps insane leader of the revolutionary party, Mao Tsetung, believed at times that the Party must maintain its roots in the people. In the 1960s he unleashed the great Cultural Revolution in order to shake up a party grown complacent and bureaucratic; this bloody process had some of the features of a Stalinist purge but was justified ideologically as the opposite of Russian elitism: a return to the people, a rejuvenation from below. In the end, however, it proved so destructive that following the Great Helmsman's death in 1976 the party repudiated Maoism. This did not mean a return to democracy but more nearly the opposite.

It seemed impossible that China could continue with both a dynamic liberalized economy and a rigidly dictatorial government. There was much speculation that with the imminent passing of its aged leader, Deng Xiaoping, the Chinese Communist Party would end its long reign and surrender to some kind of pluralism. But there were no signs of this happening, and it was hard to imagine that an elected national legislature would have the authority or prestige needed to govern this vast and now dynamic populace. So the democratic future of the world's most populous country was extremely dim.

The Chinese, it has been said, make poor democrats because the idea of pushing oneself forward to try to get elected offends traditional norms of personal behavior. Perhaps the roots of a Confucian ethic are so deeply planted in this great people that, like the people of Latin America, they will never make good democrats; it does not agree with their civic culture. There is a tendency to say, uncomfortably, that other East Asian civilizations share this Confucian cultural bias against democracy: norms of behavior crucially at odds with some of the West's political customs (arguing, contending, demanding, denouncing). Similarly, the Japanese are obviously not entirely comfortable with the electoral game; they are too solicitous about community, too concerned with consensus. High educational levels and standard of living provide favorable conditions for democracy. Moreover, like those of Germany and Italy, Japan's unhappy experience in World War II has inoculated her, for some time at least, against a reversion to military or autocratic rule. But the Japanese perform the procedures of parliamentary government like a rehearsed ceremony; it is not fully their style.

Vietnam, like China, was moving toward economic liberalization in 1995 while a decrepit, partly corrupt, and increasingly discredited Communist dictatorship appeared likely to collapse with the imminent retirement of the old leaders, who had won the war against America but failed to use the victory to improve the well-being of the people.

Iran supplies another example of total schizophrenia, if in a somewhat different way; there are two different regimes, splitting power roughly on an agreement that one can run foreign policy and the other domestic, which of course leaves large areas murky. The "fundamentalist" Islamic regime of the mullahs is an extreme case of organic democracy, which western liberal democrats regard as totalitarian or fascist; it is aggressively intolerant of everything that conflicts with the strict precepts of the Koran (see above under Algeria). Needless to say, it is hostile to the secularization that is the precondition of modern pluralist democracy, and to European culture in general. But there is another government in Iran, based on an elected parliament, with elections, however, generally subject to management and intimidation. This government has a much more pragmatic outlook and tries to preside over something like a market economy while cultivating good relations with western countries. Which one is likely to win in the long run, assuming that such antithetical principles cannot long coexist in a state (a house divided against itself cannot stand), is anybody's guess. The fundamentalists seem to have much more morale and vitality, but also to be wildly ill-adapted to economic realities. In this Persian standoff might be seen an epitome of the modern world's political contradictions.

The radical Islamicist political movement has been a powerful one throughout the African and Asian regions where the faith of Muhammad traditionally held sway. Even in Turkey, the classic example of adaptation to westernizing patterns, a rebellion against the modernizing, secularizing process, led by radical Islamicists (Refah), made startling gains in the 1990s. This "Fresh Breeze" fundamentalism of the Middle East resembled the Panyat movement of ultra-Orthodoxy in Russia and even the Christian political right in America, in dreaming of some purer, less complicated past while indignantly rejecting a corrupt, materialist present. To some extent it replaced the defunct socialists and communists in appealing to the poor and outcast. Educated people (within Islam) scorned it for its barbarity much as European intellectuals did the old village culture in the eighteenth century. Pluralist democracy was anathema to the new fundamentalists; it joined capitalism, technology, the amusement culture, and all other modernisms they hated. Their utopia would banish parliaments and party politics along with greedy businessmen, television and movies, computers, public exposure of female bodies. They threatened to become the party of the majority in many places. Then they would favor a free vote; it was their enemies, horrified at the idea of a world returned to a rural and barbarous past, who used the army, as in Algeria, to forestall this reactionary democracy.

In Bangladesh at the end of 1995, a precarious attempt at parliamentary democracy was in trouble; amid strikes and protests there was fear of the assassinations that had broken up previous governments, both elected and dictatorial, during the past two decades. The government and opposition parties could not agree on terms for new elections mandated to be held February 22, 1996.

Eastern Europe

Another type of schizophrenia is found in one of the territories left stranded by the dissolution of Yugoslavia. In the former autonomous Yugoslav province of Kosovo, Serbs and Albanians have formed separate governments. An elementary school on the outskirts of Pristina, visited and reported on by a Swiss journalist,[3] since 1992 has had a wall in it separating the Serbian and Albanian students, who enter and leave by different doors, take their recesses and gym periods at different times, and have absolutely no contact. The Serbs regard Kosovo as part of the Serbian culture and state, in their view much superior to the Albanian. The only recognized language is Serbian. As the governing power, the Serbs do not recognize the Albanian shadow republic but have thus far pretty much tolerated it. The much more numerous Albanian majority has quite extensively organized its own government, especially in education.

Kosovo, of course, resembles many other places in the sundered Yugoslav federation, some of them, like Bosnia, much grimmer. The hopeless intermixture of peoples in the mountainous Balkans, a relic of Turkish rule centuries ago, has long caused trouble. World War I might be blamed on it. The War of the Austrian Succession, as that key conflagration has sometimes been called, seventy-five years later became the war of the Yugoslav succession.

Any thought of a common democratic framework in a society so divided is of course out of the question. Democracy implies a preexisting community in which it can function. Differences of culture or class must be within the range of toleration. A democracy of dogs and cats is unlikely to succeed. The "pluralism" of late western-style democracy, insofar as it works, rests on enough common institutional and cultural elements to supply the necessary basic structure of politics. "Democratic procedures are risky in a nation in which national identity is not yet firmly established," one observer of the African political scene pointed out in a decided understatement. The separate components of the one-time Yugoslavia would have to be sorted out, by methods less horrible, if possible, than ethnic cleansing, before each of them could begin progressing toward democracy.

Scandalous as its condition is, and scandalous as was the utter failure of the rest of Europe and the United Nations to find a solution, this part of Europe is but a small and relatively insignificant one. For the rest of Europe, two main questions remained unanswered. One was whether the former Soviet Union, having overthrown communism and simultaneously liberated a number of its separate peoples, would now proceed toward something like western-style democracy. After seven decades of rule by the most formidable agency of elite rule yet devised, the Soviet Union apparently literally collapsed in the late 1980s. Party leader Mikhail Gorbachev's efforts to escape an impossible economic situation by reform of the moribund Communist party led to his use of popular opinion against the Party's entrenched apparatus and to the emergence of a modest political opposition. In March 1989 voters were allowed for the first time to vote for another candidate than the Communist party one. Amid loosening of the reins on freedom of thought, pent-up hostility to the Party's monopoly of power emerged. "Pluralism" had seemingly conquered the last bastion of monolithic dogmatism. In this sense the vast Russian empire had become democratic.

The whole amazing process was hailed as a victory of staggering proportions for democracy. "The key to the twenty-first century," *The Economist* proclaimed on the hundredth birthday of the American Republic, is "the art of making sure that people elect their governments." So at least it appeared at that moment in time.

An attempted coup by desperate old-guard elements in August of 1991 failed after it encountered resistance from masses of people in Moscow and Leningrad. A remarkable surge of opinion against the Party caused the *New*

York Times to headline "End of Communism's 74-Year Reign." A few days later (September 4, 1991) the USSR itself was declared dissolved; most of the former republics of the union regrouped as a loose confederation of sovereign states, while the three Baltic States were conceded outright independence. Ukraine soon joined them.

But, as noted earlier, to make the transition from a state-command economy to a basically free-market one required a great deal of authority. Such a major systemic change was bound to be both difficult and excruciatingly painful. The confusion emerged when, in parliamentary elections of late 1993, opponents of economic "reform" won a majority of the seats in the parliament. Earlier, in September, a clash between President Boris Yeltsin and Parliament ended in an armed attack on that body and its dismissal. Shades of the English seventeenth century, with the supposed champion of the new Russian democracy, Russian president Boris Yeltsin, cast in the role of King Charles. A new constitution approved by a majority of those who bothered to vote gave the president power to rule by decree in case of a conflict (echoes of Germany on the eve of Hitler's triumph). A fragile truce between president and parliament then broke down over Yeltsin's ordering a military attack on the small breakaway republic of Chechnya.

Polls showed the once popular Yeltsin now incredibly unpopular, but with the aid of the military and new interests attached to the emerging capitalism, and supported by the world's great powers, he managed to survive. Most people of goodwill and informed judgment probably hoped he would, since the opposition had no credible alternative. It included the extreme right-wing nationalist Vladimir Zhirinovsky, whose party members called themselves, perhaps ironically, the Liberal-Democrats, and on the other wing the ex-Communists, both groups totally opposed to all modernizing reforms. Reform parties combined had probably no more than 25 percent of the total. Zhirinovsky's program, according to one summary, was the conquest of Alaska, free vodka, and shooting criminals on sight. Russian politics was in fact a shambles: a dozen parties ranged in size from the tiny to the small, with all kinds of objectives. Several of them were led by now unemployed generals. They were probably more popular than President Yeltsin, whose favorable rating sank to a low of 6 percent during the war against the Chechens in 1994–95. It had stood at one time (1991) at 85 percent.

Democracy is somewhat irrelevant in this process. Communist rulers had to change their system, not because it was undemocratic, but because it failed to work economically. Had it delivered a rising standard of living, complaints of popular participation in politics or even failure to grant personal liberties might have been ignored. (They *were* ignored for several decades, during which most of the world labored under the illusion that

Stalinist communism was an effective, if somewhat unpleasant, road to rapid economic development. A brave and distinguished band of dissidents won world acclaim but got nowhere in the USSR, except to be committed to mental hospitals, and most of them eventually migrated.) Or these liberal amenities would have gradually crept in as danger of any basic challenge to the established order diminished.

What forced the Kremlin dictators to change course was the failure of their system to keep up with the capitalist world in production and distribution of goods. Decentralization, private initiative, the free market, greater personal freedom were responses to desperate economic conditions clearly connected to the ghastly inadequacies of centralized economic planning. The classical Stalinist regime had justified sacrifice of democracy (in any case illusory under capitalism, they thought) by the supposed enormous advantages of a socialist economy. With its failure the whole communist case against democracy collapsed.

Whether democracy would prevail was another question. Russia, and most if not all of the other components of the former Soviet Union, had never known it in its modern form. As the president of Kazakhstan said, it was a stranger knocking at the door. Urgent tasks of economic adaptation to a dynamic and risky world required the undivided attention of rulers; democracy was a luxury one could for the moment at least not afford.

Among the lands of Eastern Europe whose Communist governments collapsed as soon as the Russian one fell, Poland was the first of the East European countries to successfully rebel against its Soviet-imposed masters. Hungary had valiantly tried and failed in the spectacular 1956 uprising, led by students who battled Russian tanks with bare hands until crushed, as the West stood by and watched. Then the Prague spring of 1968 in Czechoslovakia also ended in total defeat, its "socialism with a human face" contemptuously rejected by the Kremlin. Neither of these rebellions was in vain, for they left behind important ideas and memories. There had been revolts in East Germany as early as 1953, but there seemed to be no way out of the communist prison. A police state of incredible dimensions in East Germany (the so-called Democratic Republic) testified to the persistence of Germanic efficiency.

Lech Walesa, leader of the Solidarity movement of workers, was the hero of the Polish resistance to communism that preceded the collapse of 1989. This, one might argue, was the key event in the collapse. The Kremlin had struggled with Solidarity all through the 1980s, never quite daring to use brute force openly, and the presence of this germ of freedom on its doorstep in the end doomed the Soviet system. The Polish Communist party itself offered free elections to an upper house of the Polish parliament, which resulted in a stunning rebuke to the rulers. This was the start of the whole unraveling of communism in Eastern Europe.

But in 1995 as the elected president of Poland, Walesa was unhappy and unpopular. He feuded with an elected legislature that seemed decidedly unfriendly to basic reform, and like other heads of state in postcommunist regions, he seemed to want to become a dictator to escape their influence—another Pilsudski, a benevolent dictator who would not have to deal with a stubbornly reactionary parliament. The Polish parliamentary elections of September 1993 resulted in victory for two parties, the Democratic Left alliance and the Polish Peasant party, and a rebuff to the free market and conservative (religious) parties. The Democratic Left actually had at its core the old Communists, though they no longer called themselves that; they declared themselves to be prowestern social democrats. In December 1995 Walesa was defeated for reelection. This in spite of the fact that Poland's transformation to a market economy and to democratic government had on the whole gone well. The conversion from a state-administered economy was agonizingly painful everywhere in the excommunist countries, but Poland had done better probably than anyone else. Nevertheless as the new constitution was still being written, the future shape of government had to be considered uncertain.

In elections of May 1994, Hungarians also reinstated ex-Communists, calling themselves Socialists, but now prepared to continue free-market reforms. Rising unemployment, crime, inflation had soured Hungarians on liberals (Free Democrats) elected in 1990.

Rumania, Bulgaria, and Albania had largely reverted to the old ruling class, no longer calling itself communist but not much different; sometimes converted to economic reform, just as often trying to avoid or postpone it. The president of Ukraine, Leonid Kutchma, reelected in 1994, was once a high official in the Soviet arms industry but now preached free-market reforms. Dominated by old-line Communists, the parliament opposed him. In 1995 the president was trying to get a constitutional amendment granting him greater power, and Parliament less, in order to put through a privatization program resisted by the people's representatives.

In Slovakia, which had separated (peacefully) from Czechoslovakia in another breakup of the old states, Prime Minister Vladimir Meciar muzzled the press and radio after victory in legislative elections in October 1994 and replaced officials of the privatization agency, evidently with intent to halt privatization. He named a former Communist police official as procurer-general; President Kovoc refused to invest him. In December 1995, German Chancellor Kohl in a speech about Europe's future left Slovakia off a list of prospective candidates for membership in the European Union, accusing it of becoming an intolerant, "authoritarian" state.

Such scenarios throughout Eastern Europe constituted a sorry disillusionment for those in the West who had supposed that, after the fall of the communist regimes, all would be well for democracy. "The hopes born of the fall of the Berlin Wall are dimmed," editorialized the Paris oracle *Le Monde* in May 1993, mentioning especially the two wars that, for the first time in forty years, ravaged the Old Continent (Georgia-Azerbaijan in the Caucasus, as well as Bosnia—this was before Chechnya). It is true that these peoples had repudiated the old ruling elites and attempted to install democratic institutions. But they had fallen into serious difficulties, such as almost made the dismal old order look good. These troubles sometimes extended to civil war and always brought some degree of disappointment with the new regime. Even the relatively hopeful areas, Poland, Hungary, the Czech Republic, still had to overcome doubts about the stability of their democratic processes.

Western Europe

Democracy was arguably not in the best shape in the region where, along with the United States and other lands of English inheritance (Australia, New Zealand, Canada), it was most at home. We have already described the long tradition of antidemocratic thought, the past desertions to fascist or communist totalitarianism, the periodic moods of profound disillusionment. As the twentieth century comes to an end, these tendencies are all very much alive.

There is no need to dwell again on voter apathy, and the ways in which democracy seemed to mean little to the average citizen or in which it could be said to be inoperative. All of these were much noted. It was generally agreed that political interest was at low ebb, real issues hard to find, the public politically listless. Local elections usually brought out less than half the voters (even fewer in the United States, where 25 percent was a good showing). In French municipal elections of March 1989, more than 40 percent abstained in the largest cities. Even in national elections the largest party of all was those who did not vote (a third of the registered voters in France). An apathetic and mercurial public mistrusted all politicians, hardly less so in Western Europe and the United States than in the former Soviet Union.

While each retained its own political life, European states were engaged in a project to create a European Union, which aspired in time to become a single federal state superseding the old sovereignties of Europe. The great project, launched right after 1945 by men of vision and bearing fruit in the 1957 Treaty of Rome, had grown slowly if spasmodically ever since, progressing from Economic Community to European Union, and from the original six member states to fifteen (with others knocking at the door). It did not seem to be setting much of a democratic example. The real government of the union, the Council of Ministers, which was appointed by the various member states, reached its decisions in the highly undemocratic manner of secret meetings, shrouding their minutes and records in concealment. Some members protested this secrecy, but the older and dominant states of the union, France and Germany, wanted no part of "transparency." They argued, as the framers of the U.S. Constitution had done in 1787, that delicate negotiations between sovereign states require closed doors. They also resisted suggestions that on some issues a majority vote rather than unanimity might prevail.

Also not notably responsible to the peoples of the different member states was the European Commission, the vast bureaucracy in Brussels that administered the rules and programs of the union. There was also a European parliament at Strasbourg (some distance from the Brussels center of power), but it lagged behind the other institutions of the union. Efforts to raise the status of the parliament, which since 1982 has been directly elected, seemed something of an afterthought or window dressing. Even after the Treaty of Maastricht (1992) delegated it some additional powers, the parliament felt impotent. Suggestions that it be allowed to elect the commission's president (presently appointed by the Council of Ministers), or introduce legislation, had yet to be implemented. The serious ongoing problems of the union, in trying to adjust and integrate national policies so as to prepare for a common currency, or to act on likely future candidates for admission, had to be dealt with from the top, by the existing machinery of council and commission, which had grown accustomed to operating with minimal interference from the largely ceremonial or oratorical parliament.

The European Parliament had none of the powers of a real parliament, such as to enact binding legislation and force selection of a new cabinet (council) in the event of an adverse parliamentary vote on an important question. Whether it ever would gain such powers was an open question; certainly that would not be for some time. The whole fascinating story of this emerging superstate the European Union, if such it was (there was much resistance by some of the members, who obviously did not wish the community to go that far), appeared to reveal the irrelevancy of democracy to the real issues of modern life. Its presence was more cosmetic than substantive.

Politics in the separate countries of Western Europe appeared to be in some sort of crisis, no doubt a normal condition. Parties were certainly in turmoil. Corruption was a general problem in the 1990s. Corruption affected politics in Spain, where scandal after scandal shook the long-reigning government of Felipe Gonzales; in France, where Prime Minister Balladur turned from hero to goat almost overnight, after the earlier suicide of a Socialist luminary; and even more in Italy, where it ruined major political parties. Even in England, an opinion poll showed that nearly two-thirds of the people thought MPs made money by using their office improperly, and investigations seemed somewhat to bear this out.[4]

This new venality seemed a characteristic of the times, the result of mounting *incivisme* among public servants, the vast sums of money being passed about, and the sheer growth of government that made it impossible to maintain controls. Political corruption, to be sure, was no monopoly of the West; it was found everywhere. The Soviet Union, before its collapse as well as after, was filled with it, as are China and, among other Communist-ruled countries, Vietnam, whose own leader, Du Muoi, inveighed against "debauchery, abuse of power, and embezzlement of public funds" (May 1995). But Europe was supposed to have "clean government," and Europeans often demanded it of the undeveloped world in censorious terms. Was it in process of vanishing in Europe itself? Many of these scandals were indeed brought to light by an enterprising press (keenly competing for readers). But how many more went undetected? Only 2 or 3 percent of all crimes in the United States were ever caught out and punished, it was estimated.

In Italy a wave of reform exposed the corruption seemingly endemic in Italian politics. Leaders of the Christian Democratic party as well as Socialists were implicated. The former party, for decades the leading one in Italy, was literally driven out of existence; like the Communists, it had to regroup under a different name. Meanwhile for the first time, Italy made headway in the war against the Mafia. A wave of public indignation followed the 1992 assassinations of two judges, one of whom was the most prominent anti-Mafioso, the last of many such victims of Mafia vengeance. Tens of thousands of Italians paraded in protest against the bombings. The supreme Sicilian grandfather was captured and put on trial with forty others in 1995. This was a remarkable victory for public opinion, but it threatened the very roots of politics, for Mafia corruption had penetrated the parties so that few politicians were untouched by it. A revolution seemed to be under way in Italy, not of one class against another but of all decent people against a deeply corrupt political system that had fastened itself on the Italian state.

A neo-Fascist party had risen to prominence in Italy again, though it claimed now to accept parliamentary democracy. A new center-right party called Forza Italiana, led by a wealthy and powerful Milanese entrepreneur, had a meteoric rise and an equally meteoric fall, losing 22.5 percent between June and December 1994. The Northern League, which wanted autonomy for the north and threatened a tax strike against the central government, at times found strong regional support.

Volatility was a general feature of European politics. Parties and leaders rose and fell rapidly. In France President Mitterand fell off badly after winning handily in 1988. Prime Minister Edouard Balladur was almost wildly popular in 1993–94, and he was a strong favorite to win the presidency in 1995; but early in the year his standing in the polls tumbled, and his rival Jacques Chirac outdistanced him to win the presidency; Balladur did not even make the finals. Two years earlier, a similar debacle had struck the formerly dominant Socialist party, which saw its number of representatives in the Assembly fall from 258 to 53 while many of its leaders failed to be reelected; in some of its regions of traditional strength the Socialist party was virtually wiped out. Yet in the 1995 election the Socialist candidate Jospin led a comeback, which saw him beaten only by about 47 to 53 percent of the votes cast. The experts in public opinion polling increasingly lost their ability to forecast election results, because irrational grounds of choice led to huge last-minute voting swings. The volatile electorate of a modern democracy makes extreme demands for instant gratification; patience is the least of its virtues.

The electorate's extreme volatility could not be blamed on the proverbial inconstancy of the Italians or French, for it was found elsewhere too. The British chose John Major in the 1992 general election, only to turn savagely on him in the next two years when his favorable rating in the polls came to resemble Boris Yeltsin's in Russia. The Americans turned out George Bush two years after his overwhelming popularity during the war against Iraq; his successor, Bill Clinton, rose and sank in public approval like a roller coaster. A public flooded by one sensational media event after another seemed to lose all perspective and continuity so that a politician's popularity depended on what he said yesterday or what the economic index said today.

Another common feature was fragmentation, or the dispersal of votes among numerous and diverse as well as shifting political parties. In the French presidential election of May 1995, the first round of voting found no one candidate gaining more than 25 percent of the vote, while the extremes of Right and Left, an obvious protest vote, each got about 15 percent: on one wing the National Front of the xenophobic, fascist-like Le Pen, and on the other Communists and miscellaneous minor leftists. In Italy regional elections of April 23, 1995, saw the ex-Communists, now the Democratic Party of the Left, come in first with around 25 percent of the vote. Business tycoon Silvio Berlusconi's Forza Italiana had 23 percent, while Gianfranco Fini's neo-Fascist National Alliance gained 15 percent; the Northern League and the reconstituted Christian Democrats, renamed the Popular party and divided into two factions, were also players, along with some dinosaur, unreconstructed Communists. From these fragments neither a center-left nor a center-right coalition could muster a majority. A caretaker government of "technicians" governed Italy.

The parliamentary system of requiring a government to be approved by a majority of votes in the elected legislature still could lead to hopeless stalemate. People wondered how long Italy could go on lurching from crisis to crisis as parties rose and fell, desperate coalitions were put together only to come apart, and deficits soared under governments too weak to take action. This was the scenario that had led to Hitler's dictatorship, as well as Mussolini's in the 1920s, and had caused the collapse of both the Third and Fourth French Republics, among many other cases. If it proved impossible to find a majority to support any government, the only resort was to an emergency caretaker government, as happened in 1995 in Italy. Mussolini and then Hitler had used this as a ladder to outright dictatorship.

Return to any fascist-type government seemed blocked by the past; but one could wonder whether the going order of elected party politicians could survive any really serious crisis, such as always was a possibility—a crisis of the economy, of the environment, of nuclear weapons and war, of terrorism and assassination, such as radical Islamicists were carrying to Europe increasingly, or any number of other conceivable horrors. The precarious nature of the whole modern economic and technological society lurked in the background of democratic governments. Violent voter swings were a function of many deep concerns: unemployment (related to the revolutionization of world markets by electronic communications), unease at social change, at the new Europe without national boundaries, at decay of traditional values. They were also partly the result of an ideological vacuum left by the collapse of communism and socialism, as well as the rise in special interest groups amid the fragmentation of society and values.

Greece, ancestral homeland of the democratic polis, surrendered for a while to a dictatorship but returned, a repentant sinner, to a turbulent and unsatisfactory democracy in 1974. The greatest democratic successes of the 1970s and 1980s in Europe were on the Iberian peninsula. Spain, which between 1923 and 1930 had been ruled from behind the throne by a military figure turned dictator, then experienced the turbulent republic of 1931–36 that ended in civil war, perhaps the most exciting event in the melodramatic 1930s. After 1939 the military dictator Francisco Franco became a sinister symbol for most of the world's liberals, but he kept Spain out of World War II and restored a measure of peace to a land weary of strife. He managed to remain in power until his death in 1975. In fact, Spain began its significant path of economic and technological modernization under Franco—first of the new-style authoritarian marketeers?

After the death of its longtime dictator in 1974, most observers expected Portugal to become either a left-wing dictatorship (the Communists confidently predicted this) or a right-wing military one; against all forecasts the Portuguese people in the ensuing years revealed a basic desire for personal and intellectual freedom and for parliamentary government, despite difficulties with each. Portugal had experienced earlier back-and-forth swings of this sort. In 1926 a Portuguese republic that had existed since the revolution of 1910 collapsed, largely because during its fifteen years of life there were forty-five coalition governments.

In the 1990s the Iberian peninsula, both post-Franco Spain (led back to a parliamentary regime by her king!) and Portugal, had joined the European Union and seemed safe for democracy. But who could say for sure? Anyone visiting the bustling Spanish capital of Madrid sees the fine old houses on the Avenue Castellano, once homes of the aristocrats and wrecked during the civil war, now largely converted to businesses and government offices, and wonders how that nightmare of 1936–39 could have happened. The visitor succumbs to the charm of the Spanish people and senses the presence of a wholly new Spain, the one that welcomed the world to the Olympic Games in 1992 with matchless pageantry. But an uncertain though dynamic economy, and corruption scandals as in Italy and France, cast some shadows of doubt on the future of Spanish democracy.

Perhaps the leading lesson from all this is that we should realize how imperfect and unnatural our American or European democracy is and stop presenting it to the world as if it were a model to be imitated, failing which rebukes and penalties, perhaps even armed invasion, will be inflicted on the hapless wretches who lack it. Henry B. Mayo, in an article titled "How Can We Justify Democracy?" once decided that there is no rational justification; it is an act of faith. Democracy fits somewhere into the faith of the American people, and perhaps the faiths of others. It is a word that has taken root in the structure of popular linguistic consciousness with sacred communal connotations. But it has this quality in few other societies. We believe in democracy as a kind of national faith, without rational grounds. We should refrain from temptations to force our peculiar values on others.

If civil war seems the unhappy condition of too many peoples around the world, we might note that it is not entirely absent from the older and stabler democracies; it is always a threat there. The recourse to violence always lurks just below the surface of any civilization. Politics is a war that "democratic" countries have learned, painfully, to keep at the level of a mock war but that intermittently comes close to crossing the border into real violence. In many countries today, outbreaks of fighting on the floor of national legislatures are by no means uncommon; it happened recently in Hong Kong, South Korea, Russia, Japan, and Taiwan, while the California State legislature was described recently as a seething cauldron of hatreds, barely restrained from physical battle. This apart from rioting farmers, destructive striking workers, assassinations of public officials, as common almost in Western Europe as in Russia or South America. At all times the language of politics verges on the violent. "It is a sobering exercise," Bertrand de Jouvenel wrote, "to count the expressions of anger (as against those of good will) which occur in the speeches or writings of political champions of this or that moral cause." The most democratic of politicians normally constructs his or her discourse around some sinister scapegoat-enemy, whether malignant rich people, state bureaucrats, demagogues, or bigots. "Political activity is dangerous," Jouvenel began his essay "On the Nature of Political Science" from which we just quoted. In European countries and in the United States, violence has erupted, whether in the bombing of American public buildings, French farmers blocking roads and burning trucks, German neo-Nazis attacking foreigners, Italians destroying their own great works of art—choose your own examples. Satanic cults arose among the supposedly placid Norwegians.

Perhaps western democracy suffered from the kind of global awareness that modern communications create. Faith in the ultimate triumph of democracy everywhere, belief in it as a kind of political absolute, were much easier when the world outside Europe and America was dim and distant. Today, when every day's news brings tales of misery in the Sudan, mass slaughter in Cambodia, civil war in Bosnia, anarchy in Georgia, and so on almost ad infinitum, it is hard to conceive of democracy as even very relevant to the horrifying problems of a troubled humanity.

Notes

1. Linda Wills Qammaqami, "The Catalyst of Nationalization: Max Thornburg and the Failure of Private Sector Developmentalism in Iran, 1947–1951," *Diplomatic History*, Winter 1995.

2. John Slimming, *Malaysia: Death of a Democracy* (London: J. Murray, 1969); Goh Cheng Teik, *The May 13 Incident and Democracy in Malaysia* (Oxford University Press, 1971).

3. See Cyrill Stieger, "Kosovo: Visible and Invisible Walls," *Swiss Review of World Affairs*, May 1995.

4. Maureen Mancuso, *The Ethical World of British MPs* (Montreal: McGill-Queen's University Press, 1995).

9

Conclusion

Perennial Criticisms

The dilemma or paradox encountered in the last chapter is not a new but a perennial one for democracy. "Good government means unity of action," Thiers said in 1871 during a major crisis of French government. Democracy, he thought, is "the opportunity of dismissing the authority to whom the action has been entrusted. But once you have set up an authority you must let it act and not weaken it." So the people do not decide policies; they just periodically ratify what some great man has done or else allow another great man to take his place.

People invoke democracy when they want to attack and supplant a disliked government but avoid it when, elected to office, they have to formulate and carry out programs themselves. In Poland Lech Walesa replied to criticisms that as president he was acting without consulting the rank and file of his famous Solidarity party, which had raised him to power, by saying that decisions could not wait on a vote of ten million members.

Such political decisions cannot be based on the popularity of policies; they must be made on the basis of rational, long-term considerations that rest on specialized expertise or theoretical acumen, to which the vagaries of an ill-informed public are relevant only as a limiting factor (it is hard to carry out a policy too outrageously disdainful of popular prejudices or interests).

This was a familiar point. None of the criticisms of democracy, under whatever definition of the term, that we meet today is new. They have all been heard many times before. Inefficient, a school for tyrants, an impossibility (the many cannot govern), a fraud, a trick played on the people; or a symptom of cultural disintegration, the rule of inferiors, the debase-

ment of culture and thought—democracy always received these same rebukes, however inconsistent with each other they might be. The style in
which these reproaches were expressed might change, and these new ac-
cents often gave a fresh tone to the old ideas, as they did, for example, in
the 1920s. But it is rare that we discover a new argument. The criticisms we
meet today were "fully explored in the nineteenth century," Stephen R.
Graubard remarked in 1962. "All these views have been expressed and
heard a hundred times," Jacques Ellul wrote wearily (*The Political Illusion*,
1967). Amassing examples of them lends point to the claim of structuralists
such as Roland Barthes that culture endlessly repeats itself.

Thus, remarks about the debilitating effects on policy of having to appeal
to the multitude's passions, such as Alex Comfort's complaint (in *Darwin
and the Naked Lady*) that "no Western government has any policies . . .
which extend beyond the next election," may be compared to Jacob Burckhardt writing in the 1880s that "[i]n order to get elected, the leaders of the
populace must win the excitement-craving masses . . . with consequences
that make your hair stand on end." Or protests that local interests prevail
over general ones, as in Thomas Blinder's penetrating *Hard Hearts Soft
Heads* (1988, p. 213), may be compared to many similar complaints by the
early political economists that parliamentary democracy could not see the
forest for the trees. These points are as perennially similar as analytical
ones; thus Geoffrey Gorer, in his essays "The Danger of Equality" and "A
Reconsideration of Class Distinction" in 1966, reproduced W.H. Mallock's
argument that, paradoxically, inequality is essential to democracy. Dreams
of a rational basis of policy beyond popular caprice, heard time and time
again in previous centuries, reappeared in such "behavioral scientists" as
Harold Lasswell or H.J. Eysenck.

Democracy has been prematurely pronounced dead, not once as Mark
Twain was but innumerable times, indeed in almost every decade since
the 1790s. This is still going on: we have had recent works titled *The Death
of Democracy, The Death of British Democracy, The Collapse of American
Democracy*. Not only popular tracts by the desperately disillusioned, but
serious treatments of the subject had to consider the possibility of such a
demise. Similarly, democracy is always going through a "crisis." The
year 1975 saw publication of a book about "the crisis of mass democracy"
in late nineteenth-century France and of one titled *The* [present] *Crisis of
Democracy*.

Just as often, democracy has been hailed as the hope of mankind, only to
fall shamefully—all too humanly—short of this goal. Two large themes
stand out in the history of democracy over the past two centuries. The first
is that, in some basic ways, it presses on. That irresistible tide, which all

through the nineteenth century exhilarated Americans and saddened cultured Europeans, relentlessly searches out and floods each hiding place of an inegalitarian political or social order. Once identified, the aristocratic remnant is helpless. Let it be indirect election to the United States Senate, or plural votes in England, or female suffrage in France (even in Switzerland), sooner or later they had to go. No emblem of avowed legal or political inequality can long hold out once placed under attack. More recently, equality of opportunity or access was found to be insufficient; people were still unequal despite formal, legal equality, and so ways had to be found to overcome this inequality, by affirmative action or other targeted programs to give a special boost to groups needing to catch up. But such a program threatened not only the principles of equity but the rules of state power. Writing in review of John Rawls's much-discussed *Theory of Justice* and Christopher Jencks's study of educational inequality along with other demands for "equality of condition," Robert Nisbet in 1975 (in *Commentary*) found in this drive toward uniformity the seeds of a "New Despotism."

Despite the sense in which, in the words of Jean-François Revel, the twentieth century has been on the whole a disaster for democracy, it has triumphed over its foes. As we know, in the end even democracy's most ruthless and embattled enemies have had to yield. The Soviet Union finally surrendered; thirty-five years after the death of Stalin, the whole vast edifice of centralized elite power, erected and maintained at such a frightful cost, had to be painfully jettisoned. The wave of protests that shook the old Communist regimes in 1989 included demands for elections and representative government along with assertions of rights to free speech, political opposition, individual liberties. Having attained this, of course, their peoples are not happy about it, but there is no likelihood of their returning to the old harness.

In this sense democracy seems secure: no monolithic, integral order is possible in the modernized world, no orthodoxy can enforce uniformity. Attempts to do so by terror, by mass imprisonment, by mass slaughter (consider Cambodia) have failed. Despite their enormous willpower, their charisma, and their utter ruthlessness, Hitler and Stalin failed. Today the anachronistic regime in Iran thunders its anathemas on everybody, but no one except its half-mad leaders thinks this can last long. In China and Vietnam the fading remnants of the Communist religion are gasping their last breaths. As we have seen, scores of countries struggle to attain democracy or at least to seem to do so; even the worst despotism must pay tribute to democracy by disguising itself.

The other great and obvious truth is that this democratic triumph is profoundly unsatisfactory. The feeling that democracy is an illusion or a cheat is endemic in it, not just a remedial defect. As one phase of the modern condition, democracy shares in the disenchantments of that condition: the loss of innocence and community, of religion and virtue. In any case the frustrations and imperfections are obvious. By now democracy's inherent limitations must be evident to all save the most obtuse. That any conceivable alternative is even worse is equally obvious. The unpleasantness of the alternatives that so notably emerged in the twentieth century helped keep democratic morale up. One deals with something that one must live with, even though it is not very pleasant, by ignoring it as far as possible. Elections are not valued for their own sake but because there is fear that any alternative will be worse. That has been the fate of democracy.

The larger myths or theories about democracy in human history all seem to contain some, but not total, truth. Democracy as the goal of history, as progress, has some validity. One would risk ridicule by even suggesting at this date that we can find the unifying theme of all western, if not world, civilization in the steady expansion of liberty and popular rule. Yet in a sense it *has* gone on. But just as true are the views of democracy as cultural decay or degeneration, or as part of an endlessly repetitive cycle. Vico's great myth of a remorseless quantifying and equalizing process during the Age of Men that goes on until the leveling is complete, and then explodes in chaos and leads back to an Age of Gods and then Heroes, retains its compelling power. The greatest work of imaginative literature the twentieth century produced was conceived in its image. The abysmal absurdities and crudities of popular culture in the age of the TV sitcom and the adman must now and then strike even the least critical mind as something God surely cannot permit to go on much longer, plumbing depths below depths every season.

Are any of the traditional flaws worse today, or less bad, than in former times? Some, it seems, are underlined more sharply now. The old feeling of "fatalism of the multitude" acts as it perhaps has never acted before to suggest the powerlessness of the popular will, the inability of the individual voter to influence issues. Important matters are decided from above, presented to citizens as faits accomplis. They are decided partly by implacable objective realities, the laws of economics or nature; partly by those elected to represent the people, but who of course do not do so and who may be corrupt or incompetent; partly by judges and bureaucrats, who are subject to very little popular control. Judge Max Raskin, a distinguished Milwaukee jurist, spoke for virtually all judges in saying that it would be grievous error "to shift the judicial forum into the streets where the ultimate victor is the one with the strongest pen or the loudest voice"—and where justice is decided by other peoples under other governments. "Citizens in democracy have their word to say, but fewer and fewer chances to say it," observed French columnist Claude Julien. Or they have less and less chance of having it result in anything.

The stock market paid little attention to the French presidential election of 1995, for example, thinking either that the candidates were exactly alike, the Conservative and the Socialist really the same under a veneer of rhetoric; or that whatever their inclinations, conditions would require them to do or not to do the same things in office. The French had, after all, witnessed a Socialist president quickly call off his ambitious plans for government intervention to restore full employment in 1982. (A forthcoming election was more likely to depress the market than to raise it, though it was usually assumed that, having surmounted the election, a government could take necessary decisions, which it would have feared to take before the election.) "Who are the true masters of the world?" asked *Le Monde* (May 1995), answering first that one thing is sure: they are not the governments that, elected after epic electoral battles, "find themselves powerless in the face of formidable global forces." These irresistible powers are not, as writers of political romances used to imagine, some secret clique of conspiring monopolists, but worldwide markets and economic laws. Were not half of the shares on the Paris bourse held by foreign investors, including Asians and Americans as well as other Europeans? These were not sinister Rothschilds or Morgans trying to buy up the world, but huge funds, professionally managed and highly competitive, pooling the savings of millions and millions of people and able at an electronic flash to transfer money from Paris to Singapore or Tokyo or New York. Increasingly they seemed able to buy and sell governments too; the wave of corruption scandals testifies to that. At any rate, as the French newspaper continued, the new masters of the world "have never submitted their projects to universal suffrage; democracy is not for them." This was hardly a new observation, to be sure, but is more startlingly obvious today than ever.

Testimony to the alienation of citizens and governments can be found in the tendency of peoples to blame their governments, reproaching them for their alleged failures, quite as often in the so-called democracies as in the various forms of authoritarian rule. If it is truly *their* government, a government of the people, this bitter spirit should not appear. Trouble there may be, but it should be "our" problem if it is "our" government—trouble to be faced together without recrimination. The blame for mistakes should be shared by the entire community if in fact this community has made them or caused them to be made. But people in the democracies quite commonly look upon government as an alien body, handing down its faceless decrees from afar, like Kafka's Castle. Democracy is, to be sure, manifested in the people's holding government accountable, all too often indeed creating panic in its harried objects of their hatred or scorn as they, the elected officials, scurry to try to remedy something that has gone badly wrong. But clearly the electorate views them with surly mistrust, almost as the enemy rather than the friend. Polls showed a deep distrust of all institutions—a London *Times* poll of April 30, 1974, found 27 percent having confidence in Parliament. (The press, television, the trade unions, even religion ranked lower, education not much better.) Even the judicial system was trusted by less than half of those polled—this in the land that virtually invented the independent and incorruptible law. Subsequent follow-ups of this poll show little change.

In the American capital city of Washington, only a few years ago, great numbers of visitors wandered at will through the Capitol building, the Supreme Court, the White House grounds, Arlington National Cemetery, bringing their children to marvel at the symbols of American government. Today these places are blocked off or surrounded with steel and concrete barriers as if they were hostile garrisons. Unless he or she is prepared to spend half a day undergoing security checks, the tourist is not likely to get near any of the shrines of American democracy. It would be hard to convince him or her that government has gotten any closer to the people.

The Two Democracies

We have observed two larger meanings of democracy, corresponding roughly to stages of historical development: first, the organic, "totalitarian" democracy, marked by consensus and hierarchy, that is found among people sharing a single close-knit culture and value system. Operating within the closed community it can approximate perfect democracy, with a minimum of alienating processes and institutions—as in the election, say, of a Kurdish headman. This vision of an idyllic pastoral community was the source of early democratic idealism. It persists today, in greater or less degree, among less modernized peoples, even among those who are the most modernized, as a recurring archetypal influence. (We denounce the corrupt politicians and pine for a strong, pure leader, the incarnation of Truth.) But applied to larger, multicultural societies, this spirit of family solidarity changes into the horrors of Reigns of Terror or Nazi dictatorship.

Next came the elective parliamentary system, chiefly English in origin, developed in nineteenth-century America and parts of Western Europe within the context of the nation-state, resting on a balance between pluralism and community. Disenchanting to the degree that it proved workable, assailed by rationalists and idealists for its pragmatic opportunism and concealed elitism, it was theoretically flawed but a practical success. Intellectuals might identify this kind of democracy with a capitalist economy or a lowbrow nationalist culture. It lost its glamour, was systematically denigrated, and survived only faute de mieux, it seemed; yet it presided over the most successful era in western history. In its practical application it varied from country to country, being integrated into the special customs of national cultures. Granted, it seems precarious; as the distinguished student of democracy Robert Dahl remarked, "the conditions most favorable for polyarchy [successful pluralistic democracy] are comparatively uncommon and not easily created."

The story of democracy often seems to have consisted of a long and usually acrimonious (but confused) dialogue between these two kinds of democracy, each laying claim to the word and disputing the other's title. The first kind of democracy insists that every citizen must be directly involved as an active participant in decisions affecting the community, otherwise it isn't democracy but a travesty of it. Its advocates ridicule the alleged democracy that actually gives the citizen no more than the right to cast a ballot every few years, along with thousands or millions of others, for some alleged representative in a far-off seat of government. (The long period between national elections, which can be and usually is five years in Great Britain, makes possible a situation such as existed there between 1993 and 1996, when a government clung to office for years despite being extremely unpopular according to the public opinion polls.) This is really oligarchy, the critics assert, and not a particularly attractive kind, being based on fraudulent claims to represent the people by a small group of professional politicians, a singularly unlovely caste. These politicians admittedly may on rare occasions be called to account by an aroused populace or respond to pressures from some elements of the public, but even here, you do not get the enlightened spirit of the whole community but a collection of special interests, making for the worst sort of government. It might be added that this regime is on a road to total dissolution of the organic bonds that must unite any body politic for it to be governable, and it has survived thus far only because that process of corruption has not run its full course.

The second kind of democracy replies that direct democracy is utterly impracticable in a large nation and that any serious attempt to apply it beyond an extremely local level must lead to a repressive dictatorship. Organic democracy is an obsolete tribalism, viciously intolerant even in its time and today likely to lead to the persecution of minorities on a national scale. Its main exemplar in the modern era was Hitler's Germany. Representative democracy, on the other hand, admittedly imperfect, manages to struggle along in the most advanced communities. There is nothing to replace it that is at all civilized.

The debate is a draw, since each side is obviously right in its criticisms of the other. Both kinds are imperfect. They are the two sides of a perfect democracy, a Platonic idea such as never has existed in the real world and probably never will. In the ideal world every citizen (perfectly informed) would have a direct influence on political decisions, none would be alienated, the general interest would triumph over particular interests, while each minority viewpoint would be respected and protected. With all these qualifications, government would be efficient, prompt to react to all emergencies, able to identify and respond to the sincere popular will while rejecting momentary lapses of judgment and special interest lobbies.

One might go on describing the ideal democracy while increasingly realizing how impossible such a utopia is. Probably the most remarkable experiment in combining the two democracies in recent times was General Charles de Gaulle's Fifth Republic. The French leader, who had come out of World War II with immense prestige, hated political parties and wanted to embody the general will of his people in a charismatic personality (himself). This caused uneasiness among all those who remembered the recent fascist horrors, but de Gaulle was committed not only to universal suffrage and free speech but to an elected two-house parliament and an independent judiciary. The man who had led the fight against Hitler certainly did not intend to create a Nazi-like regime. He yearned to heal the rifts in his beloved French nation, end voter alienation, somehow involve the people directly in government, as well as lead it forward to wealth and strength. Surrounded by an able group of people who shared this goal, even if they were not all of one mind about details, President Charles de Gaulle between 1958 and 1970 gave the postwar world its most interesting and impressive political regime.

But, as he realized, he did not succeed. He may have ended the *immobilisme* of the Third and Fourth Republics, too concerned with parliamentary supremacy, but he did not, except perhaps very briefly, unify France or end citizen alienation from government. It was possible for an expert observer to write in 1969 that "[i]ntegration of the workers into the economic and political life of the nation" was a remarkable feature of recent French history (Harvey Waterman, *Political Change in Contemporary France*). But many protested this kind of plebiscitary and dictatorial "democracy,"[1] and after this unique man's departure, repudiated by the same people who had given him an overwhelming mandate a decade before (and after a desperate attempt to decentralize the government, which corresponded to his desire for direct democracy but contradicted the other terms of his rule), the Fifth Republic began to look like the earlier ones. The presidents grew weaker, the parliament stronger; the parties and the divisions persisted, and an awkward gap between parliament and the presidency caused problems. After the presidential election of 1995, there was a general feeling that France was more disunited than ever before. This brave attempt to square the democratic circle by combining liberal democracy with Caesarism revealed the impossibility of doing so.

One of the few places, if not the only place, in Europe still practicing direct democracy is an area of five small Swiss cantons, in each of which all citizens assemble in the open air once a year to elect members of the local government and debate legislative proposals. Idyllic, no doubt, but these *Landsgemeinde* are now much criticized locally; people complain that it is awkward and inhibiting to have to show your hand, they'd rather have a secret ballot, and that it is inconvenient to have to leave your job or travel if you are infirm. One canton has reduced the authority of the assembly and is considering its total elimination. The event may in the end survive as one of those quaint folk ceremonies that attract tourists, like the spring migration of the cows. Meanwhile, in order to make their central government work, the Swiss have had to resort to a formula whereby the governing seven-person Federal Council must always have the same number of members from each political party—seemingly a violation of democratic principles.

A Third Democracy?

There is perhaps a third kind of democracy that is the political order of the presently emerging totally modernized, pluralized, urbanized, rationalized, consumerized, secularized, culturally homogenized global society. It is democratic because it is unable to tolerate any authority or believe in any legitimizing myths, but it has all but lost that mental discipline and community spirit without which elective government is impossible. And so it is condemned to waver back and forth between free and unfree regimes while searching for a secret that still eludes humanity: how fully autonomous individuals can live together harmoniously in a just and free community.

"The disease of our civilization on both the communist and capitalist side of the fence," a Yugoslav wrote, is the alienated helplessness of the citizen confronting a governmental machinery that is too vast and complex. We have also noted that the outcome of the debate about democracy seems to have ended in a stalemate or draw: the world wavers endlessly back and forth between democracy and antidemocracy, finding neither tolerable for long. The defects of each reveal themselves with increasing clarity. The world in general seems to be searching for a way to live without legitimation, that is, without a political myth that holds people in respectful awe. It has entered the postdemocratic phase—not necessarily nondemocratic, but searching for some "new structure in which democracy can live." T.S. Eliot had already said it in 1928: "The modern question as popularly put is: 'democracy is dead: what is to replace it?' Whereas it should be: 'the frame of democracy has been destroyed: how can we, out of materials at hand, build a new structure in which democracy can live?' " One of the Chinese students protesting against their dismally outmoded regime in the spring of 1989 said, "I still haven't found what I'm looking for"; knowing what they opposed, their attempts to formulate a positive goal did involve vaguely democratic ideas, but by no means clearly. The barely recognizable Statue of Liberty they built in defiance of their repressive and bumbling rulers exactly expressed their predicament.

It is not surprising that democracy today tends popularly to mean freedom of choice or the right to dissent, to oppose. This is so for two reasons: First, it is the essential condition of modernized man; released from authority, socially and physically mobile, he is able to perceive a greater variety of choices than in the past. Second, the discredited "totalitarian" revolutions of the twentieth century were hostile to unrestrained individual liberty, and the ideological conflict with them reenforced the right to dissent. Thus "democracy" to the American means the freedoms that fascist and Soviet citizens lacked: freedom of opinion, press, religion, economic enterprise. (It meant that also to many of those living in these unfree conditions who had the courage to protest.) It is safe to say that we are all democrats insofar as the term is taken to mean the right to basic personal liberties. The nineteenth century knew this as liberalism; most people today call it democracy.

Social democracy may be expected to continue; the continuing emancipation of individual egos from customary constraints leads to ever fiercer demands for equality, a repudiation of the old functionally unequal hierarchy, refusal to defer to any social authority. Democracy as social equality does not die, nor does the kind of cultural democracy, horrifying to some, that gives us "mass culture" in the form of television, sports, rock music, consumerism all over the world, at the expense of old high cultures or local, folk cultures, and that inundates such former repositories of high culture as the universities with demands for the admission of everybody. "The opening act of a great and still unfinished social revolution," this powerful process will certainly continue with results that cannot be foreseen. But democracy as popular government wanes because its forms rest on basic communal solidarity, transformed into understandings, conventions, practices peculiar to national political communities, now rapidly disappearing as a part of the globalization process. The new democracy drives out the old.

With their permissiveness and their rejection of authority, it is not yet clear that such societies shorn of solidarity can permanently survive; it is possible that the fully modernized society is ungovernable. Its public is too powerful to ignore, too informed to deceive, and too irresponsible to be satisfied. But if this is the natural condition of modern people, sooner or later every society throughout the earth will arrive at it. This pluralism comes about not through the triumph of democracy as a positive value but through the collapse of universal values. It is irresistible because of the globalization of culture and because of the communications revolution, rendering it impossible to prevent access to information. "A slow levelling process is going on all over the world," John Burchard noted. The global village of standardized urban mass-media culture with its styles in pop music, architecture, sports, shopping malls—knit together now by computers—becomes much the same all over the world, and areas still untouched by it diminish each year. European cities now pull down old markets and neighborhoods to build characterless high-rises, even as the Russians used to do in a cruder way. In many ways this international consumer society is profoundly democratic. Paul Robinson claimed that sexual permissiveness represents a "democratization of human sexual affairs," making erotic pleasure no longer an elite privilege. The same might be said of many consumer goods, from Coca-Cola and VCRs to automobiles and suburban houses: onetime elite prerogatives are made available to the masses in cheapened form.

This condition of late democracy may of course be seen as the aging and death of human culture—a poison that finally fills the whole bloodstream, a waste that remains and kills. It dissolves authority, hierarchy, and hence social order, culminating in a universal chaos. Successive decays occurring in elites and cities were always renewed by fresh barbarian conquests, but in the end we run out of barbarians. That civilization is a disease of this sort has been the insight of scores of historical macrotheorizers from Ibn Khaldun to Rousseau, Gobineau, and Spengler. That there is a natural progression from primitive village solidarity to civilized urban anomie has struck sociologists such as Durkheim, Tönnies, Redfield. This is far from the whole truth; there are other and countervailing processes at work, but it is one significant process always going on.

It is certain that the citizens of a modern country become ever more difficult to govern. The mass media induce a psychological as well as a material discontent—people more and more want and demand that all their wishes be fulfilled, as well as their wants satisfied. The principle of relative deprivation means that the more new products are invented, the more people feel impoverished and discriminated against if they do not have them. Television sets (with larger and larger screens, more and more capabilities) passed in a generation from a fantasy to an aspiration to a necessity; computers evolved from a monstrosity owned by a few huge corporations to something everyone carries around like a notebook. Rising rates of illegitimacy, abortion, divorce testify to the pleasure principle's steady expansion. Those who were content to keep the noiseless tenor of their way far from the madding crowd, who lived and worked as their fathers had done without thought of change, monogamous and of simple pleasures, who seldom complained and usually deferred, had always made up the vast majority of men and women; now everyone has to be upwardly and geographically mobile as well as constantly entertained.

Issues grow more complex, judgments more problematic; there is no longer any generally accepted and readily assimilable body of expertise, for example, on economics, where wild disagreements prevail among the learned. The populace is more distracted by other issues: private ones, in an age of anxiety marked by divorce, drugs, crime; or the modern version of bread and circuses, dwarfing all previous issues, in the form of entertainment via television, movies (VCRs), and so forth. Contemporary urban man or woman is preoccupied with job, leisure, sexual success, all the gadgets of an electronic civilization; he or she watches television, attends university classes, has identity problems, travels abroad, finds a mate and sheds her or him; reads incredible numbers of books on how to grow up, how to make love, lose weight, improve personality or body, get a better job, cope with stress. The sales of such books compared to those about public issues give one a fair idea of the relative importance of political democracy.

Such problems beset any kind of government, but democracy the most. "Tyranny is the natural and inevitable mode of government for the shameless and self-indulgent," Herbert Read noted (*Art and Alienation*). "To live together requires rules and a governing of the passions." And so complaints grow that, in the past, there had been better democracy because there was more virtue, more civic-mindedness, more sense of community.

Doubtless this is largely because every generation projects onto the past the myth that things were better then, *in illud tempore*, in a golden age before corruption set in. But it may be worth asking, in search of a theory of democracy, whether in fact it is not true that it has a life cycle and that it is a temporary phase in the evolution from premodern to postmodern.

Democracy as Halfway House

Examination of the long process by which democracy was created in Western Europe and the United States indicates that a successful democratic order, such as was achieved in these countries in the nineteenth century, involved a balance between traditionalism and modernism: something of both kinds of democracy, the monistic and the pluralistic; a half-modernized society, with some individual emancipation but enough remaining social cement. Lord Balfour's widely quoted dictum that an essential precondition of democracy is "a people so fundamentally at one they can safely afford to bicker" was a truism that any experienced party politician would have taken for granted. You can only play the game of parliamentary mock warfare if you know that in the end there will be no real warfare (as in the beginning there was—the width of aisles in the House of Commons had to be wider than the reach of a sword). Everyone understood not only that the majority principle is tolerable only on condition that the majority does not oppress and completely alienate the minority, but also that political discussion is fruitful only when the participants share a common set of meanings as well as a basic goodwill.

Retention of positive values, as represented by the competing political parties, was paradoxically an essential for the relativist regime of pluralist democracy. Such values had been saved from skepticism. Christians and Socialists, Tories and Labourites, Republicans and Democrats were fervent believers, though they had learned to curb their fervor sufficiently to accept the verdict of elections, and could sometimes amend their principles with amazing facility if this promised to improve their chances at the polls. Here was a precarious compromise. Strong belief in positive values was needed to create the rival programs of competing parties and inspire citizens to vote for them. This competition was the lifeblood of the democracies, and any tendency for enthusiasm to lag, for there to be "no great issues" under passionate debate, has almost always been deplored as a bad thing for democracy. Informed, intelligent, interested citizens are essential to it, and one of its main justifications is that democracy serves as a process of education, developing these sterling qualities of citizenship. When belief decays into cynicism, corruption appears. But belief is always at risk in the pluralistic society, marked as it is by skepticism and relativism.

Democracy resembles Marx's capitalism, which he saw as a dynamic but brief period, inherently unstable, its mission to destroy the old order while preparing for the new. He viewed this process as chiefly economic, but even modern Marxists concede that it is wrong to take Marxian economic determinacy too narrowly. Society is a whole, and its "great transformation" is a psychosocial one of which both politics and economics are parts. So we can think of capitalism-democracy as two facets of a single social complex.

Capitalism relied on a tenuous equilibrium of individualism within a strong social framework. The classical political economists may have thought they were advocating negative government, but they always took for granted a secure structure of law and order to enforce contracts, defend property rights, prohibit monopolies and trade unions, and in general uphold the elaborate rules on which a competitive, market-directed free enterprise economy rested. And in fact these rules were internalized in the community, so that this demanding discipline was accepted with only a minimal amount of "government." As Emile Durkheim noted, without a degree of underlying consensus, economic competition, as a peaceful process, could not exist. Even a great majority of the hardworking and underpaid poor played by the rules when capitalism was in its heyday. This was due less to propaganda or coercion than to the surviving elements of feudal solidarity. (Jürgen Habermas: "[B]ourgeois society lives parasitically off the remnants of tradition.")

A typical halfway compromise was to grant equal rights while permitting this competition to result in inequality of condition, and to assume enough social solidarity so that losers accept their fate or luck and winners are reasonably charitable and compassionate. But this equilibrium gradually is lost, and as naked egoism replaces individualism-within-solidarity, pure capitalism ceases to be workable and must increasingly be regulated or administered, whether by governmental bureaucracies or internal corporate ones. The state that was strong enough to make and enforce the rules of market competition, yet not so strong that it tilted the playing field or intervened to play a direct role—the neutral referee state, preserving contracts and preventing crime, but not administering welfare or regulating businesses—was clearly a most unstable compromise. "The state as a feeding-trough, rather than umpire or keeper of the rules," as Samuel Brittan complains in *Capitalism with a Human Face*, turns the economic order into a scramble of interest groups threatening to become a Hobbesian condition of war. But to fend off every attempt to use the state for welfare or reform purposes simply was not possible; the laissez-faire utopia existed, if at all, for one unstable moment.

In a similar way, the nineteenth and early twentieth centuries went through an urban development that at one point found rural and urban, traditional and modern cultures poised in rough equilibrium. From the time of its birth in Europe in the eleventh and twelfth centuries, the city had been a revolutionary force; there the obligations of serfdom, the traditional rules of social hierarchy, were dissolved and "the city air made men free." "A far-reaching civic equality of rights in opposition to the seigneurial order," urban historian Edith Ennen writes, appeared in the cities. But at first these places of freedom were tiny islands in a sea of peasant society. The medieval cities themselves knew too little individualism to create anything like modern democracy, though they nourished an independent spirit among the corporate bodies that could easily lead to revolutions.

By the late nineteenth century, the balance between city and country was about even, and the country was still, in places like Britain and France, the scene of a way of life hardly changed for centuries. Though we may sometimes read that the nineteenth century brought industrialization and urbanization, in Europe this process of modernization left large reaches of the traditional society still alive. Megalopolis was only beginning to corrode or swallow up the farm, the village, the craftsman. In England, Lancashire was perhaps overwhelmingly urban-industrial, but Kent and East Anglia were not much different from the way they had been two centuries earlier; at least, one could easily find areas there that were unchanged. "A morning's walk from the largest city," writes Alan Everitt, and you were in the midst of another world, where artisans followed such trades as saddler, smithy, wheelwright, miller, and shoemaker, and where town met country in the village on market day. He was referring to a date well into the twentieth century. London itself was really more like a group of small towns than a twentieth-century city, as was Paris also until well into the nineteenth century. On the fringes of London lay Kentish, Essex, Sussex, Middlesex countryside suffused with the nostalgic charm of the Middle Ages. As Eugen Weber has shown (in *Peasants into Frenchmen*, 1977), the same was true of France; ancient folkways featuring all kinds of odd practices and ceremonies survived down into the twentieth century. Those who shuddered at the very thought of all this superstition and poverty, and fled from it (like George Bernard Shaw, who, echoing Marx's slap at "rural idiocy," wrote that "[f]rom the village street into the railway station is a leap across five centuries from the brutalizing torpor of Nature's tyranny over Man into the order and alertness of Man's organized dominion over Nature"), were no more numerous than those often jaded urbanites, who found it an exquisitely charming and, above all, a living community. Both types recognized that these were different worlds.

Modern sociology was virtually born of the shock of this recognition, in works like Georg Simmel's exploration of the difference between rural and city mentalities, or Friedrich Tönnies *Gemeinschaft* versus *Gesellschaft*, or Emile Durkheim's discovery of urban "anomie." One might say, too, that American as well as European literature revolved around alternative revolts from the village and returns to it, and disgust versus fascination with the metropolitan jungle.

The point is that at some moment in time these two environments, which correspond to the organic and pluralistic modes of democracy, were in rough balance and that this provided a favorable condition for democracy in general. In a sense the direct democracy of the village provided an essential foundation for the larger pluralistic democracy of the nation. The narrow-mindedness and provincial ignorance of the village might appall the urban intellectual, but in the village or town there was more interaction between people, more use of public space, neighborhoods and community gatherings, such as provide the human interactive network of anything pretending to be democratic. The town meeting, rare and quaint as it might become, remained the leading symbol even of American democracy. When local face-to-face government is overwhelmed by the anomic impersonality of the bureaucratically governed mega-urban one, a vital component of democracy is lost.

The view of democracy as a condition poised rather precariously between two other forms of society, in transit from one to the other, enables us to grant validity to both democracy's conservative and radical critics. The former have always maintained that democracy is a phase of decadence, entailing a degree of the social dissolution that leads intellectually to skepticism, socially to individual egoism, morally to permissiveness and the decline of standards. And so it is. But it also is, or was, a defense of standards too, a conservative force (as critics on the Left claim), for total decadence is fatal to it. Democracy flourished only at that moment when there was an implicit and internalized social solidarity in which individual freedom was embedded.

Similarly in the ancient cycle of civilization, the creative zenith of Greek democracy coincided with a midway-point blending of communitarian and individualist features. The Greek cities evolved from a collection of families to an urban community, then decayed into pure individualism. Athens's creative zenith coincided with a blending of individualism and communitarianism. "In the age of Pericles Athenian political life showed a perfect equilibrium between the rights of the individual and the power of the state," from which precarious perch it soon toppled because of excessive selfishness of private interests, leading to tyranny and mobocracy in disastrous alternation (G. Glotz, *The Greek City*).

The vessel for this underlying community in modern times has of course been nationalism; virtually everyone paid usually fulsome patriotic tribute to the fatherland, worshipping its tribal symbols. Left, Right, and Center might disagree on their meaning but they all accepted these symbols. The imperfections of this larger geographic community were as obvious as its uses. But the latter should not be underestimated. The decline of patriotism is a concomitant of the decline of classical democracy. Stephen Haseler's *Death of British Democracy* (1976), a rather characteristic lament, attributed the demise to stasis; the nation had ceased to be a family and become a crowd of snarling strangers. Most of those who have seen a "legitimation crisis" (Habermas), a "twilight of authority" (Nisbet), a "crisis of democracy" (Samuel Huntington), call attention to this breakdown of a community spirit, on which every social order depends, and without which it degenerates into an ugly anarchy, manageable only by sheer force.

So either too much pluralism or not enough impairs democracy's prospects of success. For much of Western Europe, a happy if precarious medium existed by the end of the nineteenth century, a halfway house on the evolutionary road from traditional to modernized society. Robert Moss, in *The Collapse of Democracy* (1975) (concerned primarily with Britain), found the devil in the progression from liberal democracy (pre-1914) to mass democracy (since). The latter menace seems to entail chiefly egalitarianism and big government. Moss, in brief, pines for that moment of delicate equilibrium when community and personal roles were in rough harmony and a momentary consensus was based on just enough deference. He speaks of agreement on private property, personal liberty, limited government.

A successful democracy must manage the delicate problem of minority rights versus majority rule. Protection of minority rights dilutes democracy, of course. Senates or upper chambers always served this purpose, as in the U.S. Constitution, where the rights of small states were protected by giving them the same representation as large ones—Wyoming's few hundred thousand on the same plane as New York's many millions. (And the Senate becomes a more powerful and prestigious body than the House of Representatives, where areas are represented more or less equally.)

Many other special groups, in addition to geographic regions, need to be taken into account today, each demanding something like what John Calhoun wanted for the South prior to 1860, a system under which a law affecting some special interest group cannot be enacted without that group's approval. When a society is divided into innumerable special interests, racial and sexual as well as sectional and professional, getting a general law passed becomes a matter of negotiating with each of these minorities. Deadlock threatens (the stalemate society), and something the majority thinks it wants, such as health care reform or a balanced budget, gets hopelessly bogged down. Democracy will then be accused of a familiar failing, hopeless inefficiency.

In late democracy, as consensus disappears, the number of minority interests increases at the same time and by the same process. At some optimum moment for democracy, there was enough underlying unity to accommodate at least the more important minority interests, without alienating the majority. There were fewer of these interests demanding attention. It will be objected that in fact minorities were simply suppressed but have now gained some amount of recognition. This is true, but some of them scarcely existed until the modernizing process had reached a certain stage. Feminism is an example: a century or so ago only a small percentage of women conceived of themselves as having significant needs separate from those of their husbands and families. That women are now a separate interest group with their own demands on law and government is a result of the rise of feminine consciousness and of socioeconomic changes over recent decades.

Democracy's Future

"He that goeth about to persuade a multitude that they are not so well governed as they ought to be, shall never want attentive and favourable hearers." So wrote Richard Hooker in the sixteenth century, and nothing has changed. Criticism of government is bound to continue; if it becomes extreme, it may involve hostility toward the democratic political regime itself. Social cement grows weaker and weaker; bitter partisanship and extreme alienation bode ill for elected parliamentary government of the sort that was once precariously domesticated. Still, there seems little possibility that existing structures of civil liberties cum parliament-based governments will be replaced in Western Europe and the United States by any sort of authoritarian, dictatorial type of regime. The shocking nature of Hitler's attempted Caesaristic dictatorship based on cultural homogeneity inoculated the West against anything of this sort. The equally shocking failure of the attempt to impose a socialist economy by force in the erstwhile Soviet Union has killed off this option. In well-developed capitalist societies, barring some extreme emergency, civil conditions preclude a dictatorship of the Left. Germany in 1918, and Chile in 1973, indicate that a Leninist regime simply cannot arise in such societies. Even Lenin had to resort to incredible terror. Allende differed from Lenin less in lacking the will to terrorize than in living in a less primitive society. There are simply too many people and too many institutions both able and willing to resist such a process to make it feasible.

So we may expect certain features, at least, of the kind of government the West agrees to call democratic to survive there and to grow in many other parts of the world: among others, rights to property, free expression, the right to protest, to vote against a government, to make use of the courts to sue and to challenge existing laws. These will be subject to occasional abuses and misfunctions, but they will survive in principle. Whether or not this includes government via elected parliaments may be another question. The serious difficulties in managing any advanced economic society via shifting and unstable majorities in parliament could well result in evolution toward more and more powers vested in a president elected at long and longer intervals.

To be sure, in some societies democracy's hour may only just have dawned or may still lie ahead. If Western Europe and the United States are now passing beyond the moment of equilibrium in which democracy thrives, others may be just reaching it. This depends on other factors than the one mentioned, for there are other conditions probably essential to democracy, including a minimum of economic well-being. Democracy can founder on too much ethnic diversity, we know. And other lines of social evolution might overtake and distort this one.

The difficulties of making any predictions about the world today should not be underestimated. The track record of supposed experts is not impressive. The knowledgeable, well-trained, and astute core of academic Sovietologists virtually to a man failed to foresee the spectacular collapse of the Soviet Union's administered economy and Communist dictatorship. In 1987 a good historian published a book on *Germany and the Germans* in which he declared German reunification inconceivable and the Communist eastern part, the German Democratic Republic, here to stay. Undaunted, he got out a second edition in 1991; we can only hope that his prediction that the enlarged greater Germany will be stable and democratic proves more accurate.

Someone has remarked, only half humorously, that a perfect political order would be the most intolerable of all, since we would then have nothing on which to blame our personal failures. One can approach the problem of government from the individual side and say that a group of saints would make up a good democracy (someone said that the Americans of 1789 could have made any constitution work). The problem is to reform personal character or intellect. Despite the enormous growth of government, it remains as true today as in Dr. Johnson's time that forms of government are of little (Johnson said no) moment to the happiness of an individual.

> How small, of all that human hearts endure,
> That part which laws or kings can cause or cure!

Clearly democracy as a goal and ideal for humanity still suffers from the defect that it is not an end in itself. Modern people need a great many things, no doubt. To judge by the evidence of crime, aimless violence, suicide, drug addiction, alcoholism, vandalism, mental "illness," divorce, child abuse, and other indices of social dysfunction, the modern individual is far from a happy creature. The appeal of innumerable religions and pseudoreligions, domestic and imported, suggests a yearning for some kind of emotional satisfaction. There are embattled feminists, abortionists and antiabortionists, environmentalists, old-fashioned Christians, new-fashioned

Jesus freaks, orientalists, Scientologists, gay liberationists, and a thousand other seekers after salvation—salvation, one assumes, from the tragedies and discomforts of life, which include not only sickness and death but the boredom of work, the bureaucratization of the world, the impersonality, mechanization, and excessive bigness of society, the decay of traditional values, the scarcity of love. The condition is still as sad as when Matthew Arnold wrote a century and a quarter ago that

> the world which seems
> To lie before us like a land of dreams,
> Hath really neither joy, nor love, nor light,
> Nor certitude, nor peace, nor help for pain;
> And we are here as on a darkling plain
> Swept with confused alarms of struggle and flight.

To little of this does politics in general supply an answer.

The Swedes, with the highest living standard in the world as measured materially, and a nearly perfectly functioning system of political democracy, held a long national inquest a few years ago about the quality of life, which they still felt woefully lacking; all their creature comforts had not cured unhappiness. More joy in work, more beauty and art in life, better knowledge of how to live, are urgent needs today of people all over the world; these needs do not perhaps have much relevance to democracy. A dictator who could show the way to these goals would probably be welcome indeed. More concretely, if the enterprise is too large and the work too tedious, installing industrial democracy will not help much. If the bright inspiration of art and learning has vanished from the universities, student participation will not bring it back.

Whatever it is that the modern individual wants, on almost any analysis democratization does not rank high on his or her list of priorities. He or she wants productivity, equality, and liberty, Raymond Aron thought, noting that these goals clash with each other. All of them clash with other human needs, such as community, justice, peace, art, leisure.

A recent representative statement from the Left, Kim Moody's *An Injury to All: The Decline of American Unionism* (1988), expresses dismay and outrage at the collapse of a once glowing faith in the organized working class. What can be done to rescue it? Faced with the unpleasant fact that the workers are led by corrupt union bureaucrats and spurn Marxist intellectuals, one can hope for a magical conversion of the workers to socialist ideals that will lead them to overthrow the bureaucrats and establish some kind of democratic utopia; or, as the alternative to this unlikely scenario, one can dream of seizing power by revolutionary means and imposing reforms by force and terror. The choice lies between mass conversion and Stalinism. Moody talks of "massive new organization," "re-making" the working class (an ominous phrase, but he does not seem to imply a Bolshevik model). Here once more we have the true believer's acceptance of democracy only if everybody voluntarily comes around to his point of view; otherwise they must be compelled to come in (as workers must indeed be compelled to come into the closed shop in the opinion of ardent unionists). Peter Hain, in *Political Strikes* (1986), a book about British trade unionism, says, on the one hand, "new ways must be found to involve the whole membership," but on the other, Mrs. Thatcher's notion that workers should vote on every strike action was to be indignantly resisted. The treasured goal is not democracy per se but some envisioned ideal principle that needs to be realized; best if the majority adopts it, but otherwise . . .

As the principle of majority rule or government by elected officials, democracy will not correct moral defects where such defects are embedded in a civic culture. If there is inherent corruption, for example, electing and empowering a representative assembly will not cure it. If judges are accustomed to selling their verdicts (as seems to be the case, for example, in Haiti), why would legislators not sell their votes? Elected officials can be as corrupt as appointed ones; obviously the source of power does not touch the way it is carried out. It seems to be supposed that democracy will reform such defects in Haiti's politics; but in and of itself, popular elections cannot be expected to change the customs of a people. They will, obviously, only reflect these customs. The people might choose to defeat a corrupt representative at the polls, but a higher-up might just as easily have dismissed him; there is no inherent reason why the voters should be more honest than unelected rulers. If corruption is accepted and tolerated in the society, it can be cured only by some process of education and reform, which might emanate from either the electorate or a dictator, but perhaps more easily from the latter. The crucial matter is not the procedural source of the process but the will to carry it out, as a process of education. Democracy as well as every other form of government is ethically neutral. The only reason why Americans, for example, think the opposite is that they equate their own high standards of official conduct (if in fact such exist) with democracy rather than with their moral and political culture, a thing with deep roots and of long growth.

In the last analysis the formal aspect of a society, including whether or not it is more or less egalitarian, how elections are held, and so on, is surely not the most important thing about it. A democratic or classless society is worthless if it is made up of worthless people and involves lives not worth living. An undemocratic, inegalitarian one would surely be preferable if everyone in it were happy and fulfilled. We may argue that an egalitarian and democratic society must make for more happiness than the opposite kind. But the point remains that to speak of democracy or equality, or any other structural or operational feature, as if it were the end rather than the means is to confuse ends and means; what counts is quality of life for the maximum number of people, a creative and vital culture, or some other criterion that refers not to a process or a formal condition but to the conditions of human life.

The focus of interest in the more advanced nations in recent times seems to have turned more urgently toward qualities of life. Coming to some sort of viable terms with the machine, the bureaucracy, the environment, with megalopolis and anomie, with size and complexity, with too rapid change and the destruction of tradition, are the top priorities for most people. Preservation of democratic institutions and procedures takes a lower rank, probably, and if there is a conflict the latter will lose.

If we know what the good life is, from whatever source, then we will work to establish it, and we will cease to be democrats insofar as this means leaving the verdict to majority opinion whatever that may be. By the same token, if economic, ecological, military, or any sort of necessity mandates a line of action—if we must, for instance, establish a world dictator to save us from burning up due to ozone depletion—then this mandate will override democratic processes. These are means, not ends, and if some imperative end, some unquestioned good, requires their sacrifice, they will have to go. No one could approve establishing evil by democratic means, or shrink from establishing good by undemocratic means, if it is apparent to all what good and evil are. In Emil Brunner's words, "the question of just or unjust laws is more important than the question of democracy or not democracy."

Note

1. See, for example, Louis Rougier, *L'Erreur de la démocratie française* (Paris, 1963).

Bibliography

This is a selective bibliography. It is basically confined to English-language books but includes a few works in French that were especially useful to me, namely, Aron, Guy-Grand, Le Bon, Rougier, Scherer, and Vacherot.

Adam, K.M. "How the Benthamites Became Democrats." *Journal of Social Philosophy and Jurisprudence*, vol. 7, 1942.

Agar, Herbert, et al. *The City of Man: A Declaration on World Democracy*. New York: Viking Press, 1940.

Agard, Walter R. *What Democracy Meant to the Greeks*. Chapel Hill: University of North Carolina Press, 1942.

Allen, Carleton K. *Democracy and the Individual*. London and New York: Oxford University Press, 1943.

Almond, G.A., and Sidney Verba. *The Civic Culture: Political Attitudes and Democracy in Five Nations*. Princeton: Princeton University Press, 1963.

Arac, Jonathan, ed. *Postmodernism and Politics*. Minneapolis: University of Minnesota Press, 1986.

Arendt, Hannah. *The Origins of Totalitarianism*. New York: Harcourt Brace & World, 1951.

———. *The Human Condition*. Chicago: University of Chicago Press, 1958.

———. *Between Past and Future*. New York: Viking Press, 1961.

———. *Crises of the Republic*. New York: Harcourt Brace Jovanovich, 1969.

Arnold, Matthew. "Democracy." In *Mixed Essays*. London, 1879.

———. *Culture and Anarchy*. Yale University Press, 1994. Originally published London, 1869.

Aron, Raymond. *Les guerres en chaine*. Paris, 1951.

———. *Démocratie et totalitarianisme*. Paris, 1965.

Aron, Raymond, et al. *La Démocratie à l'epreuve du XX siècle*. Paris, 1960.

Austin, John. *Sense and Sensabilia*. Oxford University Press, 1962.

Bachrach, Peter. *The Theory of Democratic Elitism*. Boston: Little, Brown, 1967.

Bailey, Sydney O. *British Parliamentary Democracy*. Boston: Houghton Mifflin, 1958.

Barber, Benjamin. *Strong Democracy: Participatory Politics for a New Age*. University of California Press, 1984.

Barnes, Samuel H., Max Kaase, et al. *Political Action: Mass Participation in Five*

Western Democracies. Beverly Hills, CA: Sage Publications, 1979.

Barry, Bryan M. *Sociologists, Economists, and Democracy.* London: Collier-Macmillan, 1970.

Bayle, Pierre. *Oeuvres.* Vol. 3. The Hague, 1737.

Bealey, Frank. *Democracy in the Contemporary State.* Oxford: Clarendon Press and Oxford University Press, 1988.

Bellamy, Richard, ed. *Victorian Liberalism.* London and New York: Routledge, 1990.

Belloc, Hilaire, and G.K. Chesterton. *The Party System.* London, 1911.

Benda, Julien. "Pacifism and Democracy." In *The Foreign Affairs Reader,* ed. H.F. Armstrong. New York: Harper, for Council on Foreign Relations, 1947.

Bendix, Reinhold. *Kings or People: Power and the Mandate to Rule.* Berkeley: University of California Press, 1978.

Benes, Eduard. *Democracy Today and Tomorrow.* New York, 1939.

Benjamin, Walter. *Illuminations.* Ed. Hannah Arendt. New York: Harcourt Brace and World, 1968.

Bentham, Jeremy. *Bentham's Political Thought.* Ed. B. Parekh. London: Croom Helm, 1973.

Blake, Robert. *The Conservative Party from Peel to Churchill.* London: Eyre and Spottiswoode, 1970.

Blum, Carol. *Rousseau and the Republic of Virtue: The Language of Politics in the French Revolution.* Ithaca, NY: Cornell University Press, 1986.

Blumberg, Paul, ed. *Industrial Democracy: The Sociology of Participation.* London: Constable, 1968.

Bobbio, Noberto. *The Future of Democracy.* Trans. Cambridge: Polity Association, with Blackwell, 1987.

Bonghi, R. "La decadenza del regime parlamentare." *Nuova Antologia* (Rome), June 1, 1884.

Bouglé, Celestin. *La Démocratie devant le science.* Paris, 1904.

Briggs, Asa. *Saxons, Normans, and Victorians.* London: Historical Association, 1966.

Brittan, Samuel. *Capitalism and the Permissive Society.* London: Macmillan, 1973.

———. "Economic Conditions of Democracy." *British Journal of Political Science,* vol. 5, 1975.

Brunner, Emil. *Justice and the Social Order.* New York: Harper, 1943.

Bryce, James. *The American Commonwealth.* London and New York, 1888.

———. *Modern Democracies.* New York, 1921.

Budge, Ian. *Agreement and the Stability of Democracy.* Chicago: Markham, 1970.

Budge, Ian, et al. *Political Stratification and Democracy.* London: Macmillan, 1972.

Burchard, John. *Bernini Is Dead?* New York, 1976.

Burke, Peter. *Popular Culture in Early Modern Europe.* London: T. Smith, 1978.

Burrow, J.W. *Whigs and Liberals.* Oxford: Clarendon Press and Oxford University Press, 1988.

Carlyle, Thomas. *Past and Present.* London, 1843.

———. *Latter Day Pamphlets.* Vol 1. London, 1850.

Carpenter, Humphrey. *The Inklings.* London and Boston: Allen and Unwin, 1978.

Carpenter, L.P. *G.D.H. Cole: An Intellectual Biography.* Cambridge University Press, 1973.

Carr, E.H. *The New Society.* London: Macmillan, 1951.

Casserly, J.V. Longmead. *The Bent World.* Oxford University Press, 1955.

Caute, David. *The Fellow Travellers.* Yale University Press, 1988.

Center for Study of North Africa. *L'Afrique Politique: Yearbook.* Bordeaux, France, 1994.

Checkland, S.G. *The Gladstones*. Cambridge University Press, 1971.

Chesterton, G.K. *Charles Dickens*. New York, 1906.

Childers, Thomas. *The Nazi Voter*. University of North Carolina Press, 1983.

Christophersen, Jens A. *The Meaning of "Democracy" as Used in European Ideologies*. Oslo: Universitetsforlaget, 1966.

Cobban, Alfred. *Rousseau and the Modern State*. Hamden, CT: Archon Books, 1964.

Cohen, Carl. *Democracy*. Athens, GA: University of Georgia Press, 1971.

Cole, G.D.H. *Essays in Social Theory*. London: Macmillan, 1950.

Cole, G.D.H., and W. Mellor. *The Meaning of Industrial Freedom*. London, 1918.

Collingwood, R.G. *The New Leviathan*. Oxford: Clarendon Press, 1951.

Commager, Henry Steele. *Majority Rule and Minority Rights*. Gloucester, MA: P. Smith, 1943.

Conkin, Paul K. *Self-Evident Truths*. Bloomington: Indiana University Press, 1974.

———. *The Four Foundations of American Government*. Arlington Heights, IL: Harlan Davidson, 1994.

Cook, Terence E., and Patrick M. Morgan, eds. *Participatory Democracy*. San Francisco: Canfield Press, 1971.

Copp, D., J. Roeman, and J. Hampton, eds. *The Idea of Democracy*. Cambridge: Cambridge University Press, 1995.

Crocker, Lester G. *Rousseau's Social Contract*. Cleveland: Case-Western Reserve Press, 1968.

Crook, David P. *American Democracy in English Politics 1815–1850*. Oxford: Clarendon Press, 1965.

———. *Benjamin Kidd: Portrait of a Social Darwinist*. Cambridge University Press, 1984.

Crozier, Michael, S.P. Huntington, and Joji Watanuki. *The Crisis of Democracy*. New York University Press, 1975.

Curtis, Michael. *Three against the Third Republic*. Princeton University Press, 1959.

Dahl, Robert A. *Preface to Democratic Theory*. University of Chicago Press, 1956.

———. *Who Governs?* Yale University Press, 1961.

———. *Pluralist Democracy in the United States*. Chicago: Rand McNally, 1967.

———. *Polyarchy, Participation, and Opposition*. Yale University Press, 1971.

———. *Democracy and Its Critics*. Yale University Press, 1989.

Dahl, Robert A., and Edward R. Tufte. *Size and Democracy*. Stanford: Stanford University Press, 1973.

Dahrendorf, Ralf. *Society and Democracy in Germany*. Garden City, NY: Doubleday, 1967.

Dealy, Glen Caudill. "The Tradition of Monistic Democracy in Latin America." *Journal of the History of Ideas*, October–December 1974.

Delbrück, Hans. *Government and the Will of the People*. New York: Oxford University Press, 1923. Originally published as *Regierung und Volkeswille* (Germany, 1914).

"Democracies and War." *The Economist*, April 1, 1995.

"Democracy Works Best." *The Economist*, August 27, 1995.

Deng, Francis M. *Tradition and Modernization*. Yale University Press, 1971.

Devine, Donald J. *The Attentive Public*. Chicago: Rand McNally, 1970.

Dewey, John. *Freedom and Culture*. New York: G.P. Putnam's Sons, 1939.

"The Dictatorial Libertine." *Times Literary Supplement*, December 26, 1968.

Digeon, Claude. *La Crise allemande de la pensée française 1870–1914*. Paris: Presses universitaires de France, 1959.

Dinwiddy, J.R. "Bentham's Transition to Political Radicalism 1809–1810." *Journal of the History of Ideas*, vol. 36, 1975.

Di Palma, Giuseppe. *Apathy and Participation: Mass Politics in Western Societies*. New York: Free Press, 1970.

Disraeli, Benjamin. *The Runnymeade Letters*. London, 1836.

Divine, Francis Edward. "Absolute Democracy or Indefeasible Right: Hobbes versus Locke." *Journal of Politics*, August 1975.

Dronberger, Ilse. *The Political Thought of Max Weber*. New York: Appleton-Century-Crofts, 1971.

Duncan, Graeme, ed. *Democratic Theory and Practice*. Cambridge University Press, 1983.

Dunn, John, ed. *Democracy: The Unfinished Journey, 508 B.C. to A.D. 1993*. Oxford University Press, 1992.

Duverger, Maurice. *Modern Democracy: Economic Power versus Political Power*. New York: Holt, Rinehart, and Winston, 1974.

Eckstein, Harry. *Theory of Stable Democracy*. Princeton University Press, 1961.

———. *Division and Cohesion in Democracy: A Study of Norway*. Princeton University Press, 1966.

Eddy, W.H.C. *Studies in Democracy*. Melbourne, Australia: Cheshire, 1966.

Ellul, Jacques. *The Political Illusion*. New York: Knopf, 1967.

Elshtain, Jean Bethke. *Democracy on Trial*. New York: Basic Books/HarperCollins, 1995.

Epstein, Leon D. *Political Parties in Western Democracies*. New York: Praeger, 1967.

Eysenck, H.J. *The Future of Political Science*. New York: Atherton Press, 1963.

Farrar, Cynthia. *The Origins of Democratic Thinking*. Cambridge University Press, 1988.

Fasnacht, G.E. *Acton's Political Philosophy*. New York: Viking Press, 1953.

Feuchtwanger, E.J. *Disraeli, Democracy, and the Tory Party*. Clarendon Press, 1968.

Fink, Zera S. *The Classical Republicans*. Evanston, IL: Northwestern University Press, 1962

Finley, M.I. *Democracy Ancient and Modern*. New Brunswick, NJ: Rutgers University Press, 1973.

Fontana, Biancamaria. *Benjamin Constant and the Post-Revolutionary Mind*. Yale University Press, 1991.

Forster, E.M. *Two Cheers for Democracy*. New York: Harcourt Brace, 1951.

Fralin, Richard. *Rousseau and Representation*. New York: Columbia University Press, 1979.

Frankel, Charles. *The Democratic Prospect*. New York: Harper and Row, 1962.

Freeman, John R. *Democracy and Markets: The Politics of Mixed Economies*. Cornell University Press, 1989.

Freud, Sigmund. *Group Psychology and the Analysis of the Ego*. New York, 1921.

———. *Civilization and Its Discontents*. New York, 1930.

Friedrich, C.J. *The New Belief in the Common Man*. Boston: Little, Brown, and Co., 1942.

Furet, François. *Interpreting the French Revolution*. Cambridge University Press, 1981.

"The Future of Democracy." *The Economist*, June 17–23, 1995.

Galli, G., and A. Prandi. *Patterns of Political Participation in Italy*. Yale University Press, 1970.

Gay, Peter. *The Dilemma of Democratic Socialism: Bernstein's Challenge to Marx*. Columbia University Press, 1952.

———. *Voltaire's Politics*. 2nd ed. Yale University Press, 1988.

Giddens, Anthony. *Studies in Social and Political Theory*. London: Hutchinson, 1977.

Gilbert, Alan. *Democratic Individuality*. Cambridge University Press, 1991.

Gill, Graeme. *The Origins of the Stalinist Political System*. Cambridge University Press, 1990.

Ginsberg, Morris. *Reason and Unreason in Society*. Cambridge, MA: Harvard University Press, 1948.

Girvetz, Harry R. *Democracy and Elitism*. New York: Scribner's, 1967.

Godkin, E.L. *Problems of Modern Democracy*. 1896. Reprint. Harvard University Press/Belknap, 1966.

Godwin, William. *Political Justice*. London, 1793.

Goldman, Merle. *Sowing the Seeds of Democracy in China*. Harvard University Press, 1994.

Goodwin, Albert. *The Friends of Liberty: The English Democratic Movement in the Age of the French Revolution*. London: Hutchinson, 1979.

Goodwin, Richard N. *Promises to Keep: A Call for a New American Revolution*. New York: Times Books, 1992.

Gorer, Geoffrey. *The Danger of Equality and Other Essays*. New York: Weybright and Talley, 1966.

Grampp, William. *The Manchester School of Economics*. Stanford University Press, 1960.

Graubard, Stephen, and G. Holton, eds. *Excellence and Leadership in a Democracy*. Columbia University Press, 1962.

Guehenno, Jean. *The End of Democracy*. Minnesota University Press, 1993.

Guizot, François. *De la Démocratie en France*. Paris, 1849.

Guy-Grand, Georges. *Le Proces de la démocratie*. Paris, 1911.

Habermas, Jürgen. *The Legitimation Crisis*. Boston: Beacon Press, 1975.

Haggard, Stephen, and Steven B. Webb, eds. *Voting for Reform: Democracy, Political Liberalization, and Economic Adjustment*. Oxford University Press/World Book, 1994.

Hamer, D.A. *Liberal Politics in the Age of Gladstone and Rosebery*. Clarendon Press, 1972.

Hampson, Norman. *Will and Circumstance: Montesquieu, Rousseau, and the French Revolution*. London: Duckworth, 1983.

Haseler, Stephen. *The Death of British Democracy*. London: P. Elek, 1976.

Hegel, G.W.F. *Reason in History*. Ed. Robert S. Hartman. New York: Liberal Arts Press, 1953.

Held, David. *Democracy and the Global Order*. Oxford: Polity Press, 1995.

Herz, John. *Political Realism and Political Idealism*. University of Chicago Press, 1951.

Himmelfarb, Gertrude. "The Politics of Democracy: The English Reform Act of 1867." *Journal of British Studies*, vol. 6, 1966.

————. *Victorian Minds*. New York: Knopf, 1970.

Hobhouse, L.T. *Democracy and Reaction*. London: Macmillan, 1904.

————. *Development and Purpose*. London: Putnam's, 1913.

Hoffmann, Stanley. "Some Notes on Democratic Theory and Practice." *Tocqueville*, winter 1980.

Hofstadter, Richard. *The Idea of a Party System*. University of California Press, 1969.

Holmes, Oliver Wendell, Jr. In *The Mind and Faith of Justice Holmes*, ed. Max Lerner. Boston: Little, Brown, 1943.

Holmes, Stephen. *Benjamin Constant and the Making of Modern Liberalism*. Yale University Press, 1984.

Hopkins, Raymond F. *Political Roles in a New State*. Yale University Press, 1971.

Huizinga, Johan. *Men and Ideas*. New York: Meridian Books, 1959.

————. *America*. 1918. Trans. New York: Harper and Row, 1972.

Hume, David. *Political Writings*. Ed. Charles H. Hendel. New York: Liberal Arts Press, 1953.

Hunt, Lynn Avery. *Politics, Culture, and Class in the French Revolution*. Berkely: University of California Press, 1984.

Hunt, Richard N. *The Political Ideas of Marx and Engels*. 2 vols. University of Pittsburgh Press, 1974.

Huntington, Samuel P. *The Third Wave: Democratization in the Late Twentieth Century*. Norman: University of Oklahoma Press, 1991.

Huxley, Aldous. *Proper Studies*. London, 1927.

Huxley, Julian. *Democracy Marches*. London: Chatto and Windus, 1941.

Inglehart, Ronald. *The Silent Revolution: Changing Values and Political Styles among Western Publics*. Princeton University Press, 1977.

Jalal, Ayesha. *Democracy and Authoritarianism in South Asia*. Cambridge University Press,1995.

Jelavich, Peter. "Popular Dimensions of Modern Elitist Culture." In *Modern European Intellectual History*, ed. D. LaCapra and S.L. Kaplan. Ithaca, NY: Cornell University Press, 1982.

Jennings, J.R. *Georges Sorel: The Character and Development of His Thought*. Hampshire, England: Macmillan, 1985.

Jones, A.H.M. *Athenian Democracy*. New York: Praeger, 1957.

Jordan, David P. *The Revolutionary Career of Maximilien Robespierre*. New York: Free Press, 1985.

Jouvenel, Bertrand de. *Power: The Natural History of Its Growth*. London: Batchworth Press, 1948.

Kahan, Alan S. *Aristocratic Liberalism: The Social and Political Thought of Jacob Burckhardt, John Stuart Mill, and Alexis de Tocqueville*. Oxford University Press, 1992.

Kallen, Horace W. *Culture and Democracy in the United States*. New York, 1924.

Kallet-Marx, Lisa. "Some Recent Books on Athenian Democracy." *Journal of the History of Ideas*, April 1994.

Kaplan, Sidney. "Social Engineers as Saviors." *Journal of the History of Ideas*, June 1956.

Kater, Michael. *The Nazi Party: A Social Profile of Members and Leaders*. Harvard University Press, 1983.

Kaufmann, Walter, ed. *Hegel's Political Philosophy*. New York: Atherton Press, 1970.

Kautsky, Karl. *Bernstein und das Sozialdemokratische Programm*. Stuttgart, 1899.

———. *The Class Struggle*. Chicago, 1910.

Kelley, Robert E. *The Trans-Atlantic Persuasion: The Liberal Democratic Mind in the Age of Gladstone*. New York: Knopf, 1969.

Kelly, George Armstrong. *The Humane Comedy: Constant, Tocqueville, and French Liberalism*. Cambridge University Press, 1992.

Kendall, Wilmoore. *John Locke and the Doctrine of Majority Rule*. Urbana: University of Illinois Press, 1965.

Kent, Christopher. *Brains and Numbers: Elitism, Comtism, and Democracy in Mid-Victorian England*. Toronto: University of Toronto Press, 1978.

Key, V.O., Jr. *Public Opinion and American Democracy*. New York: Knopf, 1961.

———. *The Responsible Electorate*. Harvard University Press, 1966.

King, Preston. *Fear of Power*. London: Cass, 1967.

Kissinger, Henry. *A World Restored*. Boston: Houghton Mifflin, 1957.

———. *The Necessity for Choice*. New York: Harper, 1961.

Kojecky, Roger. *T.S. Eliot's Social Criticism*. London: Faber and Faber, 1972.

Kors, Alan C. *D'Holbach's Coterie*. Princeton University Press, 1976.

Lakoff, Sanford. *Equality in Political Philosophy*. Harvard University Press, 1964.

La Palombara, Joseph. *Democracy, Italian Style*. Yale University Press, 1987.

Lasch, Christopher. *The Revolt of the Elites and the Betrayal of Democracy*. New York: W.W. Norton, 1995.

Laski, Harold J. *The American Democracy*. New York: Viking Press. 1948.

Le Bon, Gustave. *Psychologie des foules* (The Crowd). Paris and London, 1895.

———. *The Psychology of Socialism*. New York, 1899.

———. *Psychologie politique*. Paris, 1912.

Lecky, W.E.H. *Democracy and Liberty*. 2 vols. New York, 1896.

Lefort, Claude. *Democracy and Political Theory*. Trans. David Macey, Minneapolis: University of Minnesota Press, 1988.

LeMahieu, D.L. *A Culture for Democracy: Mass Communication and the Cultivated Mind in Britain between the Wars*. Oxford University Press/Clarendon Press, 1988.

Lewis, Wyndham. *Time and Western Man*. New York, 1927.

Lijphart, Arend. *Democracy in Plural Societies*. Yale University Press, 1977.

Lillibridge, George D. *Beacon of Freedom: The Impact of American Democracy upon Great Britain 1830–1870*. Philadelphia: University of Pennsylvania Press, 1954.

Lindsay, A.D. *The Modern Democratic State*. Oxford University Press, 1947.

Linz, Stepan. *The Breakdown of Democratic Regimes*. 4 vols. Baltimore: Johns Hopkins University Press, 1979.

Lippincott, Benjamin E. *Victorian Critics of Democracy*. New York: Octagon Books, 1964.

Lippmann, Walter. *Public Opinion*. New York, 1922.

———. *The Public Philosophy*. London: H. Hamilton, 1955.

Lively, Jack. *The Social and Political Thought of Alexis de Tocqueville*. Clarendon Press, 1962.

———. *Democracy*. New York: St. Martin's Press, 1974.

Lloyd of Dolobran, Lord. *Leadership in a Democracy*. 1939.

Loubère, Leo. *Louis Blanc*. Evanston, IL: Northwestern University Press, 1960.

Lough, John. *The Philosophes and Post-Revolutionary France*. Oxford University Press/Clarendon Press, 1982.

Lovell, David W. *From Marx to Lenin: An Evaluation of Marx's Responsibility for Soviet Authoritarianism*. Cambridge University Press, 1984.

Lovett, Clara M. *The Democratic Movement in Italy 1830–1876*. Harvard University Press, 1982.

Lowell, A. Lawrence. *Public Opinion and Popular Government*. New York, 1913.

Lukes, Steven. *Emile Durkheim: His Life and Work*. London: Allen Lane, 1973.

McClellan, David. *Simone Weil: Utopian Pessimist*. London: Macmillan, 1990.

Mack, Mary P. *Jeremy Bentham: An Odyssey of Ideas 1748–1792*. Columbia University Press, 1962.

Mack Smith, Denis. *Mazzini*. Yale University Press, 1994.

Macpherson, C.B. *The Real World of Democracy*. Oxford University Press, 1966.

———. *Democratic Theory: Essays in Retrieval*. Clarendon Press, 1973.

———. *Life and Times of Liberal Democracy*. Oxford University Press, 1977.

Magnus, Philip. *Edmund Burke: A Biography*. 1939.

Maine, Henry Sumner. *Popular Government*. 1886. Reprint, Indianapolis: Liberty Classics, 1978.

Mainwaring, Scott, and Timothy Scully, eds. *Building Democratic Institutions: The Party System in Latin America*. Stanford University Press, 1994.

Mallock, W.H. *The Limits of Pure Democracy*. 4th ed. London: Chapman and Hall, 1918.

Manicas, Peter T. *War and Democracy*. Oxford and New York: Basil Blackwell, 1989.

Mannheim, Karl. "The Democratization of Culture." In *Essays on the Sociology of Culture*. London: Routledge & Paul, 1956.

Marcel, Gabriel. *Man against Mass Society*. Chicago: Regnery, 1952.

Marcuse, Herbert, ed. *The Democratic and Authoritarian State*. Glencoe, IL: Free Press, 1957.

Margolis, Michael. *Viable Democracy*. London: Macmillan, 1979.

Martini, Winfried. *Das Ende aller Sicherheit*. Stuttgart: Deutsche Verlags-Anstalt, 1954.

May, Erskine. *Democracy in Europe: A History*. 2 vols. New York, 1878.

Mayo, Henry B. *An Introduction to Democratic Theory*. Oxford University Press, 1960.

――――. "How Can We Justify Democracy?" *American Political Science Review*, September 1962.

Mazzini, Giuseppe. *Thoughts on Democracy in Europe*. London, 1847.

Meisel, James. *The Myth of the Ruling Class: Gaetano Mosca and the Elite*. Ann Arbor: University of Michigan Press, 1958.

Mencken, H.L. *Notes on Democracy*. New York, 1926.

Michelet, Jules. *The People*. Trans. J. McKay. University of Illinois Press, 1973.

Michels, Robert. *Political Parties*. English ed. New York: Hearst's International Library, 1915.

Mill, John Stuart. *Dissertations and Discussions*. Vol. 1. London, 1859.

――――. *Representative Government*. London, 1865.

――――. *On Liberty and Other Essays*. Ed. John Gray. Oxford University Press, 1991.

Miller, James. *Rousseau: Dreamer of Democracy*. Yale University Press, 1984.

Mills, C. Wright. *The Power Elite*. Oxford University Press, 1956.

Mims, Edwin, Jr. *The Majority of the People*. New York: Modern Age Books, 1941.

Mommsen, Wolfgang J. *Max Weber and German Politics 1890–1920*. Trans. University of Chicago Press, 1984.

Moore, D.C. *The Politics of Deference*. New York: Barnes and Noble, 1976.

Morley, John. *Oracles on Man and Government*. London, 1923.

Mosca, Gaetano. *The Ruling Class*. 1896.

Moss, Robert. *The Collapse of Democracy*. London: Temple Smith, 1975.

Münsterberg, Hugo. "American Democracy." In *American Traits*. Boston: Houghton Mifflin, 1901.

Myers, Francis. *The Warfare of Democratic Ideals*. Yellow Springs, OH: Antioch Press, 1956.

Naess, Arne, et al. *Democracy, Ideology, and Objectivity*. Oslo: University Press, 1956.

Naumann, Friedrich. *Democracy and Kaiserdom*. 1900.

Nelkin, Dorothy. *Technical Decisions and Democracy: European Experiments in Public Participation*. 1977.

Neubauer, D.E. "Some Conditions of Democracy." *American Political Science Review*, vol. 61, 1967.

Nicholls, David. "Gladstone on Liberty and Democracy." *Review of Politics*, vol. 23, 1961.

Niebuhr, Reinhold. *The Irony of American History*. New York: Scribner's, 1952.

――――. *Faith and Politics*. Ed. R.H. Stone. New York: G. Brazilier, 1968.

Niebuhr, Reinhold, and Paul E. Sigmund. *The Democratic Experience*. New York: Praeger, 1969.

Nisbet, Robert A. *Twilight of Authority*. Oxford University Press, 1975.

Nye, Robert A. *The Origins of Crowd Psychology: Gustave Le Bon and the Crisis of Mass Democracy in the Third Republic*. Beverly Hills, CA: Sage Publications, 1975.

――――. *The Anti-Democratic Sources of Elite Theory: Pareto, Mosca, Michels*. Beverly Hills, CA: Sage Publications, 1977.

Oakeshott, Michael. *Rationalism in Politics*. New York: Basic Books, 1962.

Ola, O. "The Cultural Basis of the Crisis of Parliamentary Government in Africa." *Civilisations* (Brussels), vol. 22, nos. 3 and 4.

Ortega y Gasset, José. *The Revolt of the Masses*. 1927.

Orth, Samuel P. *Socialism and Democracy in Europe*. New York, 1913.

Orwell, George. *1984*. Harcourt Brace Jovanovich, 1948.

Ostrogorski, M.I. *Democracy and the Organization of Political Parties*. 2 vols. New York and London, 1902.

Pareto, Vilfredo. *The Rise and Fall of Elites*. Ed. H.L. Zetterbaum. Totowa, NJ: Bedminster Press, 1968.

Parry, Geraint, and Michael Moran, eds. *Democracy and Democratization*. London and New York: Routledge, 1993.

Pateman, Carole. *Participation and Democratic Theory*. Cambridge University Press, 1970.

Payne, Harry G. *The Philosophes and the People*. Yale University Press, 1976.

Pérez-Diaz, Victor M. *The Return of Civil Society: The Emergence of Democratic Spain*. Harvard University Press, 1993.

Percy of Newcastle, Lord. *The Heresy of Democracy*. Chicago: Regnery, 1964.

Perry, Ralph Barton. *Puritanism and Democracy*. New York: Vanguard Press, 1944.

Pitkin, Hanna F. *The Concept of Representation*. University of California Press, 1967.

Plamenatz, John. *Democracy and Illusion*. London: Longman, 1973.

Pocock, J.G.A. *The Ancient Constitution and the Feudal Law*. Cambridge University Press, 1957.

Pole, J.R., ed. *The Advance of Democracy*. New York: Harper and Row, 1967.

Ponsonby, Arthur. *Democracy and Diplomacy*. London, 1915.

Poor, Harold L. *Kurt Tucholvsky and the Ordeal of Germany*. New York: Scribner's, 1962.

Popper, Karl. *The Open Society and Its Enemies*. Vol. 2. Princeton University Press, 1962.

Postan, M.M. "Karl Marx: A Democrat?" In *Fact and Relevance: Essays in Historical Method*. Cambridge University Press, 1971.

Praz, Mario. *The Hero in Eclipse*. Oxford University Press, 1956.

Prewitt, Kenneth, and Alan Stone. *The Ruling Elites: Elite Theory, Power, and American Democracy*. New York: Harper and Row, 1973.

Pugh, Martin. *The Tories and the People 1880–1935*. New York: Basil Blackwell, 1986.

Pulzer, Peter. *Political Representation and Elections in England*. London: Allen and Unwin, 1968.

Purcell, Edward W., Jr. *The Crisis of Democratic Theory*. Lexington: University Press of Kentucky, 1973.

Putnam, Robert D. *Making Democracy Work: Civic Traditions in Modern Italy*. Princeton University Press, 1993.

Pye, Lucius W., and Sidney Verba, eds. *Political Culture and Political Development*. Princeton University Press, 1965.

Rabushka, Alvin, and Kenneth A. Shepsle. *Politics in Plural Societies: A Theory of Democratic Instability*. Columbus, OH: Merrill, 1972.

Read, Donald. *Cobden and Bright*. New York: St. Martin's Press, 1968.

Redford, Emmette S. *Democracy in the Administrative State*. Oxford University Press, 1969.

Revel, Jean-François. *Democracy against Itself: The Future of the Democratic Impulse*. New York: Free Press, 1993.

Riemer, Neal. *The Revival of Democratic Theory*. New York: Appleton-Century-Crofts, 1962.

Ritter, Alan. *The Political Thought of P.J. Proudhon*. Princeton University Press, 1969.

Roberts, Brad, ed. *The New Democracies: Global Change and U.S. Policy*. Cambridge, MA: M.I.T. Press, 1990.

Roberts, Jennifer Tolbert. *Athens on Trial: The Antidemocratic Tradition in Western Thought*. Princeton University Press, 1994.

Robertson, Andrew W. *The Language of Democracy; Political Rhetoric in the United States and Great Britain 1790–1900*. Ithaca, NY: Cornell University Press, 1995.

Robinson, Paul A. *The Freudian Left*. 1969.

Robson, John M. *The Improvement of Mankind: The Social and Political Thought of John Stuart Mill*. University of Toronto Press, 1968.

Rosen, Frederick. *Jeremy Bentham and Representative Democracy*. Clarendon Press, 1983.

Rosenberg, Arthur. *Democracy and Socialism*. Boston: Beacon Press, 1965.

Rougier, Louis. *L'Erreur de la démocratie française*. Paris, 1963.

Russell, Bertrand. *Justice in Wartime*. London, 1916.

———. *Principles of Social Reconstruction*. London, 1916.

———. *Power: A New Social Analysis*. New York: W.W. Norton, 1938.

Sagan, Eli. *The Honey and the Hemlock: Democracy and Paranoia in Ancient Athens and Modern America*. New York: Basic Books, 1991.

Salomone, A.W. *Italian Democracy in the Making 1900–1914*. University of Pennsylvania Press, 1945.

Sangnier, Marc. *L'Esprit démocratique*. Paris, 1905.

Santayana, George. *Winds of Doctrine*. New York, 1913.

———. *Dialogues in Limbo*. New York, 1926.

———. *Dominations and Powers*. New York: Scribner's, 1951.

Sartori, Giovanni. *Democratic Theory*. Detroit: Wayne State University Press, 1962.

Saville, J., ed. *Democracy and the Labour Movement*. London: Lawrence and Wishart, 1955.

Schapiro, Leonard. *The Communist Party of the Soviet Union*. New York: Random House, 1960.

Schattschneider, E.E. *The Semi-Sovereign People*. New York: Holt, Rinehart, and Winston, 1960.

———. *Political Parties and Democracy*. Holt, Rinehart, and Winston, 1964.

Scherer, Edmond. *La Démocratie et la France*. Paris, 1883.

Schoenbaum, David. *Hitler's Social Revolution*. Garden City, NY: Doubleday, 1967.

Schopenhauer, Arthur. "Essay on Government." In *Parerga and Paralipomena*. Leipzig, 1851.

Schumpeter, Joseph. *Capitalism, Socialism, and Democracy*. 3rd ed. New York: Harper, 1950.

Schwartzman, Kathleen C. *The Social Origins of Democratic Collapse*. Lawrence: University Press of Kansas, 1989.

Schwarz, Gerhard. "The Market Economy and Democracy." *Swiss Review of World Affairs*, March 1989.

Scott, John A. *Republican Ideas and the Liberal Tradition in France 1870–1914*. New York: Columbia University Press, 1951.

Searle, G.R. *The Quest for National Efficiency*. Oxford: Blackwell, 1971.

Sedgwick, Arthur. *The Democratic Mistake*. New York, 1912.

Semmel, Bernard. *Imperialism and Social Reform*. Harvard University Press, 1960.

Seton-Watson, R.W., ed. *The War and Democracy*. London: Macmillan, 1914.

Shaw, Fred J. (Brougham Villiers). *Modern Democracy: A Study in Tendencies*. London, 1912.

Shaw, George Bernard. *The Intelligent Woman's Guide to Socialism*. New York, 1928.

Shils, Edward. "Political Development in the New States." *Comparative Studies in Society and History*, vol. 2.

Shklar, Judith. *Men and Citizens: A Study of Rousseau's Social Theory*. Cambridge University Press, 1969.

Siegfried, André. *America Comes of Age*. New York, 1928.

Silver, Harold. *The Concept of Popular Education: A Study of Ideas and Social Movements in the Early Nineteenth Century*. London: Methuen, 1965.

Singer, Peter. *Democracy and Disobedience*. Clarendon Press, 1973.

Slavin, Morris. "Jean Varlet. A Defender of Direct Democracy." *Journal of Modern History*, December 1967.

Smith, Bernard, ed. *The Democratic Spirit*. New York, 1941.

Smith, Tony. *America's Mission: The United States and the Worldwide Struggle for Democracy in the Twentieth Century*. Princeton University Press, 1994.

Solt, Leo F. *Saints in Arms: Puritanism and Democracy in Cromwell's Armies*. Stanford University Press, 1959.

Spearman, Diana. *Democracy in England*. New York: Macmillan, 1957.

Spencer, Herbert. *Essays*. Vol. 2. London, 1863.

————. *The Man Versus the State*. London, 1884.

Spengler, Oswald. *The Decline of the West*. Vienna, 1918.

Spitz, David. *Democracy and the Challenge of Power*. Columbia University Press, 1958.

————. *Patterns of Anti-Democratic Thought*. New York: Free Press, 1965.

Stamps, Norman L. *Why Democracies Fail*. Notre Dame, IN: University of Notre Dame Press, 1957.

Steele, Jonathan. *Eternal Russia: Yeltsin, Gorbachev, and the Mirage of Democracy*. London and Boston: Faber, 1994.

Steinhoff, William R. *George Orwell and the Origins of 1984*. University of Michigan Press, 1975.

Stephen, James Fitzjames. *Liberty, Equality, Fraternity*. London, 1873.

Struve, Walter. *Elites against Democracy*. Princeton University Press. 1973.

Sunstein, Cass R. *Democracy and the Problem of Free Speech*. New York: Free Press, 1993.

Talman, J.L. *The Origins of Totalitarian Democracy*. London: Secker and Warburg, 1952.

————. *Political Messianism: The Romantic Phase*. New York: Praeger, 1960.

Taylor, Keith. *The Political Ideas of the Utopian Socialists*. London: Cass, 1982.

Terdiman, Richard. *The Dialectics of Isolation: Self and Society in the French Novel from the Realists to Proust*. Yale University Press, 1976.

Tholfsen, T.R. "The Transition to Democracy in Victorian England." *International Review of Social History*, vol. 6, 1961.

Thompson, Dennis P. *The Democratic Citizen: Social Science and Democratic Theory in the Twentieth Century*. Cambridge University Press, 1971.

Thompson, Eric. *Popular Sovereignty and the French Constituent Assembly*. Manchester, England: Manchester University Press, 1952.

Thomson, David. *Democracy in France since 1870*. 5th ed. Oxford University Press, 1969.

Tocqueville, Alexis de. *Democracy in America*. 1838, 1840. Reprint, ed. Phillips Brooks. New York: Knopf, 1946.

Ulam, Adam. "Democracy and Marxism." In *The Unfinished Revolution*. New York: Vintage Books, 1960.

Vacherot, Etienne. *La Démocratie*. Paris, 1860.

————. *La Démocratie liberale*. Paris, 1892.
Vincent, John. *The Formation of the Liberal Party 1855–1868*. London: Constable, 1966.
Wakefield, Edward Gibbon. *England and America*. New York, 1834.
Wallace, Alfred R. *The Revolt of Democracy*. London, 1913.
Wallace, Henry A. *The Century of the Common Man*. New York: Reynard and Hitchcock, 1943.
Wallas, Graham. *Human Nature in Politics*. London, 1908.
Walsh, Correa M. *The Political Science of John Adams*. New York and London, 1915.
Waltz, Kenneth N. *Foreign Policy and the Democratic Process*. Boston: Little, Brown, 1967.
Weber, Alfred. *Abschied von der Bisherigen Geschichte*. Yale University Press, 1946.
Weber, Eugen. *Peasants into Frenchmen: The Modernization of Rural France 1870–1914*. Stanford University Press, 1977.
Weil, Simone. *An Anthology*. Ed. S. Miles. New York: Weidenfeld and Nicolson, 1986.
Wells, H.G. "The Life History of Democracy." In *Anticipations of the Reaction of Mechanical and Scientific Progress upon Human Life and Thought*. London, 1901.
————. *After Democracy*. London, 1932.
Weyl, Walter. *The New Democracy*. New York, 1918.
Wiebe, Robert. *Self-Rule: A Cultural History of American Democracy*. Chicago: University of Chicago Press, 1995.
Williams, Raymond. *The Long Revolution*. Columbia University Press, 1961.
Williamson, Chilton. "Bentham Looks at America." *Political Science Quarterly*, 1955.
————. *American Suffrage from Property to Democracy*. Princeton University Press, 1960.
Wilson, Woodrow. "Democracy and Efficiency." *Atlantic Monthly*, March 1901.
Woloch, Isser. *Jacobin Legacy: The Democratic Movement under the Directory*. Princeton University Press, 1970.
Wood, Ellen Meiksins. *Democracy against Capitalism*. Cambridge University Press, 1995.
Woodhouse, A.S.P. "Religion and Some Foundations of English Democracy." *Philosophical Review*, vol. 61, 1952.
Wrong, Dennis. *Power: Its Forms, Bases, and Uses*. New York: Harper and Row, 1979.
Young, Michael D. *The Rise of the Meritocracy*. Baltimore: Penguin, 1961.
Zetterbaum, Marvin. *Tocqueville and the Problem of Democracy*. Stanford University Press, 1967.

Index

About the Author

Roland N. Stromberg has written a dozen books, including two successful textbooks, *European Intellectual History Since 1789* and *Europe in the Twentieth Century* (both Prentice-Hall). The former is in its sixth edition, and a fourth edition of the latter is forthcoming. He has taught at the University of Maryland and Southern Illinois University, and is now retired from the University of Wisconsin–Milwaukee.